THE
EXPERT BEGINNER

DANNY ROTH is a writer, player and coach who specializes in teaching bridge to beginners and intermediates. An experienced and successful player at club, county and tournament level, he represented Great Britain in the European Pairs' Championships in 1987. He has written several other books on bridge, aimed at the more advanced player, and is author of *The Expert Improver*, also published by HarperCollins.

C O L L I N S
WINNING BRIDGE

THE EXPERT BEGINNER

DANNY ROTH

CollinsWillow
An Imprint of HarperCollins*Publishers*

First published in 1992 by
Collins Willow
an imprint of HarperCollins*Publishers*, London

© Danny Roth, 1992

**A CIP catalogue record for this book
is available from the British Library**

ISBN 0 00 218437 0

Set in Palatino by Wearset, Boldon, Tyne and Wear
Printed and bound in Great Britain
by Cox & Wyman Ltd

Contents

Introduction

'I prefer to play bridge at the top level; it is easier!'

This profound statement was made by one of the world's best, and certainly the most famous, bridge players – the film star Omar Sharif. Indeed, it holds the key to the rationale behind the teaching method recommended in this book.

At least two other classic pronouncements are relevant:

'Life is like a sewer. What you get out of it depends on what you put into it.'

This was included by the American entertainer, Tom Lehrer, in the introduction to one his songs.

'The slowest method of driving is very often the fastest.'

This apparent paradox came from one of the world's leading racing drivers, Jackie Stewart. Who can argue with his success?

We shall see how these thoughts apply in our approach to learning what must surely be one of the world's most fascinating games. Contract bridge, the form played today, was started by the famous American yachtsman, Harold S. Vanderbilt (1884–1970) and three others on a cruise in the early years of this century. Since then, it has developed into a pastime enjoyed by millions, ranging from social players to more serious tournament participants. At any level, it enables you to meet countless people and make many friends.

There are already a large number of books for bridge beginners on the market, many written by far more famous, distinguished and established names than myself. So – why another one? Is there any more to be said on the subject?

Over the last few years, I have turned semi-professional and have been involved in a fair amount of teaching and coaching while regularly playing on the tournament scene. I am therefore in regular contact with players of all levels and have noticed that the root cause of most of their problems lies in the way they have been taught.

Let me immediately emphasize again a statement I made in one of my earlier books. No bad word should be said against any bridge teacher or school. Most of the people involved are kind and patient. Almost invariably, no praise is too high. However, they are confronted with a virtually insoluble problem. Most schools and evening courses offer ten or twelve lessons for beginners and some continue a further course for intermediate players. After that, the student, thinking that he or she 'can play', goes out into the world, satisfied that there is little more to learn apart from the 'clever stuff' which is not really needed except at top level – certainly quite unnecessary for the social game, which is all that most people want.

The truth of it is that these courses do little more than scratch the surface. Worse still, they try to cover all the important aspects of the game, and therefore proceed in leaps and bounds. Consequently, students are expected to understand lesson twelve when they know little of lessons two, three, and four. The result of all this is very disappointing. There are a large number of people, playing both socially and in clubs, who proudly tell me that they have been playing for decades, some even before I was born (in the post-war birth bulge) who, to this day, can neither bid nor play the simplest of hands.

This seems such a pity when, had they only been properly taught, they could have been experts by now. Of course, many of them argue that it doesn't matter two hoots how good they are: the important thing is to enjoy the game and the social atmosphere. Doesn't the Olympic principle insist on this point? 'The important thing is not to win; the important thing is to take part.'

Very creditable, but there are two important arguments on the other side. Firstly, even at a modest social level, you will find that, if you are a good player, you will be much more in demand. In organizing club evenings, my diplomacy has been severely tested by some extremely embarrassing situations when self-centred 'good' players have refused to play with 'lesser mortals', causing considerable ill-feeling all round. These 'good' types have, of course, conveniently forgotten the days when they were beginners and better players had to play with them! Secondly, we all play games, not only for the social contacts but also for personal satisfaction and self-esteem. If you are playing a contract, it is far more fun to make it than to go down unnecessarily, even without taking into account the appreciation or rebuke you will get from your partner!

The approach to learning most games seems to be: 'Let's start playing and we will learn as we go along.' More often than not, this is a very effective and enjoyable approach. In games like football, tennis, and even chess, the rules are fairly straightforward and there should be little problem. However, in bridge, experience shows that this is a recipe for failure. I wonder how many of my readers are in the building, estate agents or architectural trades? Even if you are not, let me ask you a question. What happens if you put up a building without foundations? The answer, of course, is that it cannot stand up – certainly not in the long term, anyway. But invariably, this is exactly what bridge schools and teachers do! They put the building up beautifully and in record time, but the foundations are hardly considered. The result is inevitable. The building collapses and little more than a shell of a bridge player is left. It is the purpose of this book to lay proper foundations. Then, and only then, can the game be learnt properly through practical experience.

In order to lay your foundations, three things need to be done:

1 Familiarize yourself with a pack of playing cards. If you think I am insulting you and that you are proficient in this respect, you may well be in for a little surprise!
2 Learn the language or 'jargon', laws and procedure of the game.

3 Know the scoresheet like the back of your hand.

Make no mistake about it – this is going to take time and a great deal of hard work. All I can say is: 'Do not begrudge it! What it will save you later on is beyond calculation.'

To lay your foundations, you will need the following materials:

A pack of fifty-two playing cards – jokers are not used in bridge.
A stop-watch.
Some large sheets of plain paper and a pen.

You should be sitting at a desk or table with plenty of room in front of you – at least a two-foot square – on which you will be displaying the cards. The pen and paper should be on the side of your writing hand and the stop-watch on the other side. Notice that you do not need three other players; we are nowhere near that stage yet. You are going to do all the work yourself in a quiet, relaxed atmosphere in your own time, without either bothering or being bothered by others.

You are now ready to start the three basics.

Familiarizing Yourself with a Pack of Cards

I suggested in the introduction that this was not as simple as it sounds. Time will tell!

A game of bridge involves four players seated at a square table. For convenience, they are described by the points of the compass. If you are South, your partner will sit opposite you as North and, playing as a pair, you will be competing against the other two, sitting East and West. Your table will look like this:

NORTH

WEST   EAST

SOUTH (you)

From now on, the table will be more concisely displayed like this:

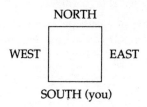

The pack of cards is based on the calendar. The year consists of four seasons, each represented by a *suit*. In decreasing order of seniority, they are:

Spades (♠),   Hearts (♡),   Diamonds (◇),   Clubs (♣).

There are thirteen lunar months, each represented by a card in each suit. Again, in decreasing order of seniority, they are:

Ace (A), king (K), queen (Q), jack (J), 10, 9, 8, 7, 6, 5, 4, 3, and 2.

There are games in which the ace is considered a low card. It is always high in bridge; the two is the lowest card and there is no number one. So there are fifty-two cards, each representing one week. If you play in upper-class circles, you may hear jacks referred to as 'knaves', threes as 'treys' and twos as 'deuces'.

The game starts by distributing thirteen cards, face downwards, to each player. Give the cards a good shuffle and cut and allocate the first card from the top of the pack to West, the second to North, the third to East and the fourth to yourself. Repeat this process clockwise for another twelve rounds to complete what is called the *deal*.

You now have in front of you four piles of thirteen cards each but at the moment, you cannot see the cards held by each player. For the first exercise, turn over the West, North and East hands but leave the South hand in front of you closed. For the three open hands, or *dummies* as we shall call them, sort the groups of thirteen cards into the four suits and set each suit out in order of seniority. I have just dealt out such a hand and my table looks like this:

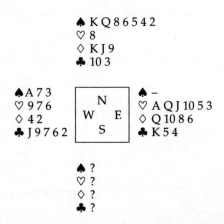

```
                    ♠ K Q 8 6 5 4 2
                    ♡ 8
                    ◇ K J 9
                    ♣ 10 3

    ♠ A 7 3              ┌─────────┐              ♠ –
    ♡ 9 7 6             │    N    │              ♡ A Q J 10 5 3
    ◇ 4 2               │ W     E │              ◇ Q 10 8 6
    ♣ J 9 7 6 2         │    S    │              ♣ K 5 4
                        └─────────┘

                    ♠ ?
                    ♡ ?
                    ◇ ?
                    ♣ ?
```

Now our aim is to read out the South hand (we shall call it the 'one closed hand exercise') without looking at the cards. Take each suit in turn and count the number of cards.

In spades, West has three, North seven and East none. There are thirteen in the pack and with ten on view, South must have three.
In hearts, West has three, North one and East six, totalling ten to leave South with three.
In diamonds, West has two, North three and East four, totalling nine to leave South with four.

Now hold it there! There is no need to go on to the clubs as we know the answer already! We have already agreed that the South hand has three spades, three hearts and four diamonds to total ten cards, and as it has thirteen cards in all, there must be three clubs. Let us now look at the clubs to check. West has five, North two and East three to total ten, leaving three for South as expected.

Having determined the suit distribution, we must look at the actual cards in more detail. In spades, working our way down from the top, we notice that the jack, ten and nine are missing so they must be with South. Similarly, in hearts, the missing cards are the king, four and two. In diamonds, they are the ace, seven, five and three and the clubs are ace, queen and eight.

One final confirmatory check needs to be made. Later on, we shall learn that we need a guide to assess how strong a hand is. The Milton point-count for the top four cards in each suit, referred to as *honours*, is generally accepted:

Ace: 4 points;　king: 3 points;　queen: 2 points;　jack: 1 point.

Let us look at our deal above:

West has the ace of spades (4) and the jack of clubs (1) to total 5 points.
North has the king and queen of spades (3+2) and the king and jack of diamonds (3+1) to total 9 points.
East has the ace, queen and jack of hearts (4+2+1), the queen of diamonds (2) and the king of clubs (3) to total 12 points.

Now, in the whole pack, there are four aces (16), four kings (12),

four queens (8) and four jacks (4) to total 40 points and
$5+9+12 = 26$ are on view. That leaves 14 for South. We confirm
that by looking at missing honours: the jack of spades (1), the
king of hearts (3), the ace of diamonds (4) and the ace and queen
of clubs $(4+2)$ to total 14 as required.

The South hand looks like this:

♠ J 10 9
♥ K 4 2
♦ A 7 5 3
♣ A Q 8

Let us review what we have done. We dealt out thirteen cards to
each player, exposed three of the four hands, set the open cards
out, sorted them into suits, lined each suit up in order of seniority
and then worked out the unseen hand by asking ourselves a
series of questions about the suits and high cards.

We are now going to repeat the process as a regular exercise
but this time introducing the pen, paper and stop-watch. I should
like you to proceed as follows:

1 Deal out four hands of thirteen cards each face down as
   above.
2 Open and sort the West, North and East hands out into suits
   and put the cards of each suit neatly in order as in the diagram
   above.
3 Start the stop-watch.
4 Write down for the closed hand:
   a the number of spades,
   b the number of hearts,
   c the number of diamonds,
   d the number of clubs *without looking at the clubs*.
   Mentally check that the number of clubs is right by looking at
   the clubs.
   e the actual spade cards,
   f the actual heart cards,
   g the actual diamond cards,
   h the actual club cards.
   Note particularly the presence of any honours in each case.

i the number of points in the West hand,
j the number of points in the North hand,
k the number of points in the East hand,
l the number of points in the South hand, i.e. 40 less the total of the other three.

Check that the number of points in the South hand ties up correctly with the missing honours you worked out in e, f, g and h above.

5 Stop the watch and look at the time.

6 Turn over the South hand and check that what you wrote down is correct.

Well, how did you get on? Before going any further, we are going to work on bringing the reading on your stop-watch down from what was probably several minutes to well under sixty seconds!

Why is this so important? The reason is that, at the bridge table, you will be doing little else! As will be explained in detail later, the game is divided into two distinct but closely related phases, bidding and play. During the bidding, you will be looking at your own thirteen cards only and trying to place the remaining thirty-nine. During the play, one other hand will be exposed and you will therefore be able to see a total of twenty-six cards. You will now try to place the other twenty-six – a much easier task but one in which a considerably higher degree of accuracy will be expected.

The first step towards these goals is to be able to look at thirty-nine cards and read out the other thirteen as we are doing here. It is going to be hard work and will need a lot of practice. I can only beg you not to begrudge the time! It will pay handsome dividends in the long run. If you are not prepared to make the effort, you will simply be jumping the gun and joining the vast majority of bridge players, including an alarming number of recognized 'experts', who spend decades effectively playing in the dark!

You will have already noticed that the number thirteen plays a considerable part in the calculations and our first job will be to analyse that number in some detail. With four suits and four players at the table, we need to be familiar with all the ways in which the number thirteen can be split up into four integral components, remembering that zero is allowed. Let us look at an example. I am going to put three numbers in front of you and ask you to give the fourth so that the total comes to thirteen:

4 4 3 ?

You would say 'Four plus four is eight, plus three makes eleven; take that away from thirteen, leaves two – kindergarten stuff!' All right, we shall see! Get your pen, paper and stop-watch ready. Sixty examples are given below. Start the stop-watch and write down the missing number to complete the total of thirteen in each example. When you have written down your sixty answers, stop the watch and go back to double-check that you have put down the correct answer for each one.

4 3 5 ?	2 4 6 ?	0 9 3 ?	5 5 1 ?
2 1 5 ?	1 1 8 ?	3 3 3 ?	3 2 1 ?
0 0 2 ?	6 4 3 ?	3 2 6 ?	6 6 0 ?
2 2 2 ?	5 4 2 ?	2 4 4 ?	7 5 0 ?
1 5 6 ?	9 0 0 ?	8 1 0 ?	1 4 4 ?
0 0 6 ?	2 1 7 ?	3 5 0 ?	6 1 1 ?
2 3 2 ?	2 4 5 ?	3 4 3 ?	2 3 4 ?
1 0 5 ?	0 4 5 ?	1 1 7 ?	4 4 4 ?
2 2 5 ?	3 0 6 ?	2 7 0 ?	1 1 1 ?
0 0 8 ?	8 2 1 ?	3 0 3 ?	2 4 1 ?
2 8 0 ?	2 9 0 ?	6 0 7 ?	2 4 3 ?
1 5 3 ?	1 5 5 ?	1 0 6 ?	4 2 2 ?
4 5 4 ?	2 6 2 ?	1 6 1 ?	2 7 4 ?
2 3 8 ?	1 0 8 ?	3 7 0 ?	4 7 0 ?
1 0 0 ?	2 0 0 ?	1 2 0 ?	0 0 0 ?

Hard work, isn't it! How long did that take? What we are aiming for is to bring your stop-watch time down to well below sixty seconds! The first step towards this is to write down all the possible combinations – there are, in fact, thirty-nine. Actually we shall list them twice: first, on the left, simply ranging from the most balanced to the most unbalanced; second, on the right, in order of frequency of appearance with the percentage probability to the nearest whole number in brackets (those without a bracket are below half a percent, though by no means impossible).

4 3 3 3	7 2 2 2	4 4 3 2 (22)	7 4 1 1
4 4 3 2	7 3 2 1	5 3 3 2 (16)	7 4 2 0
4 4 4 1	7 3 3 0	5 4 3 1 (13)	7 3 3 0
	7 4 1 1	5 4 2 2 (11)	7 5 1 0
5 3 3 2	7 4 2 0	4 3 3 3 (11)	7 6 0 0
5 4 2 2	7 5 1 0	6 3 2 2 (6)	8 2 2 1
5 4 3 1	7 6 0 0	6 4 2 1 (5)	8 3 1 1
5 4 4 0		6 3 3 1 (3)	8 3 2 0
5 5 2 1	8 2 2 1	5 5 2 1 (3)	8 4 1 0
5 5 3 0	8 3 1 1	4 4 4 1 (3)	8 5 0 0
6 3 2 2	8 3 2 0	7 3 2 1 (2)	9 2 1 1
	8 4 1 0	6 4 3 0 (1)	9 3 1 0
6 3 3 1	8 5 0 0	5 4 4 0 (1)	9 2 2 0
6 4 2 1		5 5 3 0 (1)	9 4 0 0
6 4 3 0	9 2 1 1	6 5 1 1 (1)	10 2 1 0
6 5 1 1	9 2 2 0	7 2 2 2 (1)	10 1 1 1
6 5 2 0	9 3 1 0		10 3 0 0
6 6 1 0	9 4 0 0		11 1 1 0
			11 2 0 0
	10 1 1 1		12 1 0 0
	10 2 1 0		13 0 0 0
	10 3 0 0		
	11 1 1 0		
	11 2 0 0		
	12 1 0 0		
	13 0 0 0		

I make no apology for writing it all out twice; there are two good reasons. First, it is important to note the difference in the order. The most balanced distributions are not necessarily the most frequent. This will be important later on in working out how to play a hand to give you the best chance of success. The second reason – and far more important – is that these combinations cannot be written out too often. Our next job will be to learn them backwards. You need not worry about the percentages for the moment; it is the combinations of four numbers that are vital.

How do we best go about it? There are basically two exercises to do. First, repeat the sixty-question exercise above with your stop-watch until the time comes down to two minutes at most; then get it down to one. Second, orientate the numbers you meet in everyday life towards totalling thirteen. Thus, if you get on a 236 bus, two should immediately come into your head.

Similarly, if you come across two or one digit numbers, think of all the combinations of two or three more to give you thirteen. Thus, if you get on a 72 bus, 2 2, 3 1, and 4 0 will immediately register. The six o'clock news will remind you of 3 2 2, 3 3 1, 4 2 1, 4 3 0, 5 1 1, 5 2 0, 6 1 0 and 7 0 0. Bridge is very much a game of numerical habits and the number thirteen is the base.

The next exercise concerns the adding up of honour points. Again, you should learn to do this without thinking. Let us list the possible combinations in a single suit.

We have already listed the point value of single honours as:

Ace 4,   king 3,   queen 2,   jack 1.

Thus A K is 7		A K Q	9
A Q	6	A K J	8
A J	5	A Q J	7
K Q	5	K Q J	6
K J	4		
Q J	3	A K Q J	10

If you pick up a suit with the king and queen in it, rather than saying: 'Well, the king is 3 and the queen 2, so that makes 5', you should be able to say '5' without having to think about it. This will contribute to bringing down your stop-watch time in the one closed hand exercise. It is also worthwhile being able to quickly add up points when, as very often happens, you pick up suits with only one honour in them.

Thus A A is 8		A A A	12	K K K	9	Q Q Q	6
K K	6	A A K	11	K K Q	8	Q Q J	5
Q Q	4	A A Q	10	K K J	7	Q J J	4
J J	2	A A J	9	K Q Q	7		
		A K K	10	K J J	5	J J J	3
		A Q Q	8				
		A J J	6				

and you can extend the table to four and more honours.

What I am proposing is that you put aside half-an-hour, or better still, an hour each day to do the one closed hand exercise until you are perfectly accurate in two minutes or less stop-watch time. If you can reduce your time further, so much the better! You are strongly advised not to proceed any further until you have achieved this landmark, as the whole study of the game depends on it.

Once you are familiar with your pack of cards, the tool of the trade, go on to the next section.

The Language and Procedure of the Game

This is a very big subject and could occupy a book in its own right. For the moment, however, we shall concentrate on absorbing enough to understand the scoresheet, which will be discussed in the next chapter.

Bridge is all about winning and losing *tricks*. So this is the first word to define. A trick consists of four cards, one contributed by each player. As each was dealt thirteen cards, there will obviously be thirteen tricks available during the course of play. All depends on how many of those tricks are won by North-South and how many by East-West.

Note two points in this respect. First, these two totals will always add up to thirteen and therefore the following combinations are possible:

13:0; 12:1; 11:2; 10:3; 9:4; 8:5 and 7:6.

Again, the ways in which two numbers can add to thirteen should be learnt backwards in the same way as the four-number combinations detailed in the last section. Thus, if I say '8', you say '5' without having to think about it.

Second, any trick won by either North or South is credited to the North-South total. For the purpose of scoring, it is that total which matters; how many are won specifically by North or South is irrelevant. The same applies to East-West. The contest is between the two pairs rather than individuals.

According to rules which will be explained later, one of the four players will place one of his cards (he may choose any in his hand) face upwards in the middle of the table. This is called the *lead*. The player on his immediate left makes his choice next but he must choose a card of the same suit if he is able to do so. This is called *following suit*. If he has more than one card in that suit, he may choose any one of those cards. The next player in clockwise rotation, i.e. the partner of the leader, plays the third card and finally the last player makes his choice, always following suit if possible.

Let us take an example – say West is on lead and leads the king of spades. North is next to play. He looks at his cards and if he has any spades, he must play one of them. If he has more than one spade, he may choose any of his spade cards. If he has no spade cards, he may play from any of the other three suits, the card contributed being described as a *discard*. Once the four cards have been played, the players look to see who has played the highest card *of the suit led*. (Discards, however high, cannot win tricks unless one of the other side suits has been given an overriding status, which we shall define in a moment). That player is deemed to have won the trick and it is credited to his side. He is then entitled to lead any card in his hand to start the next trick.

Before going any further, let us get the feel of playing tricks with a little practice exercise. Take your pack and pick out the thirteen spade cards, leaving the other thirty-nine on one side for the time being. Give those thirteen cards a good shuffle and dealing from the top, give one card to each player – something like this:

As you see, West has played the highest card, so he wins the trick for East-West. Remove the cards and as West must lead to the next trick, give him the next card followed by North, East and South as shown overleaf:

Here East has played the highest card and he wins the trick, again for East-West. Remove those cards and deal out four more, starting with East as he will be leading to the next trick. Perhaps something like this will come out:

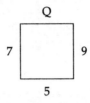

Here North has played the highest card and he wins the trick for North-South. East-West have won two tricks and North-South one.

Now do not look back in the text. Twelve cards have just been played. Can you tell which one was missing? This is an excellent exercise to test your memory and powers of concentration, both very necessary to play the game, even to a modest standard. Proceed as follows:

1 Take your thirteen spade cards and shuffle them well.
2 Start your stop-watch.
3 Place four cards face up as shown above.
4 Decide which player has won the trick and remove the cards, placing them in a neat pile face downwards by that 'player'.
5 Starting with the player who won that trick, place four more cards, face upwards, as above.
6 Repeat 4.
7 Repeat 5.
8 Decide how many tricks were won by each side. Note that it will be either 2:1 or 3:0 in favour of either East-West or North-South.

9 You still have one card face downwards in your hand. Decide
   which it is without looking at the other cards and then turn it
   over to see if you are right.

You should be able to complete this exercise in about fifteen
seconds and please do not underestimate its importance. Your
whole game depends on being able to appreciate which cards
will win tricks over others and to remember which cards have
gone and which remain outstanding. Do not be put off, feeling
that you are one of those who has 'a very poor memory'. It will
all come with practice, and that again is why you should be
prepared to give it some time before going anywhere near a
bridge table.

Assuming you are now competent with this exercise in one
suit only, we are now going to give the other cards a chance. I am
going to take the full pack and give it a good shuffle. Now I place
four cards on the table as above, assuming West, on my left, is the
leader:

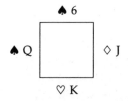

Now let us look. Spades were led and the highest card contributed *in that suit* was the queen, so West wins the trick. Note that,
although South had a higher ranked card, a king, he could not
win the trick as he was unable to follow suit. Now, if North had
been the leader, West would still have won the trick, having
contributed the highest card in the suit led, still spades. However,
had East been the leader, he would have won the trick, as nobody
else could follow to his diamond. Had South been the leader,
then he would have won the trick as nobody would have been
able to follow to his heart lead. West, having won the trick, is still
on lead.

Let us try four more cards as shown overleaf:

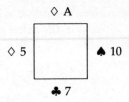

This time North wins the trick, having contributed the highest card in the suit led, diamonds. Had he been the leader, he obviously would still have won the trick as his diamond is higher than West's. But had East led, he would have won, nobody being able to follow to his spade; and had South been the leader, then he would have won, nobody being able to follow to his club.

Let us try four more cards, bearing in mind that North is now the leader.

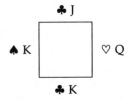

Now you will see that South wins the trick. He would also have won had he been the leader. However, if East had led, he would have won as nobody could have followed to his heart; had West led, he would have won as nobody could follow to his spade.

Now for the next exercise to be timed, I should like you to repeat this procedure throughout the whole pack:

1 Give the cards a good shuffle and start the stop-watch.
2 Assume that West is the leader and put four cards on the table face upwards as above. Decide who wins the trick but note who would have won the trick had
 a North, b East, c South been on lead.
3 Having decided who won the trick with West leading, remove the four cards and give four new ones as above, starting with the winner of the previous trick and working clockwise round the table.
4 Decide who wins this trick but also note who would have won

it had any of the others been on lead. Note that, if you deal four cards of the same suit, the same player will win, irrespective of who is the leader. At the other extreme, if each player gets a card of a different suit, the leader will always win, irrespective of the rank of the cards.

5 Continue this exercise for thirteen rounds and stop the watch. You should be able to do this exercise in well under two minutes and you are strongly advised not to proceed further until you have reached that standard. If you do, you will simply be trying to run before you can walk because we are now going to introduce an important complication.

Earlier, I briefly mentioned that, if a player was unable to follow the suit led, he is not entitled to the trick unless another suit has been given an overriding status. The word *trump* is a corruption of 'triumph' and a trump card takes precedence over all other cards.

Up to now, we have assumed that all suits are of the same status; in other words, there are no trumps. The laws allow, however, that one suit, any of the four, may be designated trumps. The rules regarding winning tricks now alter. As before, the player on lead may select any card in his hand. The others, again as before, must follow suit if they can. However, if any player cannot do so, he is entitled (though not obliged), to play a trump, i.e. a card from the trump suit if he has one and in that event, he wins the trick irrespective of the size of his trump card and irrespective of the size of the cards in the suit originally led. The only way a trump card can be beaten is by a higher card of the trump suit. Thus the ace of trumps will win the trick to which it is played in all circumstances.

This is all best illustrated with a few examples. Let us make spades the trump suit and assume West is on lead.

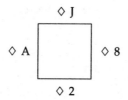

Here, everybody has followed suit and no-trump rules apply. West wins the trick and would indeed have done so irrespective of who was on lead. But now suppose South does not have a diamond in his hand. He is then entitled to play any other card. We may then have:

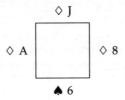

Now South wins the trick and would have done so irrespective of who was on lead. Let us go further and assume that neither East nor South had any diamonds. To be realistic, we shall exchange the positions of the ace and jack of diamonds as it is unlikely, though not impossible, that East will want to trump his partner's high card. We might then have:

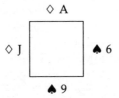

When West leads the jack, North beats it with the ace but East goes higher still by putting on a trump or *ruffing* with the six of trumps. South, however, goes one better by *overruffing* with a higher trump, the nine. Again, South would have won this trick irrespective of who was on lead. Finally, assume that West is the only one with diamonds in his hand. We might have a situation where all three of the other players are ruffing:

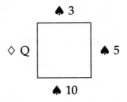

Again South, with the highest trump card on the table, wins the trick and would have done so irrespective of who was currently on lead.

We are now going to repeat the previous exercise, but consider not only who is on lead but the possibilities of any one of the four suits being trumps or there being no-trumps. Thus for any combination of four cards, there will be no fewer than twenty answers.

It is going to be a lot of work but again, please do not be tempted to skip it. Take a large sheet of paper and set out a rectangular table like this:

Player on lead:	West	North	East	South
Trumps				
None				
Spades				
Hearts				
Diamonds				
Clubs				

Now for any combination of four cards, you will put a letter (W, N, E or S) according to which player wins the trick in the conditions specified by the row and column. Remember, even if a suit is specified as trumps, if no cards from that suit appear, no-trump rules will apply.

Let us recall one of the examples we have just looked at:

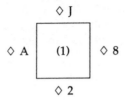

In this example, West wins irrespective of the conditions so that our table will look as follows (see overleaf):

Player on lead:	West	North	East	South
Trumps				
None	W	W	W	W
Spades	W	W	W	W
Hearts	W	W	W	W
Diamonds	W	W	W	W
Clubs	W	W	W	W

Boredom in the extreme! But in the next example, where not all players are able to follow suit, things become more interesting:

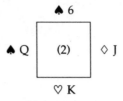

Now our table looks like this:

Player on lead:	West	North	East	South
Trumps				
None	W	W	E	S
Spades	W	W	W	W
Hearts	S	S	S	S
Diamonds	E	E	E	E
Clubs	W	W	E	S

Note again that the clubs row is identical to the no-trump row and that North can never win a trick in any circumstances.

Now see if you can fill up the table for the five examples which follow below and overleaf:

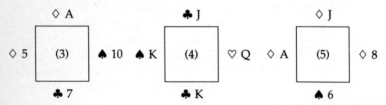

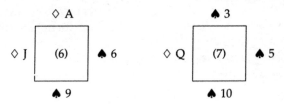

Check your answers are as follows:

(3)				(4)				(5)				(6)				(7)			
N	N	E	S	W	S	E	S	W	W	W	S	N	N	S	S	W	S	S	S
E	E	E	E	W	W	W	W	S	S	S	S	S	S	S	S	S	S	S	S
N	N	E	S	E	E	E	E	W	W	W	S	N	N	S	S	W	S	S	S
N	N	N	N	W	S	E	S	W	W	W	W	N	N	N	N	W	W	W	W
S	S	S	S	S	S	S	S	W	W	W	S	N	N	S	S	W	S	S	S

You should practise further by taking the pack of cards and dividing them up into thirteen groups of four. Start your stop-watch and, for each group, write down your twenty answers in tabular form as above. You should aim to reach the stage that you can produce the answers virtually without thinking. The whole exercise should take under three minutes. Again, the importance of this cannot be overemphasized as the whole game depends on it. Many readers will probably be fairly proficient anyway, having played such games as whist, knock-out whist and solo whist before and for them, it should be second nature.

Now that you have a full understanding of winning tricks, we can start to consider the format of the game. The four players should sit at the table with their chairs well back and cards held vertically and close to their chests so that they cannot be seen by anyone else. Before cards are played out to see how many of the thirteen tricks are won by each pair, a number of conditions have to be agreed between them:

1 Which suit, if any, will be trumps.
2 Which hand is to be exposed as the *dummy* hand. The above discussion gave the impression that all four players were in action at the same time. However, in practice, it is only three. The cards played from this hand will be decided not by the player originally holding those cards but by his partner. The partner is referred to as the *declarer* and the two opposing players as *defenders*.

The dummy hand is placed with cards face upwards on the table for all to see. The form is to arrange them in suits, with any trumps on the right of the dummy player and the highest cards in each suit nearest to him. Thus, if hearts are trumps, a dummy hand might be displayed like this:

Dummy player

♡ K	♠ J	◇ A	♣ Q
♡ 9	♠ 8	◇ 7	♣ 6
♡ 7		◇ 5	♣ 4
♡ 3		◇ 2	

3 How many tricks the pair selecting the trump suit or electing to play without trumps are promising to make.
4 Which player will lead the first card to the first trick when play commences.

Just as tennis is played best of three sets, bridge is played best of three *games*. In order to score points towards making up a game, a pair must fulfil a promise to the opposition that they are capable of making at least the majority of tricks in the *denomination* (no-trumps or a specified trump suit) of their choice. We have established that, in the course of play, thirteen tricks will be available and therefore to secure a majority, the pair will need at least seven of the tricks. Thus, for example, if North-South think they can make at least seven tricks with hearts as trumps and East-West agree to allow them to prove it, the hand will be played with hearts as trumps. Now one of three things can happen:

a North-South will make exactly seven tricks, in which case they will score according to the table in the next chapter.
b They will make more than seven tricks, i.e. they will make one or more *overtricks*, in which case they will receive that score with bonus points according to the number of overtricks.
c They will make fewer than seven tricks, in which case they will be required to pay their opponents a bonus or *penalty*, again in accordance with the table in the next chapter. The

greater the number of *undertricks*, the greater will be the penalty.

However, it is rare that a pair is allowed to play for seven tricks only. East-West may be able to say: 'Well, you may be able to make seven tricks with hearts as trumps, but we could make eight if diamonds were trumps.'

The procedure for deciding the four conditions above is known as the *auction* or *bidding* and we must now set out the manner in which this is conducted. The next word to define is *contract*. Whichever side promises to take the highest number of tricks is entitled to buy the contract. Thus, in the example above, if North-South want to play for seven tricks in hearts and East-West are happy to let them try, then North-South are said to buy a contract for seven tricks in hearts. However, if East-West say that they can make eight tricks if diamonds are trumps, and North-South are happy to let them try, then East-West are said to buy the contract for eight tricks in diamonds. The question then arises as to what would happen if North-South now think that they can make eight tricks in hearts.

We must now define the word *rank*. The denomination of highest rank is no-trumps. After that, as indicated earlier, come spades, hearts, diamonds and clubs. Spades and hearts are defined as *major* suits or *majors*, diamonds and clubs as *minor* suits or *minors*. In our example, hearts is of higher rank than diamonds and thus a contract of eight tricks in hearts takes precedence over one for eight tricks in diamonds. East-West would now have to promise nine tricks in diamonds if they are to buy the contract, but they could alternatively promise to make eight tricks in spades or no-trumps; eight tricks in clubs would not be high enough.

The auction continues until all four players are happy with final contract. We must now set out the exact procedure.

Before play commences, there are the following preliminaries:

1 The pack is spread out face downwards in front of all the four players and each player draws a card at random (it is customary to avoid any of the four at either end) and turns it face upwards. The two players with highest ranked cards

partner each other against the other two. (Suit ranks are taken into account if, for example, two or more players draw kings.)

2 The player with the highest card is the dealer for the first hand. Two packs of cards are normally used and the dealer may choose which will be used for the first deal and where he and his partner will sit.

3 The player on the dealer's left shuffles and hands the pack to the dealer, who hands it on to the player on his right.

4 The player on the dealer's right cuts, again avoiding the four cards at either end.

5 The dealer distributes thirteen cards, face downwards, to each player, one by one, starting with the player to his left and proceeding in clockwise rotation.

6 When all the cards have been dealt and not before, the players pick up their cards and look at them. The thirteen cards dealt to a player is referred to as a *hand*.

7 The dealer then starts the auction.

Saying: 'I think we can make seven tricks with hearts as trumps,' is a very long-winded way of talking and there is a specified language in which the auction is conducted. As you need to take the majority of tricks to make a contract, seven is the minimum, so the bidding is described in terms of tricks *in excess of six (the book)*.

So, if South is the dealer and thinks that he and his partner can make seven tricks with hearts as trumps, he simply says 'One heart'. This is known in bridge jargon as a *bid* or (in America) *call*. The bid then moves clockwise to West. If he thinks that East-West can make eight tricks with diamonds as trumps, he bids: 'Two diamonds'. Now the bid moves to North. If he thinks that North-South can make eight tricks with hearts as trumps, he bids 'Two hearts'. Then the bid moves to East. If East thinks that East-West can make nine tricks with diamonds as trumps, he bids 'Three diamonds'.

If, at any stage during the bidding, a player is happy with the contract last bid (be it by partner or opponent), he says so simply by saying 'No bid' or 'Pass' (more commonly used in America and the continent). The auction continues with the obvious rule that any bid must be higher than its predecessor, and closes when a bid is followed by three no-bids or passes, in other words when all four players are agreed on the final contract.

Once the auction has closed, the player who first named the denomination will *play* the contract as *declarer*. The player on the declarer's immediate left will be the leader and when he has selected his first card, the *opening lead*, he places it face upwards in the middle of the table. Then the declarer's partner, the dummy, exposes his hand as shown above. Play then continues as detailed earlier until the thirteen tricks have been completed.

Of course, South as dealer may not feel that his side is strong enough to make any contract and is not obliged to bid. If all four players feel the same way and also 'No bid', the hand is abandoned and there is a new shuffle, cut and deal. The deal passes clockwise to the next player and deals continue in that direction until a side has won the best of three games – the *rubber*.

Right from the start, you should get into the habit of making bids in a clear but deadpan voice, being careful to avoid undue quietness or emphasis. You will often be playing against elderly people who are a little hard of hearing, but at the same time, you must avoid giving your partner illegal information by distinctive intonation.

Now let us look at contracts in more detail. With thirteen tricks available, it is possible to make one, two, three, four, five, six or seven tricks in excess of six. We have already explained that there are five denominations, no-trumps and the four suits, and so there are thirty-five contracts in all. It will be helpful to list them in ascending order:

1♣	1♢	1♡	1♠	1NT
2♣	2♢	2♡	2♠	2NT
3♣	3♢	3♡	3♠	3NT
4♣	4♢	4♡	4♠	4NT
5♣	5♢	5♡	5♠	5NT
6♣	6♢	6♡	6♠	6NT
7♣	7♢	7♡	7♠	7NT

Thus the cheapest bid is one club, promising seven tricks with clubs as trumps. Then comes one diamond and so on until, most expensive, seven no-trumps, promising to take all thirteen tricks with no trumps. It would thus appear that there are thirty-five possible bids plus 'no-bid', the indication that, for the time being at least, a player does not wish to contest the auction any further. In fact, there are two other legal bids, *double* and *redouble*, but we shall discuss those in the next chapter.

Before proceeding further, I urge you to review these last two chapters and not to proceed until you are completely familiar with everything in them, being able to do the appropriate exercises in, at most, the times indicated. Everything that follows depends on it. Progress may seem slow, but much still needs to be done before you can start to learn how to play.

The Scoresheet

When it comes to scoring, I seem to be disturbingly at variance with common teaching methods. I have now lost count of the number of times I have heard bridge teachers, many of them qualified, starting off a lesson by telling their students 'not to worry about scoring for the time being.' Even when they do eventually teach it, it is done quickly in one lesson as though it was of minimal importance.

This attitude has resulted in several incidents in clubs and social evenings when players, many of whom have played for decades, come up to me and ask something like: 'I have just played three hearts doubled and went three down, vulnerable – what is the score?' I politely refrain from pointing out that it might have been a good idea if they hadn't bid quite so extravagantly and tell them the answer. I also, with unbelievable self-restraint, omit to mention that they should, of course, have known this before they started playing the game, never mind decades later!

I take the view that nothing is more important than a full knowledge and understanding of the scoresheet and to try to play without such a platform is similar to putting a brilliant footballer on to a pitch and insisting that he plays without knowing where the goal is! However fantastic his ball skills, speed and fitness may be, he will be of no use whatsoever.

Without full knowledge of the scoresheet, you cannot even begin to bid sensibly. This is surely the principal reason for the very poor standard of bidding in the world of social and club bridge; even at the top of the tree, at international level, nobody is anywhere near perfection. For that reason, we are going to spend a lot of time working on this subject and shall not proceed further until it has become second nature. In the last chapter, we set out the list of possible contracts in ascending order. Let us now reproduce it, but this time, there will be an important difference in the layout:

1♣	1♢	1♡	1♠	1NT
2♣	2♢	2♡	2♠	2NT
3♣	3♢	3♡	3♠	3NT
4♣	4♢	4♡	4♠	4NT
5♣	5♢	5♡	5♠	5NT
6♣	6♢	6♡	6♠	6NT
7♣	7♢	7♡	7♠	7NT

Three dividing lines have now appeared, one 'staircase' and two 'horizontals' and we shall learn why they are there in a moment.

For every trick you *bid and make* in excess of six, you score as follows:

Minors (clubs and diamonds)	20
Majors (hearts and spades)	30
No-trumps	{ 40 for the first { 30 for each subsequent

So let us practise using these scores for the thirty-five contracts above:

1♣ or 1♢	20	1♡ or 1♠	30	1NT	40
2♣ or 2♢	40	2♡ or 2♠	60	2NT	70
3♣ or 3♢	60	3♡ or 3♠	90	3NT	100
4♣ or 4♢	80	4♡ or 4♠	120	4NT	130
5♣ or 5♢	100	5♡ or 5♠	150	5NT	160
6♣ or 6♢	120	6♡ or 6♠	180	6NT	190
7♣ or 7♢	140	7♡ or 7♠	210	7NT	220

Yet again, these should all be at your fingertips. So, if I say 'Four hearts?', you reply: '120' without having to think about it. It should not be necessary to think to yourself 'Well, hearts is a major suit and that means thirty each and four times thirty is ... 120.' The whole exercise involves no more than registering 20 or 30 in your head as soon as you hear the suit and multiplying by the number I give you; no more is involved than the two-, three- and ten-times tables!

With no-trumps, simply treat it as a major and add ten at the end. Thus 6NT scores $6 \times 30 + 10 = 190$.

This will be a convenient point to set out the scoresheet, which looks like this:

We	They

You notice that there are two columns, for our side and the opposition, and that there is also a horizontal line across the middle. Any score for a contract bid and made is placed *under* that line.

So if we bid and make two hearts exactly on the first hand, the scoresheet would look like this:

We	They
60	

Now suppose that, on the next hand, our opponents (they) play one spade and make it with two overtricks (i.e. nine tricks in all). They get the score for their contract plus a bonus of twice the trick value for spades, i.e. $2 \times 30 = 60$. Bonuses are scored over the line so the scoresheet now looks as follows (see overleaf):

We	They
	60
60	30

Overtricks in a minor-suit contract are worth 20 points each and those in the majors or no-trumps 30 points each. Can you therefore fill in the scoresheet if, on the next hand, they play one diamond and make it with three overtricks? It would now look like this:

We	They
	60
	60
60	30
	20

One diamond is 20 below the line; the three overtricks are $3 \times 20 = 60$ above the line. To win a game, you need to score one hundred or more points *below* the line. So let us play on. Suppose on the next hand, we play one no-trump and make it with an overtrick. Our total below the line is now a hundred and we have won the first game. The score is entered and a new horizontal line is drawn like this:

We	They
	60
30	60
60	30
40	20

The new entries were 40 below the line for 1NT and 30 above the line for the overtrick. The 50 points (30 + 20) the opponents had totalled below the line are now said to be *frozen* (i.e. will be treated as bonus) and they must start again accumulating points below the new line to make a game.

At this point, we are going to define a new word. In an early paragraph of this chapter, I mentioned the word *vulnerable*, which means 'open to danger or wounding'. In bridge, a pair is said to be vulnerable if it has won one of the games needed to make the rubber. A side which is still trying to win its first game is said to be non-vulnerable. We shall see why the word vulnerable is used in a moment.

A rubber is best of three games, so it can, at any given moment, be at any one of four stages:

1 Neither side has won a game: Love all
2 North-South only have won a game: North-South vulnerable
3 East-West only have won a game: East-West vulnerable
4 Both sides have won a game: Game all

For a number of reasons, it is important to note carefully the stage that you have reached. Up to now, all the contracts bid in our sample rubber have at least been made, but it was indicated earlier that if you buy a contract and fail to make it, you will have to pay the opposition a penalty, which is scored *over* the line in their column.

The scoring in this respect, being applicable irrespective of the contract size and denomination, is as follows:

For each undertrick: 50 points (non-vulnerable)
100 points (vulnerable)

So let us assume that, on the next hand, the opponents bid four hearts but only make seven tricks. What is the penalty? We see that they have not yet won a game and are therefore non-vulnerable. The penal rate is therefore 50 points per undertrick, and as they promised ten tricks and made only seven, the penalty is $3 \times 50 = 150$. Our scoresheet now looks as follows (see overleaf):

We	They
150	60
30	60
60	30
40	20

Now assume that, on the next hand, we buy a contract of three
no-trumps but only make seven tricks. We see that, as we have
won a game, we are vulnerable and therefore the heavier penal
rate of 100 points per undertrick applies (that is why the word
vulnerable is used!). Having promised nine tricks and only made
seven, the penalty is $2 \times 100 = 200$ points. The scoresheet has
progressed to this:

We	They
	200
150	60
30	60
60	30
40	20

The time has now come to explain the inclusion of the lines in the
bidding table at the beginning of the chapter. First of all, look at
the top, staircase-type line. Notice anything special about it? All
bids above that line score less than 100 points; all bids below it
score 100 or more. Thus the bids above it do not score sufficiently
for a game in one go and are said to be *part-scores*. In our rubber,
we have had four of these already. On our side, they add up to
100; but on theirs, they only add up to 50; that is why we have a
game and they have not. All bids below the staircase are direct
game bids.

The first horizontal line rules off bids at the six-level – those involving taking twelve tricks, all the tricks bar one. If a side *bids and makes* such a contract, it is said to have won a *small slam*. Not only do they win a game under the line by virtue of having scored over a hundred, but there is an extra bonus to be scored over the line: 500 if they are non-vulnerable; 750 if vulnerable.

The second horizontal line rules off bids at the seven-level. Here a side buys the contract to take all thirteen tricks and in that case, they are said to have won a *grand slam*. Again, they win a game under the line and an even bigger bonus: 1000 non-vulnerable; 1500 vulnerable.

Before continuing our rubber, we must also explain the two outstanding bids mentioned in the last chapter – the double and the redouble.

If a pair bids a contract and one of the opponents thinks that the contract will not be made, he may, when it is his turn to bid, *double* the contract. His bid is simply one word: 'Double'. What this means is as follows:

1 If the contract is made, it is treated as twice the bid. So making one diamond doubled scores as making two diamonds, two no-trumps doubled scores as four no-trumps, and so on. Note especially that, if you double any of the following part-score contracts: 2♡, 2♠, 2NT, 3♣, 3◊, 3♡, 3♠, 4♣ or 4◊, your opponents will have won a game. However, if you double a three-level or higher contract, the opponents do *not* receive the bonus for a slam. Slams must be bid to earn their bonus.

2 Furthermore, if the contract is made, you have to pay your opponents an additional 50 points as compensation for 'insulting' them.

3 In addition, if they make a doubled contract with overtricks, each overtrick, instead of scoring its trick value, scores 100 points if the pair playing the hand are non-vulnerable, or 200 points if they are vulnerable.

This does not sound very attractive so far but now comes the other side of the coin:

4 If the contract is not made, the penalties increase substantially.

Note that I carefully avoid using the word 'double' here because, in this respect, the bid is something of a misnomer, being only applicable if the contract fails by exactly one trick. The scoring is as follows:

Number of undertricks	Non-vulnerable	Vulnerable
1	100	200
2	300	500
3	500	800
4	700	1100
5	900	1400
6	1100	1700
7	1300	2000
8	1500	2300

and so on increasing by 200 (non-vulnerable) or 300 (vulnerable) each time. There is no need to memorize this table. All you need do is to remember that, if a doubled contract fails, the penalty is expressed in hundreds, calculated as follows:

Non-vulnerable: multiply the number of undertricks by two and subtract one
Vulnerable: multiply the number of undertricks by three and subtract one

So three down doubled, non-vulnerable, scores $(3 \times 2 - 1) \times 100 = 500$. Five down doubled, vulnerable, scores $(5 \times 3 - 1) \times 100 = 1400$, as shown above.

If you compare the difference between the penalties applying if a contract is not doubled and those if it is doubled, you can see that, particularly for heavy defeats, a double can be worth a great deal. Note that it is the vulnerability of the pair that fails to make its contract that is relevant. The vulnerability of the side that doubles does not affect the score. If that isn't exciting enough, the pair buying the contract may have the last word. If, despite being doubled, one of them feels confident that their contract *will* be made, he has the option to double up again by saying 'Redouble' when it is his turn to bid. This implies the following:

1 If the contract is made, it is treated as four times the original bid. So if any of the following part-score contracts – 1♡, 1♠, 1NT, 2♣ or 2◇ – are redoubled and made, they become games. If they had only been doubled, they would still have been part-scores, albeit bigger ones.

2 Furthermore, the 50-point bonus for the 'insult' still applies.

3 If the contract is made with overtricks, each of them scores double what it would have scored had the contract only been doubled, i.e. 200 (non-vulnerable), 400 (vulnerable).

4 If the contract is defeated, the penalties are exactly double those in the table above.

In a good standard of bridge, redoubled contracts are very rare. Experts are reluctant to double unless they are fairly confident of considerable gain and in that event, a redouble is unlikely. However, the greedy persistent doubler should be wary of overdoing it.

We are now going to continue our rubber, putting into practice what we have just learnt. On the next hand, our opponents play four spades doubled and make only eight tricks. They are non-vulnerable and so the penalty for the two undertricks is $(2 \times 2 - 1) \times 100 = 300$. This brings our scoresheet to:

We	They
300	200
150	60
30	60
60	30
40	20

On the next hand, our opponents bid six no-trumps. We do not think they can make it and double. They disagree and redouble. They are right and take all thirteen tricks. They score $190 \times 4 = 760$ below the line for 6NT redoubled. Above the line they score 500 for the small slam bonus, 200 for the non-vulnerable redoubled overtrick, plus 50 for the insult, to total 750. Note that they only get the bonus for the small slam which they *bid* rather than the grand slam which they *made*. This moves the position to game-all and the scoresheet now looks like this:

We	They
	750
300	200
150	60
30	60
60	30
40	20
	760

Flushed with the success of the last hand, our opponents bid another small slam, this time six diamonds, on the next. Again we double, confident that they will not come near to making it. This time we are right and they can only take eight tricks – four down. They are vulnerable now and so the penalty is $(4 \times 3 - 1) \times 100 = 1100$. The scoresheet now becomes:

We	They
1100	750
300	200
150	60
30	60
60	30
40	20
	760

On the next hand, we play in one diamond redoubled and manage to make ten tricks, i.e. three overtricks. We score below the line $20 \times 4 = 80$ (still not game) plus, above the line, 50 for the insult and 400 for each of the three redoubled overtricks vulnerable, 1250 in all.

The scoresheet now looks like this:

We	They
1250	
1100	750
300	200
150	60
30	60
60	30
40	20
	760
80	

We now only need any part-score to complete the rubber. But the cards favour the opponents and on the next hand, they bid seven no-trumps and turn up with every high card in the pack. We cannot stop them winning all thirteen tricks. They therefore score 220 below the line and also 1500 above it for the vulnerable grand slam bonus.

In addition, there is a bonus for winning the rubber. If a pair wins it in two straight games without their opponents winning one, they score 700. In this case, where the opponents have won one game, they must be content with 500.

We have lost the rubber and the final scoresheet reads as follows (see overleaf):

We	They
	500
1250	1500
1100	750
300	200
150	60
30	60
60	30
40	20
	760
80	220
The totals are: 3010	4100

Our opponents win by 1090. It is usual to express this to the nearest 100 (50 being rounded down), so this would be an eleven hundred rubber lost. Where bridge is played for money, the stake is always expressed as so much per hundred. So, if you were playing for 50p per hundred, this rubber would cost £5.50.

Although the imaginary rubber we have just played has covered most of the important matters in respect of scoring, there are a few odds and ends to be cleared up.

First, it may not be possible to complete a rubber in time. In this case, the following credits apply:

1 If one side only has won a game, it scores 300 points. The rationale behind this is that the side that has won a game already would be more likely to win the 500 or 700 bonus for the rubber. That side is therefore awarded some compensation.

2 If one side only has a part-score (irrespective of the award or lack of it in 1, and that part-score has not been frozen, it scores a bonus of 50 points. This is a modest compensation for their greater likelihood of winning the current game. Thus, if our rubber had been abandoned before that last grand slam hand,

we would have scored 50 points in respect of the 80 we had under the line. The size of the part-score is irrelevant and if both sides have part-scores, no 50 point bonus is awarded to either, not even if those part-scores are markedly different.

Second, there is a credit for honour holdings. This is a left-over from the rules of auction bridge, the predecessor of the current game in which honour scoring played a significant part, and it is likely to be removed from the laws before very long. Nevertheless, as things stand currently, if one player (rather than the partnership combined) holds any four of the five top trump cards (ace, king, queen, jack, ten), he may announce it when play has been completed (not before!) and claim 100 points, scored *over* the line. If he holds all five, he may claim 150 points. This applies whether he is declarer, dummy or defender. If there are no trumps, a player holding all four aces may claim 150 points.

That completes the scoring but before moving on, you must be sure that you have at least the important scores at your finger tips. The first point to emphasize is that contracts fall into four categories – part scores, games, small slams and grand slams – and the distinction between the part-score and the game is the most important. In order to bid game you must reach at least:

Three-level (nine tricks) in no-trumps;
Four-level (ten tricks) in a major;
Five-level (eleven tricks) in a minor.

In practice, well over half the games bid and made are in four of a major, and most of the rest in three no-trumps. Five of a minor is relatively rare (probably under 5 per cent of all games) and we shall learn later when studying bidding that, when partnerships are strong in the minor suits, they will usually investigate the possibility of playing in three no-trumps in preference to five of a minor.

Grand slams are rare and it has been said that 'If you never bid a grand slam, you will not miss very much.' As we shall learn in the next chapter when we discuss the scoresheet in more detail, there is certainly a degree of truth in this. Small slams are, however, fairly common and bidding them will be a section for special study. For the moment, however, I should like you to do some exercises against the stop-watch to cement your knowledge of the more important aspects of scoring.

Take a large sheet of paper and divide it into five columns and as many rows as you can fit in:

Contract	Tricks taken	Result	Calculations	Scoresheet
				___
				___
				___
				___
				___

Take enough sheets of paper so that you can do 50 examples in all. The horizontal lines under the scoresheet columns enable you to fill in the results in the realistic manner. For each problem, I shall give you the following information:

1 The bid contract, e.g. 1♠, 3NT, 6♢.
2 Whether it is undoubled, doubled, or redoubled. If it is undoubled, I shall say nothing; if doubled, I shall put the letter x; if redoubled, I shall put in xx.
3 The vulnerability, where relevant: if not vulnerable, I will say nothing; if vulnerable, I shall add (V).
4 The number of tricks taken.

You will fill in the other three columns:

1 The result is the difference between the bid contract and the tricks taken. So if I say '2♡, making eight tricks', the contract will have been made exactly and your entry in the result column will be '='. Were I to say '4♠, making eleven tricks' the contract will have been made with one overtrick and your

entry will be '+1'. Were I to say '6♣ (V), making nine tricks', the contract would have failed by three undertricks and your entry in the result column will be '-3'.

2 The calculations to work out the scores going over and under the line.
3 The entry or entries on the scoresheet in their appropriate place.

So for the three examples given in 1, your sheet would look like this:

Contract	Tricks taken	Result	Calculations	Scoresheet
2♡	8	=	2 × 30	
				60
4♠	11	+1	4 × 30 + 30	30
				120
6♣ (V)	9	−3	3 × 100	300

Now start your stop-watch and fill in the answers for the following:

(1) 1♡ 7   (2) 2♢ 8   (3) 6NT 12
(4) 3♡ 8   (5) 5♣ 12   (6) 1♣ 9
(7) 5♠ 13   (8) 3♢ 4   (9) 2♣ 10
(10) 4♢ (V) 9   (11) 3♣ 11   (12) 1♢ 11
(13) 3NTx 6   (14) 6♣ 12   (15) 4NT 11
(16) 5♢x 8   (17) 1♡x(V) 4   (18) 1NTxx(V) 4
(19) 6♣xx 9   (20) 4♠x(V) 11   (21) 2♢ (V) 5
(22) 5NT 11   (23) 7♠ 13   (24) 1NT 7
(25) 4♡x 8   (26) 4♠x(V) 12   (27) 7♠(V) 13
(28) 6NT(V) 13   (29) 6♢x 11   (30) 7NT(V) 13
(31) 6♣(V) 12   (32) 6♠(V) 13   (33) 6♡(V) 12
(34) 5♣xx 10   (35) 3NTxx 7   (36) 1♠xx(V) 8
(37) 7♠x 7

On each of the following, the contract was the first of the rubber, after which there was a telephone call and one of the players had to leave. How do you score it now, and what is the payout at a stake of 20p per 100?

(38) 2♡ 8   (39) 4♣ 8   (40) 2♣x 9
(41) 6◇ 12   (42) 1♣xx 11   (43) 4♡ 12
(44) 2♠ 10   (45) 5◇ 13   (46) 2◇xx 12
(47) 1NT 10   (48) 7♣x 13   (49) 6♠xx 13
(50) 3♣ 6

Hard work, isn't it? Well, how long did it take? You should be aiming for an average of about ten seconds per example, so that the whole exercise should have taken you little more than eight minutes. In the next chapter, we shall be going through each in detail.

Calculating the Score

This chapter sets out the calculations for the 50 problems in the previous chapter. We will also consider how such results could emerge in practice, discuss the factor of probability, and introduce three new words, *par*, *sacrifice* and *phantom*. When setting out the calculations, any score under the line will be calculated first. The first two problems were part-score hands, bid and made exactly:

	Contract	Trick taken	Result	Calculations	Scoresheet
(1)	1♡	7	=	30	
					30
(2)	2◇	8	=	2 × 20	
					40

Now a non-vulnerable slam, also made exactly, where the appropriate bonus must be added over the line:

(3)	6NT	12	=	6 × 30 + 10 + 500	500
					190

Now a one-trick defeat, undoubled, non-vulnerable; remember the same penalty applies irrespective of the contract. Penalties are always scored over the line.

(4)	3♡	8	−1	50	50

Now a game contract made with an overtrick; overtricks are scored over the line. Note there is no slam bonus as the slam was not bid.

(5)	5♣	12	+1	$5 \times 20 + 20$	20
					100

Now a part-score made with overtricks:

(6)	1♣	9	+2	$20 + 2 \times 20$	40
					20

Notice that undoubled overtricks are of minimal value and are very often presented to declarers by defenders taking desperate measures to defeat a contract in preference to allowing it to make exactly. In this example, if the contract is defeated, the defenders gain 50 and save themselves the part-score 20 – a total gain of 70 in all, and that does not take into account the value of the part-score as a contribution to game. The couple of overtricks only cost 40 so the odds are at least 2:1 in favour of the desperate measures.

A game contract made with overtricks:

(7)	5♠	13	+2	$5 \times 30 + 2 \times 30$	60
					150

This would seem unlikely to occur in practice because the side could have won the game by stopping in 4♠. There is nothing to be gained by playing in 5♠ as 4♠ made with an overtrick is worth exactly the same as 5♠ made exactly. However, pairs very often go beyond game to investigate a slam and if they find it is not on, (if they have two aces missing) they can still have their game by stopping at the five-level.

(8)	3♦	4	−5	5×50	250

Notice that the defenders have lost no less than $(5 \times 2 - 1) \times 100 - 250 = 650$ by failing to double. However, this result is extremely unlikely to occur in practice and only happens when there has been a bidding misunderstanding. A double might put the pair back on the right track!

(9)	2♣	10	+2	$2 \times 20 + 2 \times 20$	40
					40

Now a part-score defeated vulnerable with the heavier penal rate applying:

(10)	4♢ (V)	9	−1	100	100

(11)	3♣	11	+2	$3 \times 20 + 2 \times 20$	40
					60

Here enough tricks for game were made but you only get the credit under the line for the part-score that was bid. The overtricks are scored above. You will still have to bid and make at least 1NT (40) to complete this game.

(12)	1♢	11	+4	$20 + 4 \times 20$	80
					20

This is very unlikely to happen but does occasionally. Normally one side or other will bid further.

(13)	3NTx	6	−3	$(3 \times 2 - 1) \times 100$	500

The doubled, non-vulnerable penalty is expressed in hundreds, multiplying the number of undertricks by 2 and subtracting one and scored over the line.

(14)	6♣	12	=	$6 \times 20 + 500$	500
					120

(15)	4NT	11	+1	$4 \times 30 + 10 + 30$	30
					130

This is an unusual contract as 3NT would have been sufficient for game. It does occur, however, when pairs investigate a possible slam in no-trumps and find they are short on high-card points.

(16)	5♡x	8	−3	$(3 \times 2 - 1) \times 100$	500

This seems ludicrous as 4♡ would have been enough for game and clearly there was no question of a slam, and yet scores like this occur quite frequently. It could be that the deal contains many very long and/or very short suits and that the opponents, perhaps already vulnerable, are capable of making a game in another suit, 4♠ or 5 of a minor. In that case, you would lose 120 or 100 plus 700 for the rubber, 820 or 800 in all. It is far better to lose 500 in the actual contract, this being described as the *par* result on the hand (the best available to either side). The 5♡ contract is referred to as a *sacrifice*. In other words, 500 points are sacrificed to prevent opponents from scoring a lot more. However, before going in for a sacrifice, you must be reasonably confident that the opponents will make their contract. If they are incapable of fulfilling it, you will have merely given them a large penalty instead of collecting a small one. The sacrifice is then referred to as a *phantom*.

(17)	1♡x(V)	4	−3	$(3 \times 3 - 1) \times 100$	800

The doubled vulnerable penalty is calculated in hundreds, multiplying the undertricks by three and subtracting one.

(18)	1NTxx(V)	4	−3	$(3 \times 3 - 1) \times 100 \times 2$	1600

The calculation is similar to (17) but the redouble doubles the final answer. This is unlikely to occur in practice, although the redouble stands to gain a great deal (80 + the value of the rubber) if the contract is made, as it is now a game and any overtricks are now worth 400 rather than 200. Against this has to be balanced the extra penalty if the contract fails. A result like this will only materialize if one of the defenders (almost invariably the doubler) turns up with a very long suit.

| (19) | 6♣xx | 9 | −3 | $(3 \times 2 - 1) \times 100 \times 2$ | 1000 |

Doubles of slams are rare and this is most unlikely to happen in practice. A slam will only be bid if the bidder is reasonably certain of making it, so heavy defeats are unlikely. We will learn later that such doubles are primarily used by the partner of the leader, to help him or her find the correct opening lead and increase the chance of defeating the contract.

| (20) | 4♠x(V) | 11 | +1 | $(4 \times 30) \times 2 + 50 + 200$ | 250 |
| | | | | | 240 |

In addition to the value of the doubled contract, there is 50 for the insult and 200 for the vulnerable doubled overtrick. There would also be 700 or 500 for the rubber, dependent on the vulnerability of the opponents.

| (21) | 2♦(V) | 5 | −3 | 3×100 | 300 |

Note that, with the heavier penal rate for vulnerable defeats applying, the defenders have lost 500 by failing to double. A double would have carried little risk as the contract, even if made, is still not game.

| (22) | 5NT | 11 | = | $5 \times 30 + 10$ | |
| | | | | | 160 |

One of the rarer contracts, affectionately known in expert circles as the 'hippopotamus'. It is usually reached by pairs searching for a minor-suit slam who realize, just in time, that they are two aces short.

| (23) | 7♠ | 13 | = | $7 \times 30 + 1000$ | 1000 |
| | | | | | 210 |

| (24) | 1NT | 7 | = | 40 | |
| | | | | | 40 |

Note the first no-trump scores higher than all the others.

(25)	$4\heartsuit x$	8	-2	$(2 \times 2 - 1) \times 100$	300

This kind of result often occurs when pairs push too hard for game and find the defenders' cards badly placed for them. This will be a convenient point to consider the odds in favour of bidding a game. Much depends on the state of the rubber, but it will be sufficiently accurate to give a game the value of 300 (non-vulnerable) or 500 (vulnerable) and assess the near-game part-score as worth its break-up value of 50. Then, if we are considering whether to stop in three of a major or to bid the game, we need a chance of about 43 per cent or better (non-vulnerable), 35 per cent or better (vulnerable). However, there is considerable debate on the true value of a part-score, particularly a high one (say 70 or more) and some experts assess it as high as 200. The chances needed now alter markedly to well over 75 per cent (non-vulnerable) and 56 per cent (vulnerable). In addition, this discussion does not take into account possible doubles and redoubles. Considering that opponents are unlikely to double unless they are fairly confident of at least a two-trick defeat, the odds needed to bid the game should be increased by about 5–10 per cent in all cases.

(26)	$4\spadesuit x(V)$	12	$+2$	$4 \times 30 \times 2 + 50$ $+ 2 \times 200$	450
					240

This is a rare result but it is better for the defenders than it would have been had the slam been bid! Rubber bonus to be added.

(27)	$7\spadesuit(V)$	13	$=$	$7 \times 30 + 1500$	1500
					210

Rubber bonus to be added.

(28)	6NT(V)	13	$+1$	$(6 \times 30 + 10) + 30 + 750$	780
					190

Rubber bonus to be added.

(29)	6♢x	11	−1	100	100

(30)	7NT(V)	13	=	$7 \times 30 + 10 + 1500$	1500
					220

Rubber bonus to be added.

(31)	6♣(V)	12	=	$6 \times 20 + 750$	750
					120

Rubber bonus to be added.

(32)	6♠(V)	13	+1	$6 \times 30 + 30 + 750$	780
					180

Rubber bonus to be added.

(33)	6♡(V)	12	=	$6 \times 30 + 750$	750
					180

Rubber bonus to be added.

(34)	5♣xx	10	−1	100×2	200

(35)	3NTxx	7	−2	$(2 \times 2 - 1) \times 100 \times 2$	600

(36)	1♠xx(V)	8	+1	$30 \times 4 + 50 + 400$	450
					120

Successful redoubled contracts at low levels are very rare. Rubber bonus to be added.

(37)	7♠x	7	−6	$(6 \times 2 - 1) \times 100$	1100

Another sacrifice, with 1100 worth conceding against a grand slam at either vulnerability.

For the remaining problems, we have to add in the 300 bonus for a game or 50 bonus for a part-score, as appropriate. We then round off to the nearest 100 (50 rounded down) to calculate the payout at 20p per hundred:

(38)	2♡	8	=	$2 \times 30 + 50$	50
					60

50 is added for the part-score to total 110 in all, rounded to 100 for a payout of £0.20.

(39)	4♣	8	−2	2×50	100

Total 100 for a payout of £0.20.

(40)	2♣x	9	+1	$(2 \times 20) \times 2 + 50$ $+ 100 + 50$	200
					80

2♣x is still a part-score, so there is a 50 bonus in addition to 100 for the doubled overtrick (non-vulnerable) and 50 for the insult. The total is 280 rounded up to 300 for a payout of £0.60.

(41)	6◇	12	=	$6 \times 20 + 500 + 300$	800
					120

Here the bonuses are 500 for the non-vulnerable slam and 300 for the game. The total is 920, rounded down to 900 for a £1.80 payout.

(42)	1♣xx	11	+4	$20 \times 4 + 50 + 4$ $\times 200 + 50$	900
					80

1♣xx is still only a part-score so the bonuses are 50 for the insult, 200 for each redoubled overtrick (non-vulnerable) and 50 for the part-score. The total is 980 rounded up to 1000 for a £2.00 payout. This could hardly happen in practice.

(43)	4♡	12	+2	$4 \times 30 + 2 \times 30 + 300$	360
					120

A game made with two overtricks for the game bonus of 300 but no slam bonus as the slam was not bid. The total is 480 rounded up to 500 for a £1.00 payout.

(44)	2♠	10	+2	$2 \times 30 + 2 \times 30 + 50$	110
					60

Although game was made, only a part-score was bid and therefore the 50 bonus only applies. The total is 170 rounded up to 200 for a £0.40 payout.

(45)	5♦	13	+2	$5 \times 20 + 2 \times 20 + 300$	340
					100

Only the game bonus applies as the grand slam was not bid. The total is 440 rounded down to 400 for £0.80.

(46)	2♦xx	12	+4	$(2 \times 20 \times 4$ $+ 50 + 4 \times 200 + 300$	1150
					160

The contract has been redoubled into game and therefore the 300 game bonus applies, as well as 50 for the insult and 200 for each redoubled overtrick (non-vulnerable). The total is 1310 rounded down to 1300 for £2.60. This would hardly happen in practice.

(47)	1NT	10	+3	$40 + 3 \times 30 + 50$	140
					40

It appears that game should have been bid but this result is surprisingly common as the defence often goes astray. The total of 180 is rounded up to 200 for £0.40.

(48)	7♣x	13	=	$(7 \times 20) \times 2 + 50$	1350
				$+ 1000 + 300$	
					280

Here the grand slam was bid and the game bonus and 50 for the insult are added. The total is 1630 rounded down to 1600 for £3.20.

(49)	6♠xx	13	+1	$(6 \times 30) \times 4 + 50$	1050
				$+ 200 + 500 + 300$	
					720

The small slam only was bid and so the 500 bonus applies along with 50 for the insult, 200 for the redoubled overtrick (non-vulnerable) and 300 for the game. The total is 1770 rounded up to 1800 for £3.60.

(50)	3♣	6	−3	150	150

Nothing scored under the line; therefore no bonus. The total of 150 is rounded down to 100 for £0.20.

Well, that was a lot of hard work and involved a great deal of repetition! However, as explained earlier, this is quite deliberate. It is vital that you have the scoresheet completely at your fingertips before you even think about starting to play. Before proceeding further, review what you have achieved so far to ensure that you are accurate in the recommended times.

The Play of the Hand: Lesson One

The play of the hand is an extensive subject and by no means a finished science. Many books have already been written on it and many more are in the pipeline. This should not put you off, because the vast majority of hands are relatively simple and any player who manages those can reach at least a reasonable standard. It is not important to master spectacular plays; what matters is that you do not fail on the straightforward ones.

Earlier, I set out rules by which a player will win a trick according to the denomination and who was on lead. In all the illustrative exercises, each player had one card only and so had no choice regarding which to play. Effectively, therefore, we were discussing the last trick in the play of a hand. In most schools, teachers use a full hand of thirteen cards and work from the beginning. I believe that it is better to work backwards from the end. The easiest tricks to play are those towards the end of a hand, when the choice is strictly limited. As we get closer to the beginning, life becomes more complicated. So we are going to extend the exercises to two cards and increase from there. We shall start longitudinally, that is, working on one suit only, and then extend latitudinally, introducing the other three suits.

Again, I am stressing the importance of having as much information as possible completely at your fingertips before going near a bridge table, and we shall try to achieve this by doing plenty of examples so that most of the work becomes second nature. You will then have added to the solidity of your platform, from which you can spring into action.

A good cross-section of suit combinations and how to play them to advantage appears in *The Official Encyclopaedia of Bridge* (published by Crown Publications Inc., New York) and similar large-scale works, and I refer to it now and then if I think I might have misplayed a hand.

It would be extremely difficult to memorize all the individual plays parrot-fashion and in any case, that is the last thing I want you to do – for two very important reasons. First, the 'correct' way to play an individual suit may or may not be correct in the context of a whole hand. Second, it is important that you should *understand how to work out* the best way to play a suit rather than merely be able to reproduce it from memory. So every step will be explained in detail and you should not proceed further until you have understood everything.

When a suit combination is put in front of you, there are a number of questions you should immediately ask yourself about the cards:

1 During the course of play, how many times is the suit likely to be led? In other words, how many *rounds* of the suit are likely to be played?
2 Of those rounds, how many are you likely to win?
3 How many are you likely to lose?
4 Bearing in mind that your answers to 2 and 3 must add up to that in 1, are the answers clear-cut or are there ifs and buts according to who leads and how the opponents' cards are placed?
5 If there are doubts in 4, to what degree are you in control of the outcome and how much rests in the hands of the opponents?

These are the five relevant questions for an individual suit. Looking ahead, you will, of course, have to do this for all four suits, always bearing in mind that the total number of rounds will be thirteen. We shall start with some very simple examples and try to answer the five questions in each case. It is a good idea to put the cards out in front of you rather than merely reading them, so that you get used to actually playing.

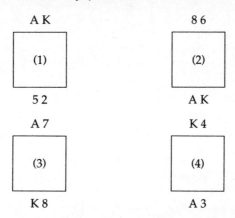

In all four cases, it is clear that two rounds of the suit will be played. Note that the maximum number of rounds of a suit on which you can insist equals the number of cards you have in the hand with the larger number of cards in that suit. So, if you have a situation where South has, say, four diamonds and North two, you might be able to insist that up to four rounds of the suit be played, but no more. It is possible, of course, that the opponents' remaining seven cards in the suit may be divided 5–2, 6–1 or 7–0 – in which case *they* may be able to insist on further rounds, but they are only likely to do so if it is in their interests. So, at least for the time being, you should concentrate on what you have in your hand.

In all four of the above examples, it is clear that you can win two tricks and lose none, to total two, simply by playing your ace and king to separate tricks. Notice, however, that there are subtle differences which you should get into the habit of registering right from the start.

In (1), you will have to finish in the North hand. In (2), you will have to finish in the South hand. In (3) or (4), however, you have an option to finish in either hand. So in (3), if you wanted to finish in the South hand, you would play the ace first and then the seven to the king; while, if you wanted to finish in the North hand, you would play the king first and then the eight to the ace. In (4), it is simply the other way about and the reversal of the positions of the ace and king are of little relevance. All this applies irrespective of the cards in the East and West hands.

Now let us remove the ace and give it to the opponents. Look at these next four examples:

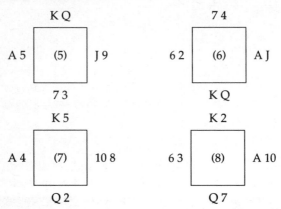

In all four cases, it is clear that, as you have the king and queen and the opponents have the ace, you will win exactly one trick and the opponents will win one. However, it is worth noting a number of other points.

First, in all four cases, the *opponents* can decide who wins the first round of the suit and who will win the second. So in (5), West has the option to play his ace or five on the first round, irrespective of who leads the suit.

Second, there are differences in respect of which hand can be reached – which may be important for the play of the remainder of the tricks. Let us look at each example in turn, considering all the possibilities, dependent on who is on lead.

(5) Here it is clear-cut that, irrespective of who is on lead, North will win one trick and West one.

(6) Similarly, South will win one trick and East one.

(7) Here it is less clear:

  a If West is on lead, he has no say: if he plays his four, South has the option to win the first trick in his own hand or in North's. If West plays the ace, South can play low from the North hand and allow that hand to win the second round, or he can play his king under the ace and allow the queen to win the second round in the South hand. In this second case, the play of the king under the ace is referred to as an *unblock* and will be discussed in more detail later on.

b If North is on lead, then West has the option to keep South off play or insist that he be put on play: if North leads the king, West may allow it to hold and win the second round; if North leads the five to the queen, West has the option to win and put North back on play or allow South's queen to hold and insist that South is now on play.

c If East is on lead, West can insist that South be kept off play but cannot insist that he be put on it. Say East leads the ten; if South puts up the queen, West has the option to win with the ace and insist that North wins the second round, but he cannot prevent North from getting the lead because, if West plays low on the queen, South has the option to allow the queen to hold or overtake it with the king.

d If South is on lead, similar conditions to (c) apply.

(8) There is a difference between this case and (7) in that, as the ace is sitting behind or *over* the king, the overtaking option has disappeared and, as we shall see, East is slightly better placed than West was just now. Let us go through it all again:

a If West is on lead, East has the option to insist on which opponent will win the trick and keep the other on lead. Say West leads the six (it does not matter which of his two low cards he chooses). Now, if North plays the king, East may win if he wants to keep South on play, or allow it to hold if he wants to keep South off lead; if North plays the two, then East may win to keep South off play or duck to insist that South will win his side's trick.

b If North is on lead, similar conditions to (a) apply.

c If East is on lead, he has no say. If he plays his ace, South can keep or unblock his king at will; if he plays the ten, South can win in either hand.

d If South is on lead, similar conditions apply to (a).

What a handful! We have only considered two tricks in one suit so far and there is already so much to discuss. What is it going to be like with thirteen tricks and four suits around, not to mention the trump element? Do not be put off; slowly but steadily, various rules of thumb or *guides* will emerge which will help you to work out the various combinations.

So far we have considered North-South dominant with ace and king, and the position if they have the king and queen against the defenders' ace. Now let us consider what happens if North-South have the ace and queen against the defenders' king. We shall see that the positions of the jack, and possibly the ten, can now be critical.

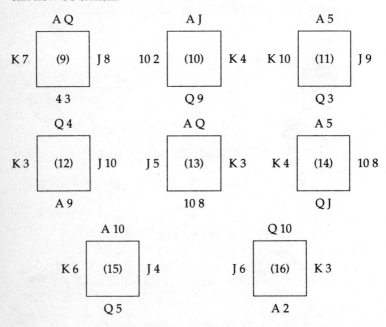

Of the two tricks to be played, North-South always have the ace and are therefore guaranteed at least one. In which circumstances will they get both?

(9) Here, if North-South are to win both tricks, the ace and king must fall to the same trick. This implies that West must be

forced to commit himself as to when he plays his king before North decides when to play his ace. Thus if East, South or West are on lead, North will be able to wait until West has decided when he is going to play his king and play accordingly. For example, if South is on play, he leads one of his low cards and if West plays the seven, North wins with the queen, cashing the ace afterwards; if West plays the king, North wins with the ace, cashing the queen afterwards. However, if North is on lead, he has to commit himself first. Now if he plays the ace, West will play the seven and the king will then beat the queen. If North starts with the queen, the king can win immediately – one trick each.

At this point I will introduce some new words to add to our bridge language. Straight runs of cards like A K, K Q, 10 9 8, 5 4 3 2, in which there are no intermediate cards missing or where any such intermediate cards have already been played, are referred to as *solid* holdings. Where intermediate cards are missing and are yet to be played, such as A Q, Q 10 8, 7 5, 8 4 2, 10 8 6 4, the holdings are referred to as *broken*. Holdings with an element of both, such as A Q J, Q 10 9, 8 6 5, are referred to as *semi-solid*. A two-card holding in which the intermediate card is in the hands of the enemy is called a *tenace* (this is the noun related to tenacious [holding] derived from the Latin *tenere* to hold; the fact that the word contains two card names (ten, ace) is no more than an amusing coincidence). In the above example, North is sitting with a tenace (A Q) over West's king. The play through the intermediate card up to the tenace just described is referred to as taking a *finesse*. When West plays low, South is said to *finesse* dummy's queen against the king.

Finessing is a considerable subject in its own right and this example is known as a *simple finesse* – certainly the most common. More complex examples may be left for the moment.

(10) Whereas in (9), the king was sitting under the tenace and could be caught, here it is sitting over the tenace (remember A J may be considered a tenace here as the queen is in the partner's hand) and is now in a better position. East can

now wait for North to play his ace and follow accordingly to ensure one trick for his side. Only in the case where he is forced to lead the suit himself, must he concede both tricks, as North can now wait for him.

(11) Here North-South have both ace and queen and the king is sitting under the ace, but as the ace and queen are in separate hands, the position is weaker. This kind of layout is a *split tenace* and the king can only be caught if West has to lead the suit himself. Otherwise, we can see that East-West must win one trick:

a If North leads, West simply puts the king on the five and the ten on the ace.

b If East leads (jack or nine), then if South puts on the queen, West *covers* with the king and although North can take his ace, the highest card outstanding, the *master* in the suit, belongs to East-West and they win one trick.

c If South leads, then West plays according to South's choice: if it is the queen, West covers to set up a trick in his partner's hand; if it is the three, West plays low and North can take his ace now or on the second round.

Given that, unless West is forced to lead, East-West must win one trick, the player who will win that trick depends on which player is in charge. Let us work it through again.

a If East leads, South is in charge. If East starts with the jack, South can insist that he stays on lead by playing low from both hands or that West will be on lead by covering the jack with the queen and allowing West's king to hold. If East starts with the nine, South can insist that East wins the second round by putting up the queen and taking West's king with the ace; or that West wins either the first or second round by putting up the queen and allowing West's king to hold, or by playing low and allowing West's ten to hold.

b If South leads, he has the option to insist that a trick shall be lost to West by leading the queen and allowing the king to hold. Note that, if he overtakes the king with the ace, the defenders have the option where they win the next trick, East contributing the jack or nine accordingly. South also has the option to insist that the second round of the suit be lost to West by starting with the three and going up with the ace when West plays low.

c If North leads, he can insist that the first trick is lost to West by playing low towards the queen, or the second by starting with the ace.

(12) Here the king is sitting over the ace and cannot be caught unless West is on lead. Otherwise a trick will be lost to West and North-South cannot force East to take a trick.

(13) This again sees the king over the ace and it therefore cannot be caught unless East is on lead. Otherwise East and North will win one trick each and the position of the jack is irrelevant.

(14) Now, with the king sitting over the queen, North-South need the jack. The king will always be caught unless North is on lead.

(15) This position is more complex and now even the ten is important:

a If North is on lead, he cannot prevent West from winning a trick but may control whether it is the first or second.

b If East is on lead, then North-South win two tricks. If East starts with the jack, South puts on the queen and the ace and ten will both win irrespective of how West plays. If East starts with the four, South plays the five and now if West plays the king, the ace and queen score separately; if West plays the six, the ten wins, followed by the ace.

c If South is on lead, each side will win one trick but South can determine which side will win it. He can insist on losing the trick to East by leading the queen, forcing West to cover. North wins with the ace and the ten forces East to win the second round with the jack.

d If West is on lead, South wins two tricks.

(16) This is similar to (15) except that the ten is now with the queen rather than the ace. Effectively this makes no difference. North-South will make two tricks if either East or West have to lead, otherwise they will make only one.

It has all been a lot of work, but slowly a pattern is emerging. You should have noticed that it is a disadvantage to have to lead away from high honours, and conversely an advantage to be able to lead towards them. In other words, the later the player with a high card has to commit himself, the better. However, note that, when considering the ace and queen, it is the position of the queen that is critical in this respect, as the ace will always win irrespective of when it is played. Generally speaking, however, the guide to follow is, where possible:

Lead from weakness through the opponents' strength towards your own strength.

You should also have noticed that, where there are solid holdings, even if split between the two defenders, who is on lead tends to matter little; whereas with broken holdings, it is often critical.

So far, we have shown examples with all the cards exposed. 'What happens,' I hear you cry, 'in actual play when you can only see your own hand and dummy's?' This is a typical illustration which crops up frequently:

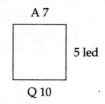

With two tricks to go and the king, jack and nine still outstanding, East leads the five. How do you play? Well, let's consider all the possibilities:

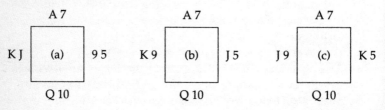

In (a), it does not matter what you do; you can only win one of the two tricks. Your ten will fetch the jack from West; if you prefer the queen, West will cover with the king. In either case, he sets up a trick for his remaining honour.

In (b), you win two tricks by putting on the ten, forcing the king from West after which your queen will be high. But if you play the queen, West will cover with the king, promoting his partner's jack.

Conversely in (c), rising with queen is the winning play, while playing the ten allows West's jack to force the ace to promote East's king.

So with (a) out of the reckoning, it appears to be a straight 50 per cent guess and indeed this may well be the case. However, I have deliberately not discussed it because to do so would simply be trying to run before we can walk. The first step is to learn how to play, seeing all four hands. Once we can do that, the next is to learn to visualize unseen cards so that we can play *effectively* seeing (in our mind's eye) all four hands. Only after that, and that is still a long way off, can we consider how best to deal with situations where we really do not know where enemy forces lie.

You have already seen how complicated the game is looking at just two cards each in the same suit and being allowed to see all four hands. I hope I have now made my point about how impossible it is to learn the game by playing full deals.

Before proceeding further, let us do some practice exercises so that we are fully familiar with two-card positions. In the layouts which follow (overleaf), you should assume that the other five cards in the suit have been played or discarded earlier. In each example, you will notice that North-South have the highest card and must therefore win at least one trick out of the two. Take pen and paper and write down for each example whether North-South will win just one trick or two with (a) West, (b) North, (c) East, or (d) South on lead.

In cases where only one trick will be won, decide whether North-South or East-West have any say in respect of which hand wins the first or second round, and whether a trick may be lost to a specified opponent. Start your stop-watch now.

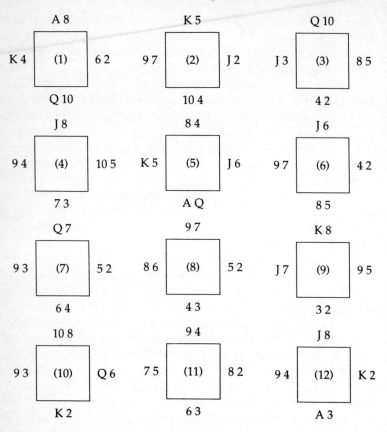

This should have taken you well under ten minutes. Let us work through the answers:

(1)   Here the Q 10 are solid and the king will always be caught unless North has to lead. In that event, he can insist that the first or second round be lost to West.

(2)   Here the jack is sitting over the king and cannot be caught unless East has to lead. North-South can insist on losing the first or second round to East.

(3)   Here North's Q 10 forms a tenace over West's jack and they will always make two tricks unless North has to lead. In

that case, he can insist on losing the first or second round to West.

(4)   Here East-West's 10 9 are solid against the jack and there will be one trick each irrespective of who leads. However, which trick is lost to whom is less clear:

 a If West leads, North has the choice of whether he wins the first or second trick, but if he specifically wants to lose a trick to East, he will have to play the eight if West starts with the four. Otherwise East can unblock the 10. North cannot force West to win a trick.

 b If North leads, he can still insist on whether he wins the first or second trick, but cannot specify who will win the opponents' trick. The lead of the jack allows East to play or withhold the 10 as he wishes, and the lead of the eight allows East or West to win the trick as they please.

 c If East leads, North can still win the first or second trick and to which hand he loses it depends on which card East starts with. If he starts with the 10, North can insist that East wins the first trick by letting it hold, or that West wins the second trick by taking the ten with the jack. If East starts with the five, North can lose the first trick to West by allowing the nine to hold or the second to East by winning and losing to the ten.

 d If South leads, similar conditions apply to (a).

(5)   Here West's king is well placed over South's A Q tenace and cannot be caught unless West has to lead. South can insist that West win the first or second round.

(6)   Here West has a tenace over South's eight and the nine cannot be caught unless West has to lead. North can insist that West wins the first or second round.

(7)   Here North's Q 7 form a tenace over West's nine, and that nine will always be caught unless North has to lead. In that case, he can insist that West wins the first or second round.

(8)   Here North's 9 7 form a tenace over West's eight and similar conditions to (8) apply.

(9)   Here East-West's J 9 are solid against the king and there will be one trick each irrespective of who leads. However, which trick is lost to whom is less clear. North can always insist on

winning the first or second trick if he is not fussy about who wins the other; but if he is, we must examine the position in more detail:

a If West leads, North is in charge and can lose the trick to either hand: if West starts with the jack, North may allow it to hold or win and lose the next round to East as he pleases; if West starts with the seven, North can win and lose the second round to West or cover with the eight and lose the first round to East.

b If North leads, East-West are in charge: if North starts with the king, West can unblock or keep his jack as he pleases; if North starts with the eight, either defender can win.

c If East leads, North can still lose to either defender irrespective of which card East chooses.

d If South leads, similar conditions apply to (a).

(10) a If West leads, North will just cover West's card and make both tricks.

b If North leads, North-South can only make one trick but have considerable power as to how to lose the other. They can lose the first trick to East by starting with the ten and allowing East's queen to hold. They can lose the second trick to East by starting with the eight and winning the first trick with the king. They can lose the first trick to West by starting with the eight and playing South's two on East's forced six, or lose the second trick to West by starting with the ten and overtaking East's queen.

c If East leads, North-South win two tricks.

d If South leads, he can insist that the first or second round be lost to East.

(11) Here East-West's 8 7 are solid against the nine and there will be one trick to each side irrespective of who is on lead. However, who wins the East-West trick and when is less clear, the situation being similar to that in (4).

(12) This is a similar situation to (10).

It will be an instructive exercise to work through these examples again, noting the situations in which East-West lose two tricks and distinguishing those in which they have some say as to whether their opponents will finish in the North or South hand.

There is no need to learn all this parrot-fashion. The important thing is that you understand each position. Automatic recognition will come with practice.

The Play of the Hand: Lesson Two

We are now going to extend our study, still in one suit, to three cards all round. In practice, it is most unlikely that the play of a hand will lead to a situation that all four players will have three cards in a suit and nothing else and therefore, this time, we shall have to discuss the possibility that the hand winning a trick can lead a card from another suit or *switch* to avoid giving an unnecessary trick away. The combinations are, of course, virtually endless so we shall confine ourselves to the more important ones.

To begin with, if North-South hold the ace, king and queen, as shown in the following six examples below and opposite, they must win all three tricks, irrespective of who leads:

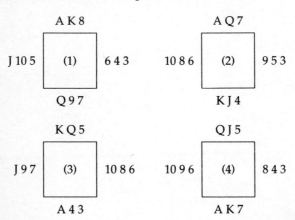

	A K 8			A Q 7	
J 10 5	(1)	6 4 3	10 8 6	(2)	9 5 3
	Q 9 7			K J 4	

	K Q 5			Q J 5	
J 9 7	(3)	10 8 6	10 9 6	(4)	8 4 3
	A 4 3			A K 7	

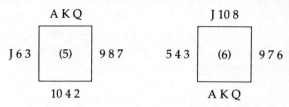

Notice, however, that there are a number of differences. In (5) and (6), all the tricks must be won in the same hand. In the other cases, North-South may choose to end in either hand. The presence of South's jack in (2) allows either North or South to win two tricks but despite the presence of the jack with North in (4), North can only win one trick. It is an instructive exercise in (1) to demonstrate that, even if West is on lead, North cannot win all three tricks. Try it after West starts with the jack.

Now let us give the queen to East-West. North-South will still win two tricks with the ace and king but regarding the third trick, the positions of all cards down to the eight could be critical. Let us first consider the position where North-South have the jack:

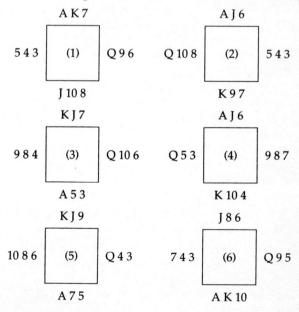

These are just a few of the possible combinations:

(1)   Here the queen is well placed behind the ace and king.
       North-South will make only two tricks unless East is on
       lead, when they will make all three.

(2)   Here North has a tenace (A J) over the queen and North-
       South will make all three tricks, irrespective of who is on
       lead. The first trick can always be won by South's king, after
       which he can take the finesse against West's queen.

(3)   Here the queen is well placed over the jack and cannot be
       caught unless East is on lead. If North starts with the jack,
       East covers with the queen to South's ace and now the ten
       cannot be caught.

(4)   With tenaces in both hands (A J with North and K 10 with
       South), the queen can be caught irrespective of whether it is
       with West, as shown, or with East. In practical play, the
       problem is, of course, to know which finesse to take but that
       only applies if North or South are on lead. If either East or
       West is on lead, North-South are assured of three tricks
       regardless of the position of the queen.

(5)   This is a relatively rare situation where the queen can
       almost certainly be caught despite being apparently well-
       placed over the jack. It will be instructive to go through all
       the possibilities:

       a If West is on lead, North will just cover whatever card
          West chooses, forcing East to play the queen, after which
          the two remaining cards in the North hand will be
          masters.

       b If North is on lead, he must start with the jack. East must
          cover to stop the jack from winning immediately and
          South wins with the ace. Now he can take a finesse
          against West's ten.

       c If East is on lead, he must lead away from his queen and
          North's jack must make.

       d The exception arises when South is on lead. Now the
          queen cannot be caught and North-South take two tricks
          only.

(6)   Here the queen is again sitting over the jack but can be

caught because South has the ten. North-South will make three tricks unless South is on lead, in which case he cannot arrange to lead through the queen.

In cases where East-West have the jack, much depends on who is on lead and whether the queen and jack are separate or together, whether North-South's ace and king are separate or together and possibly the positions of the ten, nine and even eight.

Where East-West have the ten, the Q J 10 are solid against the ace and king and at best, only two of them can be caught. North-South will make two tricks and East-West one, irrespective of the layout or who is on lead.

So we must now give the ten to North-South and there are a number of possibilities including those shown below and overleaf:

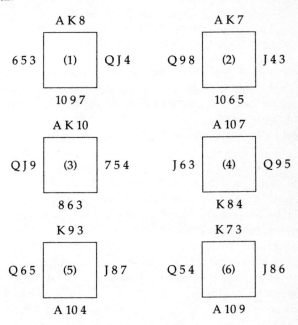

	A K 8			A K 7	
6 5 3	(1)	Q J 4	Q 9 8	(2)	J 4 3
	10 9 7			10 6 5	

	A K 10			A 10 7	
Q J 9	(3)	7 5 4	J 6 3	(4)	Q 9 5
	8 6 3			K 8 4	

	K 9 3			K 7 3	
Q 6 5	(5)	J 8 7	Q 5 4	(6)	J 8 6
	A 10 4			A 10 9	

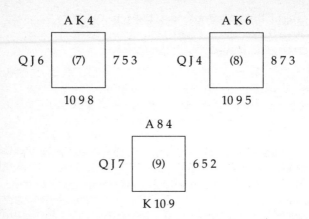

```
        A K 4                              A K 6

Q J 6    (7)    7 5 3          Q J 4    (8)    8 7 3

        10 9 8                           10 9 5


                        A 8 4

              Q J 7    (9)    6 5 2

                        K 10 9
```

We shall go through the answers in detail, firstly considering the position where these are the only three tricks left to be played and then the possible variations if we assume that they arise earlier in the play and the lead can pass from one player to another via another suit:

(1)   Here both East's honours are well placed behind the ace and king and cannot be finessed against. However, if East is on lead initially, he would have to start with one of his honours. North would win and if, later on in the play, East could be forced to lead again, North-South would win all three tricks.

(2)   Here West has a tenace (Q 9) over South's ten and East-West must win one trick irrespective of who is on lead, even if the lead is passed from one player to another.

(3)   Here if North is on lead, West will win a trick easily. If any of the others are on lead, West will play one of his honours or *split his honours*, forcing North to win with the ace or king after which North will have to lead and give a trick to West's remaining honour. However, if it is specified that the second round need not come from North, West's honours can be picked up. Say South leads to the first round. West splits his honours and North wins. If later on, South (or East or West for that matter) is allowed to lead to the second round, North has a tenace (A 10) over West's remaining

honour. This position, where North has two honours well placed over West's two honours, allows what is known as a *deep* or *double finesse*.

(4) Here East has a tenace (Q 9) over North's A 10 and East-West must win one trick, whoever is on lead. However, if it is specified that the second round need not come from the player who won the first, the position is less clear-cut:

a If North or South has to lead the first round, the king or ace will have to be played and the queen and jack will remain solid against the remaining honour. East-West are thus assured of one trick.

b If West leads to the first round, starting with the three, then if North plays the seven, East's nine will force South's king and the queen and jack will be solid against the ace. If North plays the ten, East's queen will force South's king, leaving the jack and nine solid against the ace. If North plays the ace, the queen and jack are solid against the king. In all cases, therefore, East-West are assured of one trick.

c If East leads to the first round, North-South have a chance for all the tricks. If East starts with the five or nine, West will have to play the jack to force the ace. Later, if East can be forced to lead again, North-South will have a split tenace in the king and ten. If East starts with the queen, South can win with the king after which he has a finesse against West's jack.

(5) This is similar to (4) except that North-South are strengthened by the possession of the nine. Now, if North or South has to lead, East-West are still assured of one trick. However, if East or West has to lead, a low card will force the partner to play an honour, after which there will be a finesse against the other honour. An honour will be beaten by the ace or king on the left of the lead, after which there will be a finesse against the other honour. That, however, is not the last word on this position as we shall see when we discuss (9) in a moment.

(6) This is similar to (5), the fact that the ten and nine are now together making no difference.

(7)   Assuming only these three tricks remain, East-West are safe for one trick, irrespective of who leads. However, if North is exempted from leading to either round, the double finesse illustrated in (3) is available. Note that whereas in (3), North-South need only the ten, they now need the nine and eight as well as West is sitting over the ten and nine.

(8)   Now East-West have the eight and the double finesse does not work. North-South will only win three tricks if:

   a West leads the first round and North does not have to lead the second,

   b South leads the first round (the nine or ten forcing a cover) and West has to lead the second,

   c East leads the first round (seven or eight) and either East or West is forced to lead the second.

(9)   This is similar to (5) and (6) but presents an interesting problem in practical play. Assuming that you can see the North and South cards only and an honour is led, you will not know which finesse to take. The decision involves an advanced concept and is way ahead of our study, so we shall not worry about it for the moment.

You should now satisfy yourself that you can distinguish, in the examples where a trick has to be lost, between those where North-South can insist which defender wins a trick and those where East-West have the choice:

(1)   East must win.

(2)   East-West have the choice.

(3)   West must win.

(4)   a If West is on lead, North-South have the choice: should West start with the jack, North-South can let it hold or insist that East wins a trick with his tenace. If West starts with a low card, North puts up the ten, forcing East's queen. This may be allowed to hold or South can win and lead towards the ace, forcing the loss of a trick to West's jack.

   b If North is on lead, North-South still have the choice. North starts with the ten. Now, if East covers, South has the option to let it hold or win and continue with the eight; now, if West plays the jack, it is allowed to hold; if he doesn't, the ace wins and the jack must win the third round.

c If East is on lead, he must start with the five or lose his side's trick; again North-South may let West's jack hold or insist that the trick be lost to East.

d If South is on lead, North-South cannot force West to win. Playing the four to the ace and then the ten is foiled by East covering with the queen. Now if South takes his king, West throws in his jack to promote his partner's nine.

(5)   North-South have the choice of who wins their opponents' trick simply by ducking a round into the appropriate hand.

(6)   Same applies as in (5).

(7), (8) and (9) West must win.

You should by now have grasped enough to get the general idea and you can test yourself further by doing some examples in which the North-South holdings are weaker. In all cases, they have the ace but not the king and you should answer the following:

How many tricks will North-South win if:
    a West,
    b North,
    c East,
    d South
is initially on lead and what differences, if any, are there if it is specified that the hand winning a trick can get off play in another suit? Also, which side is in control regarding who wins the various tricks and when? Start your stop-watch.

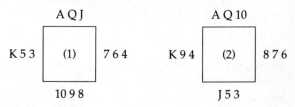

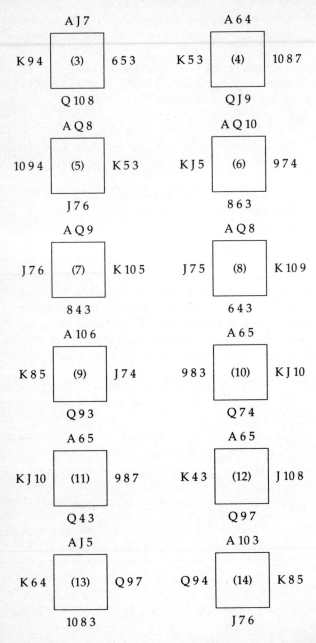

             A J 7   A 6 4

K 9 4   (3)   6 5 3   K 5 3   (4)   10 8 7

             Q 10 8   Q J 9

             A Q 8   A Q 10

10 9 4   (5)   K 5 3   K J 5   (6)   9 7 4

             J 7 6   8 6 3

             A Q 9   A Q 8

J 7 6   (7)   K 10 5   J 7 5   (8)   K 10 9

             8 4 3   6 4 3

             A 10 6   A 6 5

K 8 5   (9)   J 7 4   9 8 3   (10)   K J 10

             Q 9 3   Q 7 4

             A 6 5   A 6 5

K J 10   (11)   9 8 7   K 4 3   (12)   J 10 8

             Q 4 3   Q 9 7

             A J 5   A 10 3

K 6 4   (13)   Q 9 7   Q 9 4   (14)   K 8 5

             10 8 3   J 7 6

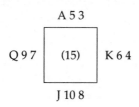

A 5 3

Q 9 7   (15)   K 6 4

J 10 8

It should take you less than a quarter of an hour to complete the discussion on these fifteen examples. Ideally, you should be aiming inside eight minutes or even less so that you are working towards a position that you can take one look at a suit combination and assess its trick-taking prospects with little or no thought. Let us work through the answers:

(1)   Here the three honours are well placed over the king but if West, East or South are on lead to start with, North will win the first round with the jack and then have to lead away from his ace round to the king. Only if North is exempted from leading to the second round of the suit will North-South win all three tricks. If North is on lead to start with, he loses a trick automatically. Neither East or South can ever win a trick and the positions of the lower cards are irrelevant.

(2)   Now North-South are better placed. If North is on lead, a trick must be lost but if anyone else is on lead, the first round is won by the jack, North playing the ten, and now South can take a finesse against West's king.

(3)   This is similar to (2). The fact that the positions of the Q 10 and jack have been exchanged makes no difference except that, whereas in (2), West (unless he has to lead) can, by covering the jack, insist that North has to win all the tricks, here he cannot prevent South from winning at least one.

(4)   This is a common position in which many players go wrong and it is therefore worth working through it in detail:

    a   If West is on lead, North-South must come to three tricks as South's J 9 tenace is well placed over East's ten, after which South can take a finesse through West (unless North is forced to lead the second round).

    b   If North is on lead, West's king must make one trick.

    c If East is on lead, South will just cover East's card and again, as in (a), North-South will make three tricks.

    d The most common situation arises when South is on lead. He must start with the queen or jack and West must play low because, if he covers, North will win, after which he will be able to finesse against East's ten. When the initial queen or jack holds the trick, East-West are now assured of a trick unless either of them can be forced to lead the second round.

(5)   Unless East can be forced to lead twice, he will make his well-placed king.

(6)   This is a double-finesse position and if any player other than North leads twice, North will be able to pick up both West's honours. Otherwise, irrespective of who is on lead, West must make one trick. If North is forced to lead twice, West makes two tricks.

(7)   The jack and ten are solid against the queen and East-West are guaranteed at least one trick in all circumstances. If North is on lead, East-West will make two tricks. However, with anyone else on lead, North will just cover West's card (i.e. put the nine on a low card or put the queen on the jack) to force East to win and return the suit round to North's tenace (A Q or A 9). Where East is exempted from leading to either round, East-West will make two tricks.

(8)   Here East-West are better placed. Unless East is on lead, when North-South will take two tricks, West can gain for his side by putting his jack on the first round. Now, if North's queen covers, East can win and his 10 9 are solid against the ace. If North ducks completely, West stays on play to lead through North's tenace and if North's ace wins the first round, he must now lead away from his queen. However, if North-South are in a position to put East on play at a later stage, the best play on the jack is indeed North's ace, so that West is kept out of the lead. Contrast this with the case where West holds 9 x x and East K J 10. Now East cannot help winning the first round if North plays low, after which he has to lead round to North's tenace.

(9) Now North-South's ace and queen are split and much, in the first place, depends on the relative positions of the king and queen.

    a If West is on lead, he must start with a low card and East must also play low. After that, East-West hold a split tenace against the queen and they are assured of one trick unless either of them can be forced to lead the second round.

    b If North is on lead, he cannot avoid losing a trick to West but he can ensure two tricks by leading low towards South's nine.

    c If East is on lead, the situation is similar to (a) in that both East and West must play low to the first round. Note also that in both cases, South is entitled to win the first round with the nine, after which North-South can dictate which defender will win a trick, either by leading the queen and letting West's king hold or overtaking the king and losing the third round to East's jack. They even have the option to lose the tricks in a different order by leading low to the second round and ducking the trick to East or rising with the ace and losing the third round to West's king.

    d If South is on lead, East-West cannot be denied one trick but North-South again have options as to who wins that trick and when.

(10) The ten is with East and there is no choice of plays. North-South need their queen to be well placed over the king and will make two tricks, irrespective of who is on lead. It is worth noting that North-South usually have the choice as to whether the queen wins its trick before or after the ace. They always have the option of winning the first round with the ace, but if they prefer to have the queen winning beforehand (may be important if other cards are out), then only if South is on lead will they be disappointed, as East can win the first round and then play the king. Note that, if East is on lead and starts with the king, North-South can still keep the desired order by ducking!

(11) Now the tenace is over South's queen but West is actually a

little too strong; as they have the nine, it would be better if the ten or jack were with East:

a If West is on lead, he has to lead away from his tenace and North-South take two tricks.

b If North, East or South are on lead, North-South must play low from both hands. West is forced to win and must lead away from his tenace. Where other cards are still out and West cannot be forced to lead either round, East-West will take two tricks.

(12) Now the K J 10 tenace is split against South's queen, but the presence of the nine provides some compensation:

a If West is on lead, he has to lead round to South's queen and North-South take two tricks.

b If North is on lead and starts with the ace, East-West will win two tricks unless West can be forced to lead the second round. It is better for North to start with a low card. Now if East plays low, South's nine will force the king to give North-South two tricks; thus East must split his honours. South must now play low and his side wins two tricks unless East is exempted from leading the second round.

c If East is on lead, the eight will concede two tricks immediately as South's nine will force the king, so East must start with an honour. Now South has a choice of plays. If there are no other cards outstanding, he may duck completely, forcing East to continue after which South will just cover East's card. Otherwise, he may cover with the queen, take West's king with the ace and lead towards the nine from the North hand.

d If South is on lead, he cannot avoid losing two tricks if there are no other cards outstanding. Even if there are, he will have to play to North's ace now and arrange for West to be on play for the second round.

(13) The jack and ten are split and the position becomes more complicated, the position of the nine becoming relevant as explained in this and the next example. It will be instructive to work through every combination:

a If West is on lead, North-South will make two tricks. If

West starts with the king, North wins, after which the jack and ten become solid against the queen. Note, however, that North is forced to win (otherwise East-West win two tricks) and now East-West are in charge of who wins the second North-South trick and when. Once North's ace has won, if he continues with the jack, East has the option to allow it to hold or win and let South have the last trick; if North plays the five after the ace, East may win and lose the third trick to the jack or play low, allowing South to win the second round. If West starts with a low card, North can always arrange for a trick to be lost to East by playing low. After that, North will win the other two tricks (unless he is forced to lead the second round). However, if it is important for South to get on lead, North might try his jack. Now if East wins, South will just cover East's next card and cannot be denied one of the tricks. East can be sure of keeping South out of the lead by allowing the jack to hold the first round. With North on lead, East-West have the choice of who wins their trick.

b If North is on lead, East-West must make two tricks.

c If East is on lead, North-South must make two tricks and have the option to keep West out of the lead by, if East leads the queen, letting it hold; or if East plays low to West's king, winning with the ace, after which East-West will have the choice regarding to whom they lose the other trick.

d If South is on lead, North-South can take two tricks if South starts with the three. West must play low, otherwise the J 10 become solid against the queen and North's jack is played, forcing East's queen. Now South just covers East's next card and West's king is trapped. Note that, if South starts with the ten, West covers with the king and now East's Q 9 form a tenace over North's jack and North-South will only be saved if East can be forced to lead the second round. You should satisfy yourself that starting with the eight does not work either.

(14) Here the eight has been given to East, the nine to West and

the positions of the ten and jack reversed, as well as those of the king and queen. It will be useful to see what differences these changes make:

a If West is on lead, North-South will still make two tricks but note now that West must start with a low card if he wants to keep South off play.

b If North is on lead, East-West will make two tricks as before.

c If East is on lead, North-South will also make two tricks as before; note that East-West have the option to keep South off lead whether East starts with the king or a low card.

d The major change arises when South is on lead – North-South can only take one trick. If South starts with the jack, West covers. If South starts low, West also plays low and now his Q 9 form a tenace over the jack.

(15) Now the J 10 are together opposite the ace:

a If West is on lead, North-South will make two tricks. If West starts with a low card, North plays low forcing East's king. Now the J 10 are solid against West's queen and a finesse wins the other two tricks. If West starts with his queen, North wins and now the J 10 are solid against the king. In all cases, North and South will take one trick each and East the other.

b If North is on lead, East-West will take two tricks as in the last two examples.

c If East is on lead, North-South make two tricks. If East starts with the king, North-South have the option to let it hold or win, leaving South's J 10 solid against the queen. This way North-South can a lose a trick to either hand. East can reduce the opponents' options by starting with a low card to West's queen. North must win and now East has the option to win the second or third round.

d If South is on lead, East-West will make two tricks. South must start with an honour (otherwise West's nine forces North's ace) and West must play low; North ducks and East wins with the king, after which West's Q 9 form a tenace over South's J 8. Note that, if West covers the first honour from South, North-South make two tricks by taking the ace and leading through East's king towards the jack. In all circumstances, East and West will win one trick each but North-South can force West to win the first round if North is on lead and East to do so if South is on lead.

This analysis has been very detailed because I want you to get used to the idea of juggling cards in one suit around and be fully familiar with the various situations in it before we go on to complications arising from the introduction of the other suits, the effect of designating one of them as trumps and the difficulty of not being able to see all the cards. Do not begrudge spending quite a long time on this chapter and making sure you understand everything in it before proceeding further. We have already covered some quite advanced plays – the important thing is to understand, rather than memorize, every situation.

The Play of the Hand: Lesson Three

So far we have only considered positions where all the players have the same number of cards in one suit. Inevitably, that meant confining ourselves to three situations with each player having one, two or three cards. This is, of course, unrealistic in practice as there are thirteen cards in each suit and they must inevitably be divided unevenly, 4 3 3 3 being the nearest we can get to an equitable distribution.

We are now going to consider the various distributions involving all thirteen cards, placing emphasis on the most common ones. We shall start by being allowed to see all four hands and then consider how best to play certain combinations given the limited knowledge when seeing only two.

Let us remind ourselves of the basic questions:

1 During the course of play, how many times is the suit likely to be led? In other words, how many *rounds* of the suit are likely to be played?
2 Of those rounds, how many are you likely to win?
3 How many are you likely to lose?
4 Bearing in mind that your answers in 2 and 3 must add up to that in 1, are the answers clear-cut or are there ifs and buts according to who leads and how the opponents' cards are placed?
5 If there are any doubts in 4, to what degree are you in control of the outcome and how much rests in the hands of the opponents?

With a 2–1 split, you can only insist on two rounds and similar conditions apply to having two cards in one hand, except that you do not need the defenders to lead the first round – you can do it yourself.

Let us pause there; you should see the idea by now. The above cases are likely to arise if you are playing in a no-trump contract and the opponents attack what is likely to be their longest suit. From now on, we shall concentrate on suits where you and your partner have the majority and your side will be attacking the suit. We shall take a sample of the hundreds of combinations and rather than set out the line of play, parrot fashion, we shall work out in detail the best plan of campaign. In each case, we shall be asking ourselves the following questions:

1 How many cards do we have between us?
2 How many does that leave for opponents?

Note that the answers in 1 and 2 must total 13.

3 How are the enemy cards most likely to be divided?
4 How many tricks do we need from this particular suit to contribute to our contract?
5 How do we best tackle the suit to win the required number of tricks safely, remembering that it is only to the good if we make more, but we must avoid making less, normally being prepared to forgo overtricks for the safety of the contract.

We shall assume that there are no problems in crossing from one side of the table to the other in other suits and start with the case where we have all four top honours:

A K Q J 9 x
x

Here North has six cards and you (South) have one, making seven in all. That leaves six for the opponents and the probabilities of their divisions are as follows (in percentages rounded to the nearest whole number).

3:3	36
4:2	48
5:1	15
6:0	1

Note that, with an even number of cards missing, the uneven 4:2 break is more likely than the even 3:3 break. Before you memorize these percentages, a word of caution is appropriate. These only apply *a priori*, i.e. at the beginning of a hand with no other information available. As soon as opponents make a bid or reveal their distribution in other suits, these odds are liable, indeed almost certain to change, possibly quite dramatically. We shall learn more about that later on.

With six cards in the North hand, we can insist on six rounds of the suit being played and we can see that, if we simply cash our winners from the top, we shall swallow up the opponents' cards comfortably when the suit breaks 3:3 or 4:2 and even if they are 5:1 with the ten being the singleton. If we need six tricks, this is clearly the best line of play. If we only need five tricks, we are still all right if the suit breaks 5:1 as we shall only lose the ten and must therefore consider the situation where all six opposing cards are in one hand. We can work out that, if they are all with East, there is nothing to be done (unless East can be forced to lead the suit) but if West has them, then a low card from South to North's nine ensures five tricks – if the nine loses to the ten, then we have had no worse than a 5:1 split. If East is void, the nine will hold and we still have the four top honours to come.

Now let us make a change to give North-South eight cards:

K Q J 8 x

A x x

Now five cards are missing and the distributional percentages are:

	3:2	68
	4:1	28
	5:0	4

Note now that, with an odd number of cards missing, the most equitable split is the likeliest. We can see that, provided neither opponent has all five missing cards, the top four honours will swallow all their cards and five tricks will be easy. Note, however, that it is wise to play the ace on the first or second round and be sure that the third round is won in the North hand so that you can continue the suit. If the ace is played on the third round, there will be no more cards in the South hand and you will have to cross to North in another suit to be able to cash the last two tricks.

The question remains as to whether anything can be done if a defender holds all five outstanding cards. If that is East, the 10 9 are solid against the ace and cannot be caught, so one trick must be lost. But if West holds everything, then, if the ace is played first, we shall be in a position to take a double finesse against the 10 9 by leading twice from the South hand. The play will go: ace, on which East discards, revealing the position. South then plays one of his low cards and West puts on the nine or ten to force the jack. North wins and must return to the South hand in another suit in order to take another finesse against West's remaining high card. This is a good point to introduce a new word in our language. A winning card in another suit which is used by one of the partnership to gain access to the opposite hand is referred to as an *entry*. In this situation, an entry is needed to the South hand after the second round of our suit has been played so that the third round can be played from the weakness of South through the strength of West to the strength of North. Note that exchanging the positions of the ace and one of the other honours does not materially alter the position. If North-South have nine or more cards between them, the defenders are left with four or less and North-South must win as many rounds as they can play.

Now let us give the defenders the jack. Starting with seven cards between North-South, suppose the layout is like this:

A K Q 10 9 x

x

To take all six tricks, we have the choice of cashing from the top or playing the low card from South and finessing the ten. It will be instructive to work out the percentages. Cashing from the top will work when the opponents' cards split 3:3 or when they are 4:2 with the jack in the doubleton or when they are 5:1 with the jack being the singleton. The total chance is $36 + 1/3(48) + 1/6(15)$, about 54 per cent. Taking the finesse first time works when the suit breaks 3:3, or 4:2 with the jack in the West hand or 5:1 with the jack singleton in the West hand. The total chance is $1/2(36 + 48 + 1/6 \times 15)$, about 43 per cent, thus cashing from the top is the better line. Note that five tricks are certain unless the suit breaks 6:0. If West follows to the first card from South, five tricks can be ensured by finessing the ten.

Now let us consider a more common distribution of the North-South cards:

$$A K x x x$$
$$Q 10$$

To make five tricks, we again have the choice of cashing from the top, (queen first then the other two to avoid entry problems) or starting from the North hand and finessing the ten. Cashing from the top wins on a 3:3 break = 36 per cent; finessing the ten works on a 3:3 or 4:2 break with the jack in the East hand – $1/2(36+48) = 42$ per cent. Note, however, that if the nine is in the North hand, the odds swing back in favour of cashing from the top because a doubleton jack in either hand is good enough. In the above layout, you can be more than 90 per cent certain of ensuring four tricks by finessing the ten on the first round.

Let us now give North-South eight cards. Consider this layout:

$$A K Q x x x$$
$$10 x$$

For six tricks, we must obviously cash from the top. This works with any 3:2 break or 4:1 with the jack singleton. The total is $68 + 1/5(28) = 73$ per cent. If you only need five tricks from the combination, the best line is to go to the North hand and lead a small card towards the ten. Only the overtrick will be lost if the suit does break 3:2 after all, but you will still be all right if the suit is 4:1 and will gain when East has all five outstanding cards as he must either go up with the jack, and allow your ten to make separately from the top honours, or play low and let the ten win. If West has all the cards, you cannot win five tricks unless North's fourth highest card is the eight, in which case you will be able to take a finesse against West's nine after the ten has lost to the jack. East will have discarded on the first round and so the finesse is certain to succeed and is referred to as a *marked* finesse.

Where North-South have nine cards between them, only a 4–0 break will cause any trouble. This is unlikely but happens occasionally, the relevant percentages being:

2:2	40
3:1	50
4:0	10

Consider this layout:

A Q 9 x x x
K x x

We can see that, if East has all the outstanding cards, the J 10 are solid against the king and cannot therefore be caught, but if West has them, there is scope for a double finesse. The king should therefore be cashed first. If West discards, that's too bad, but if East fails to follow, we can now play towards the A Q 9. West must split his honours and we shall then need an entry back to the South hand in another suit in order to take the second finesse against West's remaining honour. Note that, if North-South have ten or more cards, they cannot lose a trick.

Now we are going to improve the defenders' holding and give them the queen. Starting with North-South having seven cards between them, we shall consider two situations, illustrating contrasting techniques:

A K J 10
x x x

We have a choice of playing the ace and king, hoping that the queen drops in two rounds. This will ensure four tricks if the suit breaks 4:2 with the queen in the doubleton, or 5:1 with the queen being the singleton. The total chance is $1/3(48) + 1/6(15)$, about 18 per cent. A much better play is the finesse (repeated if necessary) against West, which will ensure four tricks 50 per cent of the time. However, you can improve your chance still further by cashing the ace and then taking the finesse. This covers the (admittedly remote) possibility that East has a singleton queen, improving your odds by about 1 per cent. It is a small gain, but these petty trifles add up in the long run so that it is wise to be aware of them from the start.

Having grasped the idea, how would you play this combination:

A K J 10 x
x x

This time, as there are only two cards in the South hand as opposed to three in the previous example, you should refrain from cashing a top honour, preferring to take the finesse imme-diately. As we have just learned, cashing a top honour gains if

East has a singleton queen but loses if West has four to the queen, which is about fifteen times more likely.

Now let us give North-South eight cards:

A K x x x

J x x

If North-South need five tricks from this combination, the best hope is to cash the ace and king. Note that you gain nothing by playing the jack from South, hoping to play low from North if West plays low. If West has the queen, he will simply cover the jack, leaving the ten or nine as a master for the third round. This type of finesse is referred to as a *fool's* finesse (whether it is taken on 1 April or any other date!).

A 10 x x

K J x x

Here, we have the option to play either defender for the queen. If we decide that East is more likely to have the queen, then we should cash the ace first in case West has the queen singleton and then play a low card to the jack. Conversely, if we decide that West is more likely to have the queen, then we should cash the king first to cover the possibility that East has the queen as a singleton and then play a low card towards the ten. These lines of play give a slightly better than a 50 per cent chance of catching the queen, whereas simply banging down the ace and king needs a 3:2 break with the queen in the doubleton – a much poorer bet. Note two other points: if we do not have the nine or eight, one trick will have to be lost if the suit breaks 4:1 (unless the queen is the singleton) or 5:0. Also, if the jack and ten are together in either hand, North-South are better placed in that they can take two finesses against Q x x x in the hand sitting under those honours.

Increasing the North-South holding to nine cards leaves the opponents with four, and now playing for the drop is a far more serious proposition. There is an old saying among bridge players (notably of the weaker brethren!) in respect of finessing against a missing queen: 'With eight ever; with nine never!' My advice is to bear it in mind but refer to it only as a very last resort, as there are so many other considerations to be noted. Let us look at this layout, an additional low card having been added to the North hand from the last diagram:

A 10 x x x

K J x x

We can play one of our top cards without risk. Suppose we start with the king and both defenders follow low. Now we play a low card from South and West plays low again. At this point, there is one more card in the East hand than in the West and the odds favour going up with the ace, i.e. playing for the drop. But note the following points:

1 If we go up with the ace and it turns out to be wrong, we are still on lead – that might be important.

2 Against that, if it is important that one defender or the other should be kept off lead, we can ensure this by taking a finesse in preference to playing for the drop. Thus if it is vital to keep East off lead, we can start with the ace and then play a low card from the North hand, intending to play the jack if East plays low. This way, if a trick must be lost, it will be to West.

These considerations usually override the small extra percentage offered by the 'eight-ever, nine-never' philosophy.

If North-South have ten cards between them the percentages for the relevant splits are:

2:1	78
3:0	22

Most of the time the queen will be swallowed up by the ace and king, but if all the defenders' cards are in one hand then much depends on whether the ace and king are together or separate and possibly on who has the ten:

(1) K 10 x x x
     A J x x x

(2) K x x x x
     A J x x x

(3) A K J x x
     x x x x x

(4) A K x x x
     J 10 x x x

In (1), the queen can be caught irrespective of its position but there is no play to guarantee five tricks. We need to guess which defender is likely to have the length. If we decide it is West, we start with the ace and take the marked finesse against his queen if East discards. Conversely, should we decide it is East, we start with the king and take the marked finesse if West discards.

In (2), the ten is missing and we must appreciate that, if East is void, West's Q 10 form a tenace over South's jack and cannot be caught. Thus we must hope that if anyone has the length, it will be East and we start with North's king, intending to take a marked finesse against East's queen should West discard.

In (3), we note that, if East has all three outstanding cards (whether they include the ten or not), the queen is well placed over the ace and king and cannot be caught. Thus we cash the ace and should East discard, we return to the South hand in another suit to take a marked finesse against West.

In (4), again Q x x with East cannot be caught but if they are all with West, as will be revealed on the first round when the ace is cashed, we can return to South in another suit to take the marked finesse against West. Note, however, that if South does not have the ten, West's Q 10 will form a tenace over the jack and cannot be caught.

If North-South have eleven or more cards, the queen will always be swallowed up in two rounds.

Let us now give the opponents the queen and jack. Often this will mean the loss of at least one trick and much will depend on the positions of the ten and nine and how many tricks are needed. Where North-South have seven cards, there are chances of five tricks in this layout:

A K 10 9 x

x x

Here, if West has Q J or Q J x, playing low from the South hand, intending to play the ten if West plays low, secures all the tricks. Note, however, that if West has Q J x x, he can ensure one trick by splitting his honours on the first or second round. Where only four tricks are needed, the play becomes more debatable. Three lines of play are worth considering:

1 Cash the ace and king, then play the ten. This works on any 3:3 break or a 4:2 break where at least one honour is in the doubleton. The total is $36 + 9/15(48) = 65$ per cent.
2 Play towards the ten and then return to South to play towards the nine. This works if West holds both honours, irrespective

of his length or if he has one honour in a doubleton, trebleton or four card suit. The total comes to about 66 per cent.

3 Play towards the ten and if it loses, cash the ace and king. This wins if West has both honours, irrespective of length or if he has a doubleton or trebleton honour. This also comes to about 66 per cent.

So there is little to choose between them and again the choices of to whom we want to lose tricks and when, are likely to be of overriding importance.

In contrast, the best we can hope for is three tricks here:

A x x x

K x x

Now the opponents have both ten and nine and they are assured of at least one trick. Our only hope for three rests in a 3:3 break, after which the fourth card in the North hand will be master by virtue of being the only card left after everyone has followed to three rounds. Note two important points:

1 If we play the ace and king followed by a third round and they do indeed break 3:3, we shall still need an entry to the North hand in another suit to be able to enjoy the thirteenth *established* card.

2 If we play this way and it turns out that the suit breaks 4:2, the opponents will be able to cash their second trick as soon as they have won their first, as here:

A x x x

J 10   Q 9 x x

K x x

After the ace and king, the queen and nine will both be masters.

For these reasons, it is often a good plan to play low from both hands on the first round or cash the king (the high card from the shorter hand) and then low from both hands on the second round. This ensures easy access to the North hand by using its ace on the third round (the round after which South runs out of cards in the suit) and also prevents the opponents from cashing their second trick immediately. The technique, referred to as *ducking* an early round, is an important part of play and we shall see later that it is just as important to the defenders.

Where North-South have eight cards, again much depends on the position of the ten. Where it is in enemy hands, they are assured of one trick as Q J 10 are solid against the ace and king. Where North-South have it, there may be chances to escape a loser:

K 10 x x x

A 9 x

If five tricks are needed, there is no other hope but that a defender has Q J doubleton; there is no double finesse position, as illustrated earlier, because the ace and king are split. However, if four tricks will suffice, we need to realize that these will be safe on any 3:2 break and must therefore consider protecting against Q J x x in one hand. The crucial point here is that, if West has the length, we shall need to play low towards the ten, but if East has the length, we must play towards the nine. Which is it to be?

In fact, we can have the best of both worlds by observing the guide of concentrating on the hand with the shortage first. Play a low card and put in the nine. If East has the length and both honours, the nine will hold. If the nine loses, we cash the ace. If both follow, we have had a 3:2 break and can cash the rest of the tricks. If it turns out that West has the length with both honours, East will now discard, after which a marked finesse can be taken against West. This line of play works about 90 per cent of the time and only fails if the nine loses to a singleton honour with West or if there is a 5:0 split. You should satisfy yourself that playing towards the ten first does not work so well as you cannot take a finesse against East after cashing the king on the second round.

Where only three tricks are needed, only a 5–0 split is dangerous and you should again satisfy yourself that, if you cash the ace and then lead a low card from the North hand towards the nine, there is no lie of the cards that can prevent you from success. Take your time – these are quite advanced plays, but understanding the principles will give you a much firmer base from which to start playing.

Where North-South have nine cards, there is the chance of a 2:2 split as well as finesse possibilities and again the positions of the ten and nine may be important, as follows:

$$K\ 10\ x\ x\ x$$
$$A\ 9\ x\ x$$

To take five tricks, we start by cashing one of the tops. If both defenders play low, there is no hope but the 2:2 break. If an honour appears, however, from the hand to the right of the first winner, there is scope for debate. Say we start with the ace. If West produces an honour, we have no choice but to hope he has the other as well. But if East plays an honour and West plays low on the second round, it becomes debatable whether we should play for the finesse or the drop. If East actually has both honours (i.e. the drop is the winning play), he would have had a choice of which of them to play on the first round, the queen and jack being equals in the same hand. Had he only a singleton honour (i.e. the finesse is the winning play), he would have had no choice of card. This latter case is therefore more likely (even taking into account that East has more cards in his hand at the moment of decision) and we should take the finesse.

Where only four tricks are needed, these may be ensured by playing a low card from either hand and putting in the ten (or nine) if the defender playing second produces a low card. This protects against a 4:0 split. If that defender discards, we will rise with an honour and take a marked finesse against the other defender to ensure the loss of only one trick. Lay out the cards in any combination to ensure you understand this point.

Let us now alter the layout, giving the nine to the opponents:

$$K\ 10\ x\ x\ x$$
$$A\ x\ x\ x$$

Now, for five tricks, we must start with the ace. If East plays an honour, we still have the option to take a finesse against West. If we only need four tricks, we note that these cannot be guaranteed. If East holds Q J 9 x, they form a tenace over the ten and cannot be caught. If West holds them all, we can lead towards the K 10 twice to ensure the loss of only one trick.

Where North-South have ten cards, the defenders will only take one trick if they hold all of the remainder. In that event, they are unlikely to be caught. Where North-South have eleven or more cards, all the tricks are assured.

The Play of the Hand: Lesson Four

Let us now give the defenders the king rather than the queen and jack. Where North-South have seven cards, there are certain combinations which will provide the possibility of all the tricks, particularly if we are in possession of the ten. This is an example in which many players often go wrong:

A Q 10 x

J x x

Here, obviously, if we are going to make four tricks, the king will need to be with West and it is tempting to lead the jack and run it if West plays low so that we can stay in the South hand to take a further finesse if it holds. However, if West holds a singleton king or K x, he can cover the jack and promote a trick for his partner's nine (or even the eight, as in this layout):

A Q 10 x

K 9   8 x x x

J x x

For this reason, provided there are adequate entries to both hands, it is better to play a low card towards the ten, return to the South hand and play another low card towards the queen. This gives the chance of four tricks, with our four honours all making separately. Notice that there will always be three tricks, even if the king is with East. If North-South do hold the nine, we can start with the jack without risk.

If the ten is missing, we need a fair amount of luck:

Q J 9 8 x

A x

Obviously the king will need to be with East and fall in two rounds and the only hope is to find K 10 doubleton in that hand. We lead the queen from North and if East covers, we cash the jack rather than take a finesse against West, playing East for the ten. If West has four or more cards, the ten cannot be caught. If he has three or less, that implies that East had three or more, in which case, he simply holds back his king. He cannot be caught as the ace must fall in two rounds.

To make four tricks with this combination, it is best to accept the loss of a trick to the king and try to arrange for the ace, queen and jack to be played to separate tricks. It is silly to lead the queen from North now as it will be wasted against a singleton king in either hand. It is best, therefore, to start with the ace and lead low towards North's holding. If either defender produces the king or ten on the first round, there is no further problem. If both play low and West follows low to the second round, then we must consider whether to finesse against the ten or go up with the queen or jack.

There will be no chance if either defender started with K 10 x x x. If West started with K 10, K x or 10 x, his honour will appear and there will be nothing further to think about. Finessing against the ten succeeds if West started with 10 x x x and East K x (this can happen in four possible ways) or if West started with K 10 x x and East x x (which can happen in six possible ways). Going up with the queen or jack succeeds when West started with K x x (six possibilities) or K x x x (four possibilities) and therefore there is little to choose between them. Note that, if West started with K 10 x, either line will work.

Where North-South have eight cards, this is a common position:

A x x x

Q J x x

The first point to note is that there is no play for four tricks. Even if the king is a singleton, the ten will win the fourth round. It is therefore futile to start with the queen and indeed this will cost if either defender has a singleton king. It is thus better to start with the ace and then play low from the North hand towards the Q J, ensuring three tricks unless East has a small singleton or void.

Where North-South have nine cards, much will depend on how many tricks are needed if the ten is missing, as here:

A 9 x x x

Q J x x

If we need all five tricks, the king will have to be credited with West (a 50 per cent chance against the much smaller probability that he is singleton with East) and that West will have exactly K x, K 10 or K x x. We thus start by running the queen. This will cost when West has the king singleton but is still the line offering the best chance.

However, if only four tricks are required, a low card towards the queen guarantees them. Set out the cards with either East or West having a void and you will see that this is the only foolproof line.

Even if North-South have ten cards between them, the finesse offers a better percentage than the drop. Consider this position:

A Q 9 x x

J x x x x

Three cards are missing. The critical case arises when West has all of them. If you start by playing a low card to the queen, West's K 10 will then form a tenace over the jack and cannot therefore be caught. We must therefore start with the jack, noting now that, even if West has the singleton king, nothing is lost as North-South have so many cards between them. On the jack, West has to cover and when East discards, we return to the South hand via another suit and take a marked finesse against West's ten.

Where North-South have eleven cards between them, we have an exception to the rule. It was mentioned earlier that, where an even number of cards are missing, the uneven break is more likely. This case is the exception, with the percentages being:

1:1   52

2:0   48

and thus playing for the drop is just fractionally a better bet than the finesse.

Where North-South have twelve cards between them, the king is the only missing card and must fall under the ace in one round.

We are now going to strengthen enemy forces by giving them the jack in addition to the king, and start with North-South having seven cards between them. The number of tricks required often dictates the line of play. This is a classic example:

A Q 10 9 x x

x

Here we are entitled to insist on six rounds but the only hope of taking all six tricks rests in West's holding exactly K J doubleton. If he has any more, at least one trick must be lost as we can only take one finesse. Where we only need five tricks, the best line is to finesse the queen on the first round and play the ace on the second. This gives the chance of dropping a doubleton jack with East. Note that this is better than finessing the ten on the first round as, even if East has a doubleton king, the jack, three times protected, cannot be caught. If the suit breaks 3:3, it is an even money bet on which finesse to take.

If only four tricks are needed, the best line changes yet again. When South leads a low card, it is all right to try the queen if West produces the jack but if he plays low, the best card is the ace followed by the queen. This protects against a singleton king with East without diminishing the chances of four tricks in other cases.

Where North-South have eight cards between them, again the number of tricks required is likely to dictate the line of play, as in this example:

Q x x x x x

A 10

We must first realize that there is no chance of six tricks. There are, however, two possible lines for five. One is to play the ace first and then the ten towards the queen, succeeding if the suit breaks 3:2 with the king with West, or exactly K J doubleton with East. This totals about 37 per cent. The alternative of playing low from North towards the ten succeeds if the suit breaks 3:2 with East having the jack or K x, or West has a doubleton K J. That totals a superior 47 per cent.

Where four tricks only are required, we can cope with a singleton king with West by cashing the ace first and then leading towards the queen, failing only if East started with K J x x. The line gives an 88 per cent chance.

Where three tricks only are required, we are able to cope with a 5–0 split in either hand; the play of a low card from the North hand deals with both eventualities. If East follows low, we put in the ten; if he discards, we rise with the ace and lead towards the well-placed queen.

Where North-South have nine cards between them, there are chances for six tricks even if the ace and queen are split, provided the ten and nine are present, as here:

A 10 9 x x x

Q x x

Here all the tricks are available if West has a singleton king (by playing the ace and then finessing against East's jack) or leading the queen, hoping that East has a singleton jack. The two lines are equally likely and thus we must decide who is likely to be longer or stronger on points.

If only five tricks are needed, they cannot be absolutely guaranteed but the ace followed by low to the queen covers the maximum number of distributions, losing only to K J x or K J x x with West for a 78 per cent chance.

Where North-South have ten cards, the probability that the jack will drop in two rounds alters the best line of play, as here:

A 10 9 x x

Q x x x x

With nine cards, it was explained that cashing the ace and running the queen were equally good bets but now, as the ace works if the king is singleton on *either* side, this is twice as good.

Where only four tricks are needed, these can be guaranteed against any 3–0 split, either by leading low towards the queen or low from South, intending to play the ten if West plays low. This latter line is superior as it still gives the overtrick if West holds the singleton king. Leading low to the queen is bound to involve the loss of exactly one trick.

Where North-South have eleven cards, the play of the ace is slightly superior to the finesse (available if the ace and queen are in the same hand) as explained earlier.

Let us now give the defenders the king and queen. Now, unless North-South have eleven cards between them and get a 1:1 split, one trick is certain to be lost as the K Q are solid against the ace. We shall therefore aim for the maximum, bearing that in mind.

Where North-South have seven cards between them, much depends on how many finesses we can take

A J 10 x x x

x

We can insist on six rounds and if we need five tricks, we shall need to find West with K Q or K Q x and thus we lead low and finesse the ten. However, if we only need four tricks, taking the finesse is a common error. Any 3:3 break will suffice as well as any 4:2 break in which at least one honour is in the doubleton. Note that we cannot catch K Q x x in the West hand even if we do finesse the ten. The best line, therefore, is to play the ace first and then a low card, keeping the J 10 intact.

A J 10 x

x x x

Here we can take two finesses by leading twice from the South hand and this is the best line for three tricks.

Where North-South have eight cards, we can still take two finesses if an extra card is added to the above layout but the number of tricks required may be crucial:

A 10 x x x

J x x

If four tricks are needed, we need to find West with K Q x, K x, Q x or K Q doubleton and play small towards the ten, cashing the ace if this loses. However, if three tricks will suffice, we can afford to protect against either defender holding a singleton honour by starting with the ace and playing a low card towards the jack, failing only if there is a 5–0 split.

Where the ten is missing, we must place the missing cards to give us the best chance of catching it:

A 9 x x x x

J x

For five tricks, we need to find East with K 10 or Q 10 doubleton. We start with a low card from North towards the jack and if East produces an honour, we play the jack from South hand next, finessing against the other honour in the West hand, while catching or *pinning* the ten at the same time. Note that we cannot win five tricks if either defender has K Q doubleton as the ten cannot be caught. Leading towards the jack is also the best line for four tricks. Now, if the ten appears from East, we shall lead small towards the nine next to protect against West having started with K Q x x.

Where North-South have nine cards between them, we approach the position where playing to drop honours rather than finessing against them becomes a more serious proposition. It will be instructive to work out the percentages here:

A J 10 x x x

x x x

We shall start with a low card from South and if West plays an honour, we shall win and return to the South hand to play towards North's holding to ensure five tricks if West started with K Q 9 8. If West plays low on the first round, we put in the ten or jack and if that loses to East, we shall return to the South hand to play another round. If West plays low again, it becomes debatable whether to play for the finesse or drop of the remaining card. As was indicated earlier, if East started with a doubleton K Q, he would have had a choice which honour to play; if he started with a singleton, he would have had no choice. We are more likely to be in the position where he had no choice and thus the finesse is the better bet.

However, with

A 9 x x x

J x x x

the absence of the ten rules out finessing possibilities and the ace followed by a low card towards the jack is the best line for four tricks, succeeding on any 2:2 break or if West started with a singleton honour. Where only three tricks are needed, we can protect against a 4–0 split either way by starting with a low card from North. If East has everything, he will have to rise with an honour, West discarding. Now the ace followed by another low card towards the jack ensures three tricks. If East discards on the first round, West will beat the jack, but now the A 9 will form a tenace over West's remaining K 10 x and we shall lead twice from South towards the ace to ensure the loss of only one further trick.

Where North-South have ten cards between them, two tricks will only be lost if all the outstanding cards are behind the ace, or if K Q 10 sit under the ace but over the jack. Otherwise, it is a simple matter to protect against a void over the ace as here:

A 10 x x x x

J x x x

where we will lead a low card from the South hand and put in the ten if West plays low.

Where North-South have eleven cards, there is now a chance for all the tricks if the king and queen are both singletons. The play of the ace will reveal the position immediately.

Well, we have scarcely scratched the surface and could go on for hours. First of all, it will do no harm to repeat a number of important points:

First, the recommended way to play an individual suit may be 'correct' in the context of the suit considered in isolation; that does not necessarily mean it is correct in the context of a whole hand.

Second, we have, up to now, assumed unlimited access to either hand to play our combinations to best advantage; the necessary entries may not be available in practical play in which case a (possibly markedly) different approach may be required.

Third, we have assumed that North or South are always starting to attack the suit; particularly if North and South have a modest number of cards between them, it may be possible to arrange for the defenders to open it up, which will usually be to our advantage.

Fourth, we have assumed that we are talking about a trump suit or suit to be attacked at no-trumps. If we have these combinations in a non-trump or *side suit*, with another suit as trumps, the picture will often change considerably.

Fifth, we have assumed that there is nothing in the bidding or early play before this suit has been touched to indicate a skew distribution or a concentration of high-card points in one hand or the other.

However, the paramount concern for the time being is to learn to walk before we can run. For the exercises in this section, I should like you to assume that everything hangs on this suit being played correctly. In each of the following, I shall show you a suit combination and the number of required tricks (possibly more than one such number for a given combination) and ask how you would play it in each case. There is no need to work out the actual percentage figures; the best line of play is what matters. Start your stop-watch.

(1)	K J 10 x x x x	(a) 3	(b) 2	
(2)	K x x x x J 10 x	(a) 4	(b) 3	(c) 2
(3)	K x x x x J 10 x x	(a) 4	(b) 3	
(4)	K 10 x x x J x x x x	4		
(5)	A 10 9 x x x x	2		
(6)	A 9 x x x 10 x x	(a) 3	(b) 2	
(7)	A 9 x x x 10 x x x	(a) 4	(b) 3	
(8)	Q J x x x x x	(a) 2	(b) 1	
(9)	J 9 x x Q x x x	(a) 2	(b) 1	
(10)	J 10 8 7 x Q x x x	(a) 3		

You should be able to work these out in well under ten minutes and aim to get under five. Let us look at the answers:

(1) Four rounds are possible but with the ace missing, three tricks is the maximum for which we can hope. This means that West will have to hold A Q, A Q x, or Q x x and we must lead towards the jack and then to the ten. We lose out if East has a singleton queen but that is much less likely. If we need only two tricks, we can lead twice towards North's holding, succeeding if either honour is with West, irrespective of the distribution. It could be argued that we should duck one round completely to cover the position where East started with A Q doubleton but that loses in the more likely

contingency that he started with a trebleton including one of the honours and we guess wrong on the second round.

(2) For four tricks, we need to find West with A Q doubleton and we should therefore lead a small card towards the king. Note that leading the jack gains nothing. West will simply cover with the queen or ace and we will have achieved nothing. Where we need three or two tricks, we can afford to lose to the ace and queen and it is better to concentrate on leading towards the short hand first. Thus we start with a low card from North so that, if East has a singleton honour or four to both honours, he will not capture one of our honours. Two tricks are guaranteed unless East is void.

(3) With nine cards, it seems debatable whether to play towards the king, succeeding if West has A x, or run the jack, succeeding if West has Q x. The former is the better play as it gains if East has a singleton queen while running the jack does not gain if East has a singleton ace because now West's Q 9 will form a tenace over the ten and cannot be caught. This is also the best line for three tricks, succeeding if West is void.

(4) We are clearly going to lead towards the king and the question arises as to how to play if West plays a low card. If that is a singleton, two tricks must be lost; if it is a doubleton, West is just as likely to have the ace as the queen. However, playing the ten gains in the case where East is void, i.e. West has both honours.

(5) One trick is certain and there is a chance of a second if the suit breaks 3:3 or in a number of 4:2 splits. The best chance is to hope that West has two or more honours under the ace and therefore we play low towards the nine and then low towards the ten, capturing any honour from West with the ace or playing the ace on the third round if the nine and ten both lose to East.

(6) For three tricks, we need a 3:2 break but we can handle certain 4:1 distributions as well. If East has K Q J x, there is no hope, but if either defender has one of the honours as a singleton, the play of the ace followed by a low card towards the ten will suffice. Against that, an immediate low

card towards the A 10 will deal with K Q J x with West. Which is the better play? We can see that a singleton honour in either hand can happen in six ways, while a small singleton with East can happen in only two and thus it is better to start with the ace.

However, if only two tricks are needed, a 4:1 break is no problem and we consider handling a 5:0. Now a low card towards the ten will ensure two tricks. If East has the *stack*, he will be forced to rise with an honour, after which we can return to North and lead towards the ten again, forcing East to produce another honour. After that our 10 9 are solid against the third honour and one of them must score. If West has the stack, he will beat the ten but now we can go to the South hand and lead twice towards the A 9 tenace to ensure a second trick.

(7)   Where we have one extra card, we will take four tricks if there is 2:2 division and the ace may be played on the first or second round. Three tricks are assured if the suit breaks no worse than 3:1. A 4:0 stack with East cannot be caught but if West has everything, we can hold our losses to two tricks by starting with a low card towards the ten or low towards the nine. Either play will reveal the position in time and we can subsequently play twice towards the ace to ensure catching one honour.

(8)   For two tricks, we need a 3:3 break with West having one honour at least or a 4:2, 5:1 or 6:0 with West having both honours. In any event, it is obviously best to observe the usual rule of leading from weakness through strength to strength, i.e. playing twice towards the North holding. If only one trick is needed, any 3:3 break will suffice but we can cover the position where East has A K doubleton by ducking the first or second round. The latter is slightly better as it ensures overtricks if West has the honours after all.

(9)   Here we have the possibility of finessing against the ten if West has it but there is no need to do so immediately. For two tricks, we should start by leading low towards the queen in case East has both ace and king or a singleton ten.

Should the queen lose, we play towards the nine next, this being preferable to playing towards the jack, gaining if West started with A K 10 x. If only one trick is needed, we can allow for a singleton honour with West by starting with a low card towards North. If West plays low, either the nine or the queen guarantees one trick but the nine gives a better chance of an overtrick. Should it lose to the ten, we lead another round towards one of the honours and there is no layout that can deny us one trick.

(10) Here we are clearly not going to lose more than two tricks if there is a 2:2 or 3:1 break; the problem arises on a 4:0. In order to keep a tenace position in both hands against the nine, we must keep an honour in both hands and start by leading towards the jack. If either defender discards or *shows out*, the other will be marked with the nine which can then be caught.

This has been a lot of work and we have still hardly scratched the surface. Again, it is more important to understand the logic behind each recommended play rather than to memorize every combination. If you can manage that, you will be able to work out for yourself how to play other combinations, bearing in mind the long list of provisos listed earlier. It is, however, worthwhile getting your time for this exercise down to the suggested minimum so that, when it comes to playing, you can see your trick-taking potential for each suit with the minimum of effort.

The Play of the Hand: Lesson Five

We are now going to consider the effect of a trump suit and assume that our various combinations are in a side suit while another suit is trumps. As before, we can still insist on the same number of rounds of our suit being played but, on the assumption that there are ample trumps available, we shall see that the number of winners and losers are often going to be different. This especially applies where there is an imbalance between the North and South hands so that one or other runs out at an early stage.

This was a position we looked at in the last chapter:

Q J 9 8 x

A x

We observed that, if West has the king, it cannot be caught (except in the most unlikely event that it is a singleton). We also saw that, even if it is with East, we could catch it only if it were a singleton or one of a doubleton, as the ace was bound to fall in two rounds. But if there is a trump suit, the picture changes. Suppose the full layout is like this:

Q J 9 8 x

10 x x   K x x

A x

Now we lead the queen from North. There is no point in East's covering as the ace is going to have to be played on the second round, so he plays low and the queen is allowed to hold. We now play a low card to the ace, return to the North hand in another suit and lead a third round. East only has the king left and must play it and, as South has now run out, he is entitled to put a trump on, winning the trick. If we can return to the North hand, again in another suit, we can cash the last two cards in this suit (nobody else having any more left) and we shall have made four tricks without loss.

Let us consider other positions where we can establish or *set up* a suit without loss:

A K x x x x

x x

We have eight cards between us and if the suit breaks 3:2, two rounds will leave one defender with a winning card, probably the queen or jack. We play a third round and ruff it to eliminate that card and then return to the North hand to enjoy the remainder, making five tricks without loss. If the suit breaks 4:1, we shall have to ruff two cards in the South hand to establish the suit and can only enjoy four tricks – but again without loss.

A x x x x x

x

South runs out after the first round, which is won by the ace. Now a second round is ruffed, the North hand is re-entered in another suit and a third round is ruffed. If the suit breaks 3:3, it is now established. If it breaks 4:2, a further round will be needed and a 5:1 break will require a still further round. According to the break, we shall, respectively, make four, three or two tricks – but notice again that it will be without loss. You should, however, be aware of three important points:

1 We need plenty of entries to the long suit to set it up and cash its established winners.
2 We need spare trumps in the short hand to ruff the losing rounds.
3 The option to ruff is also available to opponents and we cannot enjoy our established winners unless all opposing trumps have been drawn.

Let us alter the position slightly and introduce a new technique, the *ruffing finesse*.

Q J 10 x x x

x x x   K x x

A

We cash the ace and all follow. Now we enter the North hand in another suit and lead the queen. If East covers, we ruff and the rest of the suit is established; if he plays low, we simply discard a losing card in another suit, referred to as a *loser*, from the South hand and stay in the North hand to lead a third round. This forces the king and we ruff, returning to the North hand in another suit to enjoy our established winners.

This is another example:

                    K Q J 10 x x

    x x x   A x x x

                        —

We are lacking the ace but can still enjoy five tricks without loss. Lead the king from the North hand. If East covers, simply ruff and return to the North hand in another suit to enjoy five established winners. If East refuses to cover, discard losers from the South hand and carry on with high cards from North until he does.

We can even have a double ruffing finesse:

                    Q J 10 9 x x x

    x x   A K x x

                        —

We lead the queen from North, ruffing East's king whenever he feels like playing it. Then return to North and lead another high card, catching East's ace in a similar manner for five established tricks without loss. Note, however, that West will run out of the suit after two rounds and his trumps must be exhausted early unless South is prepared to ruff with trumps higher than those in West's hand. Notice that this is still in line with the principle of leading from weakness through strength to strength. North has the weak holding, East has the strength and South's trumps are stronger still.

Note that ruffing finesses can be taken against lower-ranking cards. This was another combination we looked at in the last chapter:

                    A Q 10 9 x x

                        x

We observed that we could only take six tricks if West held exactly K J doubleton and that indeed still holds here. We also saw that there were plays for five tricks, but with no trumps available, that would involve the loss of one trick. Now with the option to ruff, there are many chances for five tricks without loss.

A Q 10 9 x x

K x   J x x x

x

Here we could play low to the queen and follow with the ace. When the king falls, the 10 9 are solid against the jack and we can take a ruffing finesse. However, beware! The position could be:

A Q 10 9 x x

K J x   x x x

x

Once we have played a low card to the queen, the K J are solid against the ace and West can easily (and indeed should!) drop the king under the ace on the second round. Now we would have to ruff the third round to ensure five tricks without loss. The decision on how to play the combination at the table with only the North and South hand exposed rests on a number of considerations including the view we take about the distributions of suits and points.

If we only need four tricks and particularly if it is essential to avoid the loss of a trick in the suit, the best play is to start with the ace and then ruff a low card. If no honour has appeared, we return to the North hand in another suit and ruff another low card, hoping for a 3:3 break. If an honour appears from West on the first or second round, there will be the option to take a ruffing finesse against East on the third.

Let us re-examine some more positions we looked at in the last chapter.

Q x x x x x

A 10

If the king is a singleton, no trick will be lost. The ace wins the first round and the queen the second, after which two low cards from North ruffed by South will bring down the jack to establish the remaining two cards for four tricks in total. If the king does not appear under the ace, only one trick will be lost as the third and subsequent rounds can be ruffed until the suit is established.

A J 10 x x x

x

In this case, the ace covers the singleton and no trick need be lost. An interesting problem arises if we try to establish the suit by ruffing. Say the ace draws two low cards and the second round, when ruffed, pulls an honour from West. We now have a similar position to

A Q 10 9 x x

x

which we discussed earlier – whether to take a ruffing finesse on the assumption that East has the other honour, or whether to play for the 3:3 split. As indicated earlier, there are a number of considerations which may sway the decision one way or the other.

A 9 x x x x

J x

Here, one lost trick cannot be avoided and it is likely that it will be advisable to lose it on the first round if we are short of entries to the North hand. Let us illustrate this point with an example. Suppose we have a friendly 3:2 break as here:

A 9 x x x x

K 10 x   Q x

J x

but that there is only one entry available to the North hand in another suit. Now let us try playing it both ways. Suppose we take the ace on the first round and play low to the second, won by East's queen. East plays another suit and we win in the South hand. Now we use our sole entry to the North hand to play a third round of our long suit, ruffing in the South hand to bring down West's king. The remaining three cards in the North hand are now established, but we cannot get back there to cash them. But suppose we duck the first round of the suit. One of the opponents wins (they have the choice) and plays another suit. South wins and plays a second round of our suit to North's ace. Now we are in the North hand to play the third round, ruffing to establish the suit. But observe the difference. The side entry has not been used and we can use it to return to the North hand to cash our established winners.

An obvious point arises here for East-West. Attacking North's entry at an early stage is one of the defenders' major priorities and books on advanced play give examples where it is worth giving a trick away (typically leading an unsupported king to an ace) to remove an entry to a long suit in this kind of situation.

Indeed, it is time to consider the defenders' position in respect of establishing tricks in long suits in some detail. Let us look at a basic position which crops up frequently:

K Q J 10 9 x

x x x   A x

x x

South plays a low card to North's king. If East wins this, South, when he next gets in, will lead his other low card and will be able to enjoy five tricks. But let us try the effect of East's refusing the first round and winning the second. Now South is exhausted and will need a side entry in the North hand to be able to enjoy the rest of the tricks. If there isn't one, East's play of *holding up* to the second round will have saved his side four tricks, in that South will make one trick in the suit instead of five. Note that this all applies whether there are trumps around or this is a suit at no-trumps. If this suit is trumps, five tricks cannot be prevented but even now, it might still be worthwhile for East to hold up. If North has no entry outside, he may well be inconvenienced in being unable to draw West's third trump immediately.

When to win and when to refuse is a considerable subject on its own and often critical decisions have to be taken. Put yourself in the West position with this side suit in a trump contract:

K Q 10 x x

A x x x   J x x

x

South plays his low card and what are you to do? If you go up with the ace, you will establish four tricks for North (assuming he has one entry). Against that, if you play low, North's king will win. Now any subsequent round can be ruffed by South and you will never make your ace! It seems that you are faced with having to choose between the frying pan and the fire! What you should ask yourself is 'Would I prefer to win one trick and lose four or win no trick and lose one?' The decision will obviously rest on what is happening in the other suits, but a general guide is that it usually pays to duck in these situations. You will have to be prepared to look silly occasionally but the trick you have sacrificed usually comes back in another suit and very often with interest. The loss to the opponents is likely to be more serious than that to your side.

The question of winning or ducking does not only apply to aces. You can be faced with a similar decision with lower cards, as here:

$$Q J x x x$$
$$K 10 x x \qquad\qquad 9 x$$
$$A x$$

Again, this is a side suit in a trump contract and South might well have tried to avoid losing any tricks in the suit by running the queen. Often, however, entries to the North hand may be at a premium and in practice, South leads the ace and follows with his low card. How do you play? It is the same problem again. If you rise with the king, the rest of the suit is set up and you will win one trick and lose four. Hold him up, however, and although the queen will win and any subsequent round can be ruffed, North-South will probably only take two tricks in the suit, needing a large number of entries to ruff out your king to establish a third. Again ask yourself the question 'Would I prefer to win one trick and lose four or win no trick and lose two?' Again, it usually pays to duck. We can go lower still:

$$J 10 9 x x x$$
$$Q x x x \qquad\qquad K$$
$$A x$$

South starts with the ace, dropping your partner's king. Now the low card follows and what are you to do as West? Unless the North hand has several entries, you are weighing up winning one trick and losing five against winning no tricks and losing two! Ducking is almost certainly going to be better. Very often, North will win with the jack and play the ten, South discarding rather than ruffing, and you will get your queen anyway. That way, the opponents ensure that the suit is established. It may well be that South tries to establish this suit early in play before trumps are drawn – likely to happen if North's entries are in trumps. In that case, East can ruff the second round and you can keep your queen intact without loss!

Another important use of trumps is to ruff losers. Often this has to be done before trumps are drawn. Let us, for the first time, introduce two suits, spades being trumps, hearts being the side suit:

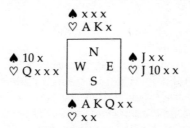

♠ x x x
♡ x x

♠ 10 x
♡ Q x x x

♠ J x x
♡ J 10 x x

♠ A K Q x x
♡ A K x

South plays the ace and king of hearts and then his third heart and as North has no more, he can ruff while the others are still following. After that, trumps may be played from the top and you will see that North-South make six trump tricks and two heart tricks – eight in all. But observe what happens if South draws out all the trumps first. Three rounds will be needed, after which North will have run out. He will now not be able to ruff South's third heart and a trick in that suit will have to be lost to East-West. South may draw two rounds of trumps before taking the heart ruff, but no more. Ruffing of this type normally gains when the hand ruffing is, or will become, shorter in trumps than his partner. A couple of further examples will illustrate:

♠ x x x
♡ A K x

♠ 10 x
♡ Q x x x

♠ J x x
♡ J 10 x x

♠ A K Q x x
♡ x x

Here North-South gain nothing by taking a heart ruff in the South hand. They can take five top trump tricks and two top heart tricks but no more.

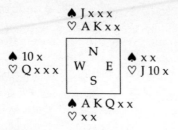

This time, however, there is something to be gained by ruffing in the hand with long trumps. North cashes the two top hearts and ruffs a third in the South hand. A low trump is won by North's jack and now North's last heart is ruffed by South (East may ruff if he wishes, but he will be overruffed by South's higher trumps) and now the North hand is longer in trumps than South. North-South thus make four top trumps, two ruffs and the two top hearts – eight tricks in all. If they simply played out all the trumps, they would only make five top trumps and the two hearts to total only seven.

The third important use of trumps is to prevent opponents from making tricks with their high cards and thus cut down losers. Let us examine this diagram:

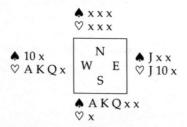

Spades are still trumps and West, on lead, plays the ace of hearts and everybody follows. When he persists with the king of hearts, South, who has now run out of the suit, is entitled to play a trump and wins the trick. It is important now for South to refrain from playing out all his trumps. If he does and West regains the lead later on in one of the minor suits, he will be able to cash his queen of hearts, as South will not have a trump to play on it. The usual guide therefore is to use trumps when necessary, viz. to draw opponents' trumps, establish side suits or ruff losers where it will gain but to hold on to the remainder as *controls* to prevent opponents from enjoying their tricks.

We are going to conclude with eight examples illustrating some of the principles I have set out in these last few chapters. Throughout, I am going to allow you to see all four hands because we are still very much at the walking stage. Playing in real conditions involves visualizing the unseen hands and *then* playing as though you can see all four, but that is going too far ahead at this stage.

The procedure you should adopt is to decide:

1 How many rounds are likely to be played in each suit, bearing in mind that there will only be thirteen tricks played in all.
2 How many you are likely to win.
3 How many you are likely to lose.
4 Will that be enough for the contract?
5 Are there any problems?
6 How are they to be solved?

Use your stop-watch and aim to do each in under five minutes. It will also be useful revision to fill in the scoresheet when you have completed your contract. Assume each hand is the first of a new rubber and that you are the declarer, sitting South.

No-trump contracts

(1) The contract is 3NT and West leads the king of spades.

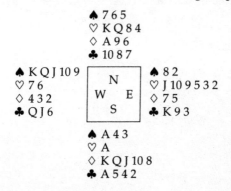

```
                    ♠ 7 6 5
                    ♡ K Q 8 4
                    ◇ A 9 6
                    ♣ 10 8 7
  ♠ K Q J 10 9                      ♠ 8 2
  ♡ 7 6            ┌─────────┐      ♡ J 10 9 5 3 2
  ◇ 4 3 2         │    N    │       ◇ 7 5
  ♣ Q J 6        │ W     E │        ♣ K 9 3
                  │    S    │
                  └─────────┘
                    ♠ A 4 3
                    ♡ A
                    ◇ K Q J 10 8
                    ♣ A 5 4 2
```

(2) The contract is 3NT and West leads the five of hearts to East's queen.

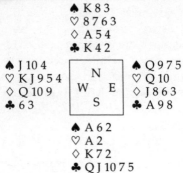

```
                    ♠ K 8 3
                    ♡ 8 7 6 3
                    ◇ A 5 4
                    ♣ K 4 2
  ♠ J 10 4                        ♠ Q 9 7 5
  ♡ K J 9 5 4        N            ♡ Q 10
  ◇ Q 10 9       W        E       ◇ J 8 6 3
  ♣ 6 3              S            ♣ A 9 8
                    ♠ A 6 2
                    ♡ A 2
                    ◇ K 7 2
                    ♣ Q J 10 7 5
```

(3) The contract is 3NT and West leads the queen of spades.

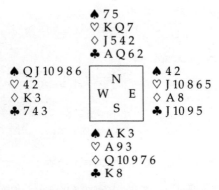

```
                    ♠ 7 5
                    ♡ K Q 7
                    ◇ J 5 4 2
                    ♣ A Q 6 2
  ♠ Q J 10 9 8 6                  ♠ 4 2
  ♡ 4 2              N            ♡ J 10 8 6 5
  ◇ K 3         W        E        ◇ A 8
  ♣ 7 4 3            S            ♣ J 10 9 5
                    ♠ A K 3
                    ♡ A 9 3
                    ◇ Q 10 9 7 6
                    ♣ K 8
```

(4) The contract is 6NT and West leads the jack of spades.

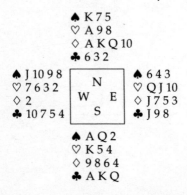

```
                    ♠ K 7 5
                    ♡ A 9 8
                    ◇ A K Q 10
                    ♣ 6 3 2
  ♠ J 10 9 8                      ♠ 6 4 3
  ♡ 7 6 3 2          N            ♡ Q J 10
  ◇ 2           W        E        ◇ J 7 5 3
  ♣ 10 7 5 4         S            ♣ J 9 8
                    ♠ A Q 2
                    ♡ K 5 4
                    ◇ 9 8 6 4
                    ♣ A K Q
```

Trump contracts

(5) The contract is seven hearts and West leads the ace of spades.

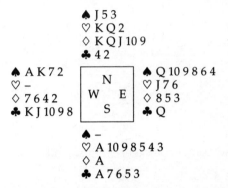

```
              ♠ J 5 3
              ♡ K Q 2
              ◊ K Q J 10 9
              ♣ 4 2
♠ A K 7 2                  ♠ Q 10 9 8 6 4
♡ –            N           ♡ J 7 6
◊ 7 6 4 2    W   E         ◊ 8 5 3
♣ K J 10 9 8   S           ♣ Q
              ♠ –
              ♡ A 10 9 8 5 4 3
              ◊ A
              ♣ A 7 6 5 3
```

Have you any other comment to make on this hand?

(6) The contract is six spades and West leads the ace of clubs and continues with the ten of clubs. There now follows the most important piece of advice in respect of bridge play – work out the whole hand before playing to the first trick – this cannot be overemphasized!

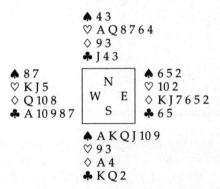

```
              ♠ 4 3
              ♡ A Q 8 7 6 4
              ◊ 9 3
              ♣ J 4 3
♠ 8 7                      ♠ 6 5 2
♡ K J 5        N           ♡ 10 2
◊ Q 10 8     W   E         ◊ K J 7 6 5 2
♣ A 10 9 8 7   S           ♣ 6 5
              ♠ A K Q J 10 9
              ♡ 9 3
              ◊ A 4
              ♣ K Q 2
```

Have you any other comment to make on this hand?

(7) The contract is five clubs and West leads the ten of spades.

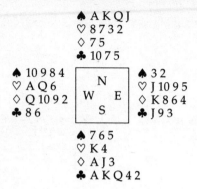

♠ A K Q J
♥ 8 7 3 2
♦ 7 5
♣ 10 7 5

♠ 10 9 8 4   ♠ 3 2
♥ A Q 6   ♥ J 10 9 5
♦ Q 10 9 2   ♦ K 8 6 4
♣ 8 6   ♣ J 9 3

♠ 7 6 5
♥ K 4
♦ A J 3
♣ A K Q 4 2

Have you any other comment on this hand?

(8) The contract is six hearts and West leads the king of diamonds.

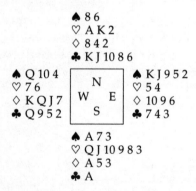

♠ 8 6
♥ A K 2
♦ 8 4 2
♣ K J 10 8 6

♠ Q 10 4   ♠ K J 9 5 2
♥ 7 6   ♥ 5 4
♦ K Q J 7   ♦ 10 9 6
♣ Q 9 5 2   ♣ 7 4 3

♠ A 7 3
♥ Q J 10 9 8 3
♦ A 5 3
♣ A

Solutions to the no-trump contracts

We are now going to discuss the recommended line of play for each problem and I should like you to set out the cards in front of you and turn them over as we play them together. We shall be going very slowly and you will particularly notice that most of the discussion will take place before we play a single card to the first trick.

Up to now, I have referred to cards in words – ace of spades, ten of hearts, and so on. For compactness, I shall, from now on, call them ♠A, ♡10, etc.

(1) The contract is 3NT and West leads the ♠K.

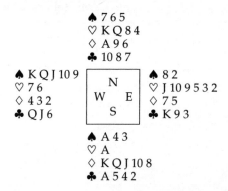

```
              ♠ 7 6 5
              ♡ K Q 8 4
              ◇ A 9 6
              ♣ 10 8 7

  ♠ K Q J 10 9    ┌─────┐    ♠ 8 2
  ♡ 7 6           │  N  │    ♡ J 10 9 5 3 2
  ◇ 4 3 2         │W   E│    ◇ 7 5
  ♣ Q J 6         │  S  │    ♣ K 9 3
                  └─────┘
              ♠ A 4 3
              ♡ A
              ◇ K Q J 10 8
              ♣ A 5 4 2
```

First of all, note the very obvious opening lead. No-trump contracts often involve a race between the two sides to see who can set up their long suit first. Once such a suit has been established, the absence of trumps implies that long cards cannot be beaten. Here West has a solid five-card suit and it is usual to lead the top card of a sequence. You should lead the ace from A K, king from K Q, queen from Q J, jack from J 10, and so on. This informs partner that you do not hold the card immediately above, but promises the card immediately below. Admittedly declarer can also take advantage of this information but as he knows what forces are against him anyway, it usually pays to give information to both partner and declarer rather than to neither.

We are now going to count the number of rounds, potential winners and losers in each of the four suits and gather some idea of where we stand:

Spades: We have three cards in each hand and could there-
           fore insist on three rounds. Of those, we will clearly
           win one trick with the ace but lose the others. Worse
           still, as West holds five, if he gets the lead after the
           ace has been played, he can cash four tricks in the
           suit.

Hearts: We can insist on four rounds, winning three (ace, king and queen) and losing one. Note that East has six, so he must not be allowed to get the lead after those high cards have gone otherwise he will be able to cash three long cards in the suit.

Diamonds: Five rounds, clearly winning all five and losing none.

Clubs: Four rounds, winning one with the ace and losing two more to the king and queen but the fourth card will be a winner as the suit is breaking 3:3.

Now let us collate what we have so far:

	Rounds	**Winners**	**Losers**
Spades	3	1	2
Hearts	4	3	1
Diamonds	5	5	0
Clubs	4	2	2
Total	16	11	5

There are only going to be thirteen tricks in all, so we must be careful about the choice of suits on which to concentrate. We note that there are eleven winners, which should be sufficient as we only need nine. However, we must discount the possibility of establishing that long club. To do so would involve losing the lead twice and if West gets in, he will be able to cash four spade tricks, which, in addition to the club, will add up to five to leave us one trick short. So we must be content with our ten top winners and consider if there is any problem in cashing them. It is usual to concentrate on long suits first but if we were to win the spade and cash the five diamond tricks immediately, there will be no entry to the North hand (dummy) to cash the two heart honours. For that reason, the ♡A must be *unblocked* first. The order of play is therefore as follows:

1   ♠K won by the ace, North playing the five and East the two.
2   ♡A to West's six, North's four and East's two.
3   ◊8 to West's two, North's ace and East's five.

4   ♡K to East's three, South discards the ♠3, (it is usual to discard cards which are unlikely to make tricks or help higher cards in the same suit to do so); West follows with the seven.

5   ♡Q to East's five, South discards the ♠4, West discards the ◇3.

6   ◇9 to East's seven, won by South's ten, West following with the four.

7   ◇K, West discards the ♠9, North follows with the ◇6, East discards the ♡9. Note that East hangs on to his ♠8 and tries to protect his ♣K so that, if he gets in with that card, he can lead the spade to his partner's high cards in that suit.

8   ◇Q, West discards the ♠10, North discards the ♠6, East discards the ♡10.

9   ◇J, West discards the ♠J (note that he tries to protect his ♣Q in case South has the ace and king, nothing being lost if East has one of those cards), North discards the ♠7, East the ♣3 (he may also discard the ♡J as he can see that there is no danger of South being able to reach dummy to cash what would then be an established ♡8).

10   South cashes the ♣A to West's six, North's seven and East's nine.

11   South leads the ♣2 to West's jack, North's eight and East's king.

12   East returns his ♠8, South discards the ♣4, West wins with the ♠Q, North discards the ♡8.

13   West leads his ♣Q to the ten, East discards the ♡J and South follows with his last card, the ♣5.

North-South have won ten tricks against East-West's three and score 100 under the line and 30 over.

(2) The contract is 3NT and West leads the ♡5 to East's ♡Q.

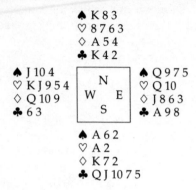

```
              ♠ K 8 3
              ♡ 8 7 6 3
              ◇ A 5 4
              ♣ K 4 2
♠ J 10 4                      ♠ Q 9 7 5
♡ K J 9 5 4      N           ♡ Q 10
◇ Q 10 9      W     E        ◇ J 8 6 3
♣ 6 3            S           ♣ A 9 8
              ♠ A 6 2
              ♡ A 2
              ◇ K 7 2
              ♣ Q J 10 7 5
```

Let us first consider that opening lead. We learnt that it is usually unwise to lead away from broken holdings like KJ x; it is obviously better for the suit to be led towards such tenaces. However, we also emphasized that no-trump contracts usually involve a race to set up long suits and in practice, it is usually worth risking giving up an unnecessary trick for that purpose. On this occasion, West is lucky to find his partner with the queen so that he has, in effect, led from a combined solid holding K Q J and they have got the ten and nine as well.

When leading a low card from a long broken suit, the usual choice is the fourth highest card. This enables partner to work out the position in the suit, which may help him to judge how best to defend the hand. The method is known as the *rule of eleven*.

Take any spot card and call it x. With the two being the lowest card in the suit, there will be (x − 1) cards lower than that spot card and therefore 13 − (x − 1) = (14 − x) cards higher. As the x is the fourth highest card, there are (14 − x − 3) i.e. (11 − x) higher cards still unaccounted for. The player in the East position therefore deducts the spot card from eleven, looks to see how many cards higher than the spot card are in his own hand and the remainder must be in the declarer's hand.

Let us take, as an example, the position here. The five is led: 11 − 5 = 6. So there are six cards higher than the five unaccounted for and East can see two in his own hand and three more in the dummy. So he knows that there is only one card higher than the five in the closed declarer's hand and once that card has been played, the rest of the suit can be run for tricks to the defenders.

Now let us go through the four suits again and see where we stand as regards rounds, winners and losers:

Spades: Three rounds, winning two and losing one. But note that, if East gets in after the ace and king have been played, he will also have an established fourth round to cash.

Hearts: Four rounds, winning one and losing three and West has a long card to cash if he is allowed to get in so we could indeed lose four.

Diamonds: A similar position to spades.

Clubs: Five rounds, winning four and losing one.

The collation:

	Rounds	**Winners**	**Losers**
Spades	3	2	1
Hearts	4	1	3
Diamonds	3	2	1
Clubs	5	4	1
Total	15	9	6

So it appears there are nine tricks to be taken, but we shall have to lose the lead to set up the clubs and now there is a danger that the defenders will take their four established heart tricks to make five in all for a one-trick defeat or (as they say in America) *set*.

In situations like this, we have to hope that the ♣A and the long hearts are in different hands and that we can arrange to lose the trick to that ace when the hand holding it is out of hearts. To achieve this, we must refuse the first trick, win the second, and only then attack clubs. East will win but West now has no quick entry to be able to cash his hearts and we shall be able to make nine tricks before the enemy can make five. The play goes as follows:

1   ♡5 from West to ♡6 (it does not matter which card North plays and costs nothing to cover) from North, ♡Q from East and ♡2 from South.

2   ♡10 from East to ♡A from South, ♡4 from West and ♡3 from North.

3   ♣5 from South, ♣3 from West, ♣K from North and ♣8 from East. As the South hand has plenty of entries and spades and diamonds, it makes little difference whether East wins or not, but it is worth his while holding up to third round if only to make South use one of those entries as East-West have potential tricks in those suits. Note South observes the guide of playing the high card from the short suit first. (Note that East-West did the same thing in hearts!)

4   ♣4 from North, ♣9 from East, ♣10 from South, ♣6 from West.

5   ♣Q from South, West discards ♠4 (trying to keep his winning hearts and protect his ◇Q), ♣2 from North and ♣A from East. East is now on play and his partner's discard of a low spade suggests that he is not interested in the suit and therefore he might have something in diamonds.

6   ◇3 from East (fourth highest again), ◇K from South, ◇9 from West, ◇4 from North.

7   ♣J from South, West discards ♠10, North discards ♡7 (of no possible use), East discards ◇6. Notice that each defender keeps one suit guarded – West the diamonds and East the spades; if both discarded from the same suit, it is likely that they would allow North-South an extra trick in that suit.

8   ♣7 from South, West discards ♠J, North discards ♡8, East discards ◇8. South will now make his three top cards – the order does not matter.

9   ♠A from South, West discards ♡9 (he must keep his ◇Q protected), North follows with ♠3, East plays ♠5.

10   ♠2 from South, West discards ♡J, North wins with ♠K, East plays ♠7.

11   ◇A from North, ◇J from East, ◇2 from South, ◇10 from West.

12   ◇5 from North, East discards ♠9, South plays ◇7, West wins with ◇Q.

     (You now see why he had to hold all his diamonds.)

13   West cashes ♡K, North discards ♠8, East discards ♠Q and
     South discards ♠6.

North-South have taken nine tricks to East-West's four and the
former score 100 under the line.

(3) The contract is 3NT and West leads the ♠Q.

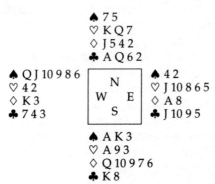

```
                    ♠ 7 5
                    ♡ K Q 7
                    ◇ J 5 4 2
                    ♣ A Q 6 2
   ♠ Q J 10 9 8 6              ♠ 4 2
   ♡ 4 2          ┌─────────┐  ♡ J 10 8 6 5
   ◇ K 3          │    N    │  ◇ A 8
   ♣ 7 4 3        │  W   E  │  ♣ J 10 9 5
                  │    S    │
                  └─────────┘
                    ♠ A K 3
                    ♡ A 9 3
                    ◇ Q 10 9 7 6
                    ♣ K 8
```

West has made the obvious long solid-suit lead and he has an
outside entry to his suit. Let us go through the suits as usual:

Spades: Three rounds, winning two and losing one. But if
          West gets in after the ace and king have gone, he will
          have four long cards to cash.

Hearts: Three rounds, winning three and losing none. Note,
          however, that East will have two long cards to cash if
          he is allowed to get in after the ace, king and queen
          have gone.

Diamonds: Five rounds, winning three and losing two.

Clubs: Four rounds, winning three and losing one.

The collation:

	Rounds	Winners	Losers
Spades	3	2	1
Hearts	3	3	0
Diamonds	5	3	2
Clubs	4	3	1
Total	15	11	4

There seem to be enough winners but not without setting up the diamonds, which will involve losing the lead twice. Looking from the defenders' point of view, they need to set up their long spade tricks to defeat the contract. This also involves losing the lead twice, but as they have the opening lead, they are a step ahead. Suppose we win the first spade and attack diamonds. The defenders will arrange that the hand with the shorter spades, i.e. East, will win the first round so that he can return his remaining spade. South will win and when West gets in with the second diamond, he can run the rest of the spades to complete six tricks for a two-trick defeat. Can anything be done?

As in the previous hand, we have to exhaust one of the defenders, obviously East, of spades before he gets in with a diamond. Obliged to switch to hearts or clubs, he will put his side a step behind in the race and our diamonds will get in first. South must, therefore, refuse to win the first spade. The play goes:

1   West's ♠Q to North's ♠5, East's ♠2 and South's ♠3.
2   West's ♠J to North's ♠7, East's ♠4 and South's ♠A.
3   South's ◇6 to West's ◇3 (note that he tries to hold his king as entry to the spades), North's ◇J and East's ◇A.
4   East switches to ♡J (although his clubs are more solid, there is clearly nothing to be gained by leading round to an A Q tenace in dummy and in practice, he might play hoping to find his partner with the ♡A), to South's ♡3, West's ♡2 and North's ♡K.
5   North leads ◇2 to East's ◇8, South's ◇9 and West's ◇K.

We have now reached an interesting position. West can, of course, persist with spades but he knows that he will lose to the king and has no entry in a side suit to enjoy the rest of the suit. In practice, therefore, he might well return his partner's heart, which would indeed defeat the contract if East started with ♡ A J 10 or longer. Let us work on that assumption:

6   West returns ♡4 to North's ♡7, East's ♡10 and South's ♡A.
7   South cashes ◇Q, West discards ♠6 (no longer of any possible use), to North's ◇4 and East discards ♡5 (also of no possible use – there may still be a chance in clubs).

8   South cashes ◇10, West discards ♠8, North follows with
     ◇5, East discards ♡6.
9   South cashes ◇7, West discards ♠9, North discards ♣2,
     East discards ♡8.
10   South cashes ♣K (high from the shorter hand first) to
     West's ♣3, North's ♣6 and East's ♣5.
11   South plays ♣8 to West's ♣4, North's ♣Q and East's ♣9.
12   North cashes ♣A to East's ♣10, South discards ♡9, West
     follows with ♣7.
13   North cashes ♡K, East discards ♣J, South discards ♠K,
     West discards ♠10.

North-South score ten tricks and concede three to score 100
points under the line and 30 over it. Note that last trick. South
discarded the king of spades, which could easily have made a
trick in its own right. As the play went, North-South had a trick
to spare or *burn*. Go over the play again and satisfy yourself that,
if South wins the first trick, he will be defeated even if he tries to
recover by holding up the second round. However, you should
also satisfy yourself that, if he does make that mistake, he can
cash three tricks each in hearts and clubs which, with the top
spades, will total eight tricks for a one-trick set as opposed to the
two-trick set he will suffer if he persists in trying to set up the
diamonds. It will pay you to spend the time going through these
variations to be sure that you understand them. More difficult
hands are based on these principles.

(4) The contract is 6NT and West leads the ♠J.

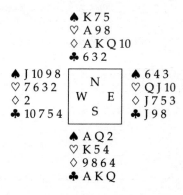

```
                    ♠ K 7 5
                    ♡ A 9 8
                    ◇ A K Q 10
                    ♣ 6 3 2
   ♠ J 10 9 8                      ♠ 6 4 3
   ♡ 7 6 3 2        N              ♡ Q J 10
   ◇ 2           W     E           ◇ J 7 5 3
   ♣ 10 7 5 4       S              ♣ J 9 8
                    ♠ A Q 2
                    ♡ K 5 4
                    ◇ 9 8 6 4
                    ♣ A K Q
```

The Expert Beginner

Again, West has chosen the top of a sequence in a long solid suit. Let us do our trick count:

Spades: Three rounds, winning three, losing none.
Hearts: Three rounds, winning two, losing one.
Diamonds: Four rounds, winning three, losing one.
Clubs: Three rounds, winning three, losing none.

The collation:

	Rounds	Winners	Losers
Spades	3	3	0
Hearts	3	2	1
Diamonds	4	3	1
Clubs	3	3	0
Total	13	11	2

Looks like we are doomed! It is unlucky to say the least: a 3:2 break in diamonds is much more likely than the actual 4:1, and even in the latter case, the jack could have been a singleton or West could have had the length or *stack*, in which case his jack could be caught by a finesse, leading the suit from the weak South hand through his holding to the strong North hand. Before we curse our ill-luck, let us look at those diamonds more closely. The jack is three times protected and well placed over the ace, king and queen and therefore cannot be caught *unless East can be forced to lead the suit*. Now the ten will score. Can this be arranged?

Defenders are, by nature, very uncooperative people and East will not touch diamonds unless he has to. His hand will therefore have to be stripped down to nothing but diamonds and his heart winner, and then he will have to be given that heart winner. Fortunately, his distribution is identical to that of North and South, so there is a chance. The play goes as follows:

1   West leads ♠J to North's ♠5, East's ♠3 and South's ♠A.
2   South leads ◇4 to West's ◇2, North's ◇A and East's ◇3.
3   North leads ◇K to East's ◇5 and South's ◇6, West discarding ♡2.

In practical play, it would be at this point that South would discover the bad news. However, it is an excellent habit to anticipate these problems before they arise. In more difficult hands, you may well have to prepare for these contingencies long before they are revealed. The next job is to eliminate the black suits (the exact order does not matter).

4 North leads ♣2 to East's ♣8, South's ♣A and West's ♣4.

5 South cashes ♣K to West's ♣5, North's ♣3 and East's ♣9.

6 South cashes ♣Q to West's ♣7, North's ♣6 and East's ♣J.

7 South cashes ♠Q to West's ♠8, North's ♠7 and East's ♠4.

8 South plays ♠2 to West's ♠9, North's ♠K and East's ♠6.

9 North plays ♡8 to East's ♡10, South's ♡K and West's ♡3.

10 South plays ♡4 to West's ♡6, North's ♡A and East's ♡J.

11 North plays ♡9 to East's ♡Q, South's ♡5 and West's ♡7.

East is now on play with only ♢ J 7 left and has the choice of leading either round to North's ♢ Q 10, while West has to discard his two black tens. So North-South make twelve tricks and concede one to score 190 under the line and 500 over for the non-vulnerable small slam. You should note that, if West has any of East's three heart honours, the contract cannot be made. Let us clarify this by looking at three examples:

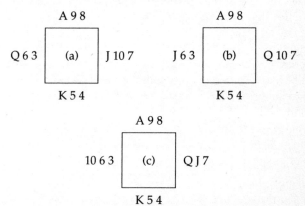

(The ♡2 was discarded on the second round of diamonds.)

In an earlier chapter, we discussed at some length the importance of distinguishing situations where North-South or East-West could dictate which rounds of a suit were won or lost and which opponent would win that or those rounds. This hand is a beautiful illustrative example. From North-South's point of view, it is vital that the *third* round be lost, (as opposed to the first or second). If they lose the first or second, the defenders can simply return this suit and now East cannot be forced to lead diamonds to his cost. The second point is that this third round must be lost to East rather than West, the latter having his two black tens to cash.

Now, with the hand as it was, East had all three honours and could not avoid being thrown in or *endplayed*. But give West just one and the defence prevails. In (a), West simply hangs on to his queen. In (b), East must play his queen on the first or second round, i.e. under the ace or king so that his partner wins the third trick. In (c), East must play both his queen and jack on the first two rounds to make way for his partner's ten to win the third. This is quite an advanced defence but it is important for a beginner to realize from the start that high cards are not always assets and indeed may be serious liabilities which have to be discarded early.

We are now going to turn to the trump contracts and note the differences in technique.

Solutions to the trump contracts

(5) The contract is seven hearts and West leads the ♠A.

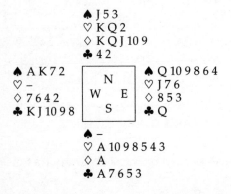

```
              ♠ J 5 3
              ♡ K Q 2
              ◇ K Q J 10 9
              ♣ 4 2
♠ A K 7 2      ┌───────┐      ♠ Q 10 9 8 6 4
♡ -            │   N   │      ♡ J 7 6
◇ 7 6 4 2      │ W   E │      ◇ 8 5 3
♣ K J 10 9 8   │   S   │      ♣ Q
              └───────┘
              ♠ -
              ♡ A 10 9 8 5 4 3
              ◇ A
              ♣ A 7 6 5 3
```

West has led an ace backed up by the king, usually a good lead against a trump contract. Let us do our trick count:

Spades: Three rounds which will all be trumped. But we notice that even after that, South will still be longer in trumps than North, so that taking those ruffs is unlikely to achieve very much.

Hearts: Seven rounds, winning seven (as the jack drops in three rounds) and losing none.

Diamonds: Five rounds, winning five and losing none.

Clubs: Five rounds, winning one and losing one, subsequent rounds could be ruffed in the North hand but not before a trick has been lost. Thus trying to ruff clubs in dummy is a non-starter and we need only worry about the first two rounds.

The collation:

	Rounds	Winners	Losers
Spades	3	0	0
Hearts	7	7	0
Diamonds	5	5	0
Clubs	2	1	1
Total	17	13	1

Notice that, with trumps around, the winners and losers in each suit do not necessarily tally up with the rounds played.

Thirteen tricks seem to be available and we can avoid playing a second round of clubs by discarding the four clubs in the South hand on four winning diamonds in dummy. Is there any problem? The order of play is critical because, as East has only three diamonds, we cannot enjoy the fourth and fifth round until trumps have been drawn. However, if we draw trumps immediately and then start on diamonds, we will be able to cash the ace but will have no entry to get to the others. Consequently, that ace must be cashed while one high trump is still in dummy. The play goes as follows:

1   West's ♠A to North's ♠3, East's ♠4 and ruffed by South's ♡3.

2   South plays ♡4, West discards ◇2 (cannot possibly win a trick with five higher solid cards in dummy), North wins with ♡K, East follows with ♡6.

3   North plays ♡2 to East's ♡7, South's ♡A, West discards ◇4.

4   South cashes ◇A to West's ◇6, North's ◇9 and East's ◇3.

5   South plays ♡5, West discards ◇7, North wins with ♡Q, East plays ♡J.

6   North cashes ◇K to East's ◇5, South discards ♣3, West discards ♣8.

7   North cashes ◇Q to East's ◇8, South discards ♣5, West discards ♣9.

8   North cashes ◇J, East discards ♠6, South discards ♣6, West discards ♣10.

9   North cashes ◇10, East discards ♠8, South discards ♣7, West discards ♠7.

At this point, South's hand is *high* with the ♣A and nothing else but trumps – all unbeatable cards. Let us play it out to the end.

10   North plays ♣2 to East's ♣Q, South's ♣A and West's ♣J.

11   South plays ♡10, the others discarding as they please; it makes no difference.

12   South plays ♡9, the others discard.

13   South plays ♡8, the others discard.

North-South have taken all thirteen tricks without loss to score 210 under the line and 1000 over it for the non-vulnerable grand slam.

I asked whether you had any other comment to make on this hand. The North-South score totalled 1210 and the 'break-up value' of a non-vulnerable game is 300, so the whole hand is worth 1510. East-West could have saved themselves a great deal if they had sacrificed in 7♠. Shall we play it?

Let us assume that East is declarer, so South is on lead. Doing our usual trick count, we see that, at the worst, East-West should lose three diamond tricks and the ace of clubs to go four down. However, it may not even be as bad as that. In the play of the grand slam in hearts, we noticed that North-South had a problem in respect of the diamond blockage and that this could only be overcome by crossing to the dummy at the right moment in hearts. Now, with spades as trumps, this is impossible because West is void of hearts and can ruff. As a result, East has a chance to discard some of his losing diamonds on the high clubs once the ace has been knocked out. The play goes like this:

1   South cashes ◇A; this is the most urgent trick for the defence so that North can cash more diamond tricks if he can get in. West follows with ◇2, North with ◇9, East with ◇3.

2   South plays ♡A, West ruffs with ♠2, North follows with ♡2 and East with ♡6.

East-West must now set up their club tricks before drawing trumps. It is a similar situation to North-South's problem with the diamonds. West's trumps will serve as entries to cash the clubs.

3   West plays ♣K. Notice he can afford to do this. With the queen in the East hand, the East-West holding is solid (K Q J 10 9 8) and by playing the king, they can stay in the West hand if South chooses to duck. North follows with ♣2, East with ♣Q and South has a problem. He has two possible lines of defence. He can win now, allowing the whole suit to be set up for West, or refuse this and the next round so that his partner can ruff the third. We will try it both ways and observe that it makes no difference. Let us first assume that South wins.

4   South plays ♡3, West ruffs with ♠7, North follows with ♡Q, East with ♡7.

5   West leads ♣J, North follows with ♣4, East discards ◇5, South follows with ♣3.

6   West leads ♣10, North ruffs with ♠3, East overruffs with ♠4, South follows with ♣5.

Now North's trumps are reduced to the same length as West's and they can be drawn, after which West can enjoy the other two clubs unhindered.

7   East plays ♠6, South discards ♡4, West wins with ♠K,
     North follows with ♠5.
8   West cashes ♠A, North follows with ♠J, East with ♠8,
     South discards ♡5.
9   West cashes ♣9, North discards ◇10, East discards ◇8,
     South follows with♣6.
10   West cashes ♣8, North discards ◇J, East discards ♡J,
     South follows with♣7.

The last three tricks are all won by East's trumps, which nobody
can beat. All East-West have lost are the two minor aces – 300
over the line, a tremendous result when compared with the loss
they would have suffered on the grand slam. Even vulnerable,
the penalty would only have been 500, still a comfortable save.

   Let us go back to the point where South was offered the club
trick. Suppose he refuses it. West would now lead ♣J and East
discards a losing diamond. If South refuses again, West leads
♣10 and North ruffs. East may now either overruff and ruff two
hearts in dummy or simply discard his last diamond, later ruffing
the two hearts in dummy. You should replay it to satisfy yourself
that, either way, East-West still only lose two tricks in all.

(6) The contract is six spades and West leads the ♣A and
continues with the ♣10. There now follows the most important
piece of advice in respect of bridge play – work out the whole
hand before playing to the first trick. This cannot be
overemphasized!

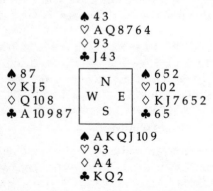

```
                    ♠ 4 3
                    ♡ A Q 8 7 6 4
                    ◇ 9 3
                    ♣ J 4 3
      ♠ 8 7           ┌───────┐      ♠ 6 5 2
      ♡ K J 5         │   N   │      ♡ 10 2
      ◇ Q 10 8     W  │       │  E   ◇ K J 7 6 5 2
      ♣ A 10 9 8 7     │   S   │      ♣ 6 5
                    └───────┘
                    ♠ A K Q J 10 9
                    ♡ 9 3
                    ◇ A 4
                    ♣ K Q 2
```

Let us first do our trick count as usual:

Spades: Six rounds, winning six and losing none.
Hearts: Six rounds, with the king with West (as it must be if
            we are to have any hope), we can set up the suit
            without loss and enjoy five winners as one will have
            to be ruffed.
Diamonds: Two rounds, winning one and losing one.
Clubs: Two rounds, winning two and losing one (to the ace
            on the opening lead).

The collation:

	Rounds	Winners	Losers
Spades	6	6	0
Hearts	6	5	0
Diamonds	2	1	1
Clubs	3	2	1
Total	17	14	2

So there appear to be enough tricks available but a problem in
how to avoid the diamond loser. Clearly this will have to be
discarded on dummy's long hearts. However, we must ask
ourselves whether there is any problem in establishing and
cashing those hearts. We can easily play a low heart from the
South hand and when West plays low, finesse the queen, follow
by cashing the ace and ruffing a third round. That will leave three
more hearts in dummy, all high – but how are we to get back
there to cash them?

Clearly the only conceivable entry lies in the ♣J. However, if
we play the obvious two under West's ace, the king and queen
will both be too high for the jack. For that reason, we must play
one of our honours under the ace, keeping that precious two to be
able to get to the jack later on. This is another illustration of the
importance of considering which hand wins specific rounds of a
suit and when. The play goes as follows:

1   West leads ♣A to North's ♣3, East's ♣5 and South's ♣Q.
2   West leads ♣10 to North's ♣4 (keeping the jack for later as
    explained), East follows with ♣6 and South's ♣K.

3   South cashes ♠A to West's ♠7, North's ♠3 and East's
     ♠2.
4   South cashes ♠K to West's ♠8, North's ♠4 and East's ♠5.
5   South cashes ♠Q, West discards ♣7 (of no possible use),
     North discards ◊3 (also of no possible use), East follows
     with ♠6.

Trumps are now drawn and South can set about establishing
North's hearts.

6   South leads ♡9 to West's ♡5, North's ♡Q and East's ♡2.
7   North cashes ♡A to East's ♡10, South's ♡3 and West's ♡K
     (now that the queen has been played, the king and jack are
     equals against the ace and West plays the card he is known
     to have. This gives away no information about the position
     of the jack).
8   North leads the ♡4, East discards ◊2, South ruffs with ♠9,
     West follows with ♡J.

The hearts are now established and only now does South use his
carefully preserved entry to enjoy them.

9   South leads ♣2 to West's ♣8, North's ♣J, East discards
     ◊5.
10   North leads ♡8, East discards ◊6, South discards ◊4, West
     discards ♣9.

We can see now that the South hand is high with the ◊A and two
trumps. There are also two winning hearts in the North hand so
North-South have two tricks to 'burn'.

11   North leads ◊9 to East's ◊7, South's ◊A and West's ◊8.

South now cashes his two trumps, the others discarding as they
please. North-South have won twelve tricks and conceded one to
score 180 below the line and 500 above it for the non-vulnerable
small slam. South also scores 150 above the line for his top five
honours in trumps.

    I asked whether you had any other comment to make on this
hand. You should have realized that, because of the club position,
the ♣A is the only lead to give away the contract. Had he led

anything else, West could have waited with his ace to put on South's ♣2 to ensure that the jack could never be used as an entry to the hearts. Play how he might, South is now one trick short and cannot avoid a diamond loser to give East-West 50 over the line.

The lead of an unsupported ace against a small slam is very much a double-edged proposition. On the one hand, if you cash it as here, you may give the position in the suit away and release tricks for the opposition in any order or place they care to take them. On the other, if you do not cash it, losers in the suit may be discarded and you may never live to enjoy it. It is often a very close judgment but statistics suggest that more slams are presented to declarer by cashing an ace than by failure to cash one. And while we are on the subject, more slams are given away by failure to lead away from an unsupported king than by leading away from one.

(7) The contract is five clubs and West leads the ♠10.

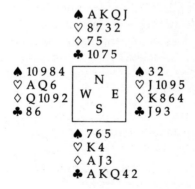

```
                    ♠ A K Q J
                    ♡ 8 7 3 2
                    ◇ 7 5
                    ♣ 10 7 5
    ♠ 10 9 8 4                      ♠ 3 2
    ♡ A Q 6          N              ♡ J 10 9 5
    ◇ Q 10 9 2    W     E           ◇ K 8 6 4
    ♣ 8 6            S              ♣ J 9 3
                    ♠ 7 6 5
                    ♡ K 4
                    ◇ A J 3
                    ♣ A K Q 4 2
```

Let us do our trick count as usual:

Spades:　　Four rounds, winning four and losing none. But note that trumps will have to be drawn before we can enjoy more than the first two rounds.

Hearts:　　Four rounds, winning none and losing four. But as we can ruff in the South hand, we should, in practice, only lose two tricks.

Diamonds: Three rounds, winning one and losing two. But third
            round can be ruffed in the dummy for positive gain
            as North is shorter in trumps than South. So we are
            entitled to count two winners and one loser in the
            suit, but note that the ruff will have to be taken
            before trumps are drawn.

Clubs: Five rounds, winning five and losing none.

The collation:

	Rounds	Winners	Losers
Spades	4	4	0
Hearts	4	0	2
Diamonds	3	2	1
Clubs	5	5	0
Total	16	11	3

So there appear to be eleven winners, but there are also three
losers. One of the heart losers, however, may be discarded on the
fourth round of spades. So we can now summarize the problem
which lies in the order of play. We have already agreed that we
cannot enjoy all the spades until trumps have been drawn but the
diamond ruff must be taken before trumps are drawn. We cannot
take our diamond ruff without losing one trick in the suit first to
exhaust dummy.

That means that the diamond trick will have to be lost before
the spades can be cashed for the heart discard, i.e. while the two
heart losers are kept intact. We must therefore look at the heart
suit in closer detail. The ace is sitting over the king and thus two
tricks in the suit will be lost *unless West has to lead them*. In that
event, we need lose only one trick in the suit. We must therefore
arrange that, if we are to lose a diamond trick, it must be to West
rather than East. With that in mind, we look at the diamond suit
in more detail. If East held both king and queen, they would be
solid against the ace and there would be nothing we could do to
keep him out of the lead. However, here he has only one of the
honours and provided we keep the ace sitting over that honour,
we can keep East off play.

To achieve this, we must force East to commit himself in front of South's ace, i.e. we must observe the usual rule of leading from the weakness in dummy through East's strength to South's strength. When we lead a low card from North, we shall watch East's play with interest. If he puts up the king, we will win with the ace and continue with the jack, ensuring the loss of the trick to West's queen. In practice, East will probably play low and the full play will go as follows:

1   West's ♠10 to North's ♠J, East's ♠2 and South's ♠5.
2   North leads ◇5, to East's ◇6 (once the five is played, the six and four become equals so it costs nothing to cover), South's ◇J and West's ◇Q.
3   West plays ♠9 to North's ♠Q, East's ♠3 and South's ♠6.

South can now afford to draw one round of trumps but no more as he needs to be able to return to his hand after the diamond ruff to draw the rest of the trumps.

4   North plays ♣5 to East's ♣3, South's ♣A and West's ♣6.
5   South cashes ◇A to West's ◇2, North's ◇7 and East's ◇4.
6   South plays ◇3 to West's ◇9, North ruffs with ♣7 and East follows with ◇8.
7   North plays ♣10 (note that, had South drawn two rounds of trumps before taking the diamond ruff, North would now be left with nothing but major cards and he would now be forced to play hearts for the loss of two tricks or spades, which would be ruffed as there would be one trump still at large). East covers with ♣J (note again, with the ten played, the jack and nine become equals so this cannot cost). South wins with ♣K and West follows with ♣8.
8   South cashes ♣Q, West discards ♠4 (cannot possibly be of any use), North discards ♡2 (also of no value), East follows with ♣9.
9   South plays ♠7 to West's ♠8, North's ♠K, East discards ◇8.
10   North cashes ♠A, East discards ♡5, South discards ♡4, West discards ♡6.
11   North plays ♡3, East plays ♡J (top of a solid sequence) to South's ♡K and West's ♡A.

South's last two cards are trumps and they win, irrespective of what West leads. North-South have thus won eleven tricks and conceded two to score 100 below the line.

I asked whether you had any other comment on this hand. You should have noticed that 3NT is a far easier contract. If South plays the hand, North-South will make at least five tricks in clubs, four in spades and one in diamonds for ten in total and if West chooses to attack hearts (his best lead actually is his fourth highest diamond), the ♡K will bring the tally up to eleven. Even if North plays the hand and East finds the obvious solid heart lead, the defenders can, at best, take four heart tricks but not more and to ensure that much, West must be careful to play his queen rather than the six if South plays low to the first trick.

(8) The contract is six hearts and West leads the ◇K.

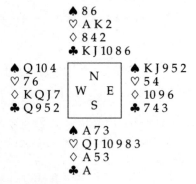

```
                    ♠ 8 6
                    ♡ A K 2
                    ◇ 8 4 2
                    ♣ K J 10 8 6
     ♠ Q 10 4                    ♠ K J 9 5 2
     ♡ 7 6          ┌─────┐      ♡ 5 4
     ◇ K Q J 7    W │  N  │ E    ◇ 10 9 6
     ♣ Q 9 5 2      │  S  │      ♣ 7 4 3
                    └─────┘
                    ♠ A 7 3
                    ♡ Q J 10 9 8 3
                    ◇ A 5 3
                    ♣ A
```

Let us do our trick count:

Spades: Three rounds, winning two and losing one; the third round can be ruffed in the short trump hand for positive gain.

Hearts: Six rounds, winning six and losing none.

Diamonds: Three rounds, winning one and losing two.

Clubs: Two rounds, winning two and losing none. However, we shall look at this suit more closely in a moment in that there is the possibility of ruffing out two more rounds and setting up a long card if entries permit.

The collation:

	Rounds	Winners	Losers
Spades	3	2	1
Hearts	6	6	0
Diamonds	3	1	2
Clubs	2	2	0
Total	14	11	3

Looks pretty grim, doesn't it – but let us see whether we can do something more with those clubs. We could cash the ace early, cross to dummy with a high trump, cash the king of clubs, discarding one of our losing diamonds, and ruff a club in hand. Now cross back to dummy with another high trump (clearing the opponent's trumps in the process) to ruff a fourth round of clubs in hand, bringing down West's queen and setting up dummy's fifth club, on which we hope to discard our second losing diamond. However, in order to get back to dummy to cash that winning club, we need the spade ruff, which involves losing the lead in that suit first. Now the defenders can cash a winning diamond to take two tricks before we can win twelve – one off.

No – we shall have to try something else – a technique known as *loser on loser*. Let us look at that club suit again. We see that the best way to be selfish is to be unselfish. Suppose we allow West to have that queen. That would give us four tricks in the suit for one lost and miraculously, we can discard all our losers in spades and diamonds. Now the collation looks like this:

	Rounds	Winners	Losers
Spades	2	1	1
Hearts	6	6	0
Diamonds	3	1	2
Clubs	5	4	1
Total	16	12	4

That looks better. We play as follows:

1   West leads ◊K to North's ◊2, East's ◊6 and South's ◊A.
2   South cashes ♡Q (we shall not take a spade ruff so we can

afford one round of trumps immediately – but no more as the ace and king are needed as entries to the clubs). West follows with ♡6, North with ♡2 and East with ♡4.

3　　South cashes ♣A to West's ♣2, North's ♣6 and East's ♣3.

4　　South leads ♡3 to West's ♡7, North's ♡A and East's ♡5.

5　　North cashes ♣K to East's ♣4, South discards ◊3, West follows with ♣5.

6　　North leads ♣J to East's ♣7, South discards ◊5 (this is the loser discarded on the loser; note that this play amounts to a winning ruffing finesse should East hold the ♣Q), West wins with ♣Q.

South has now exhausted his hand of diamonds and still has the ♠A as guard to his two losers, which will be discarded in a moment. Note that, if West had originally led spades rather than diamonds, North would have discarded losing spades rather than losing diamonds on the early clubs, keeping the ◊A to guard the diamond losers which would be discarded later on the remaining clubs.

7　　West leads ◊Q (hoping that South had started with four or more diamonds), North follows with ◊4, East with ◊9, South ruffs with ♡8.

8　　South leads ♡9, West discards ◊7, North wins with ♡K, East discards ♠2.

9　　North cashes ♣10, East discards ♠5, South discards ♠3, West follows with ♣9.

10　　North cashes ♣8, East discards ◊10, South discards ♠7, West discards ♠4 (keeping ◊J to beat the ◊8 on dummy – it is obvious that his partner is guarding the spades).

The South hand is now high.

11　　North leads ♠6 to East's ♠9, South's ♠A and West's ♠10.

South's last two cards are trumps and the others may discard as they please. North-South thus have won twelve tricks against the one they lost to the ♣Q. They therefore score 180 under the line and 500 over it for the non-vulnerable small slam.

You will have noticed that I made a number of comments regarding defence but have not so far gone into the subject in any great detail. This is deliberate as we must discuss bidding first, the two being very closely related.

Before we proceed, however, I strongly advise you to play and replay the above hands over and over again until you can do them virtually without thinking. The next step is to repeat the exercise with the East and West hands closed. Make sure you understand the methods used and appreciate that alternative lines fail and why! The more learning you have at your fingertips, the easier life will be when you get to the table.

The Auction

Let us refresh our memories regarding the purpose of the auction. Three things are decided:

1 Which suit, if any, will be trumps.
2 Which player will declare the hand – and therefore which hand will be dummy (i.e. the declarer's partner) and which of the defenders will lead the first card (i.e. the one sitting *over*, or to the left of, declarer and *under*, or to the right of, dummy).
3 How many tricks out of the thirteen (and it will have to be at least seven) does the declarer promise to take and are the stakes to be simple, doubled or redoubled?

The bidding involves two simultaneous conversations between the two pairs (conducted of course, with impeccable politeness in that the four players take turns to speak in clockwise rotation).

Whereas play (with twenty-six cards on view) tends to be fairly clear-cut, bidding (when you can only see thirteen) leaves much more scope for judgement and opinion and there are also several ways or *languages*, or what we shall call *bidding systems*, by which partners can communicate with each other. Each player must try to make a realistic valuation of the trick-taking potential of his hand and tell his partner so that the partnership can decide what their best contract is, bearing in mind the rewards for success and the penalties for failure as laid down in the scoring system which we learnt earlier and now know backwards! During the bidding, whatever your style or bidding system (and there are many) there is one overriding consideration:

What final contract do you have in mind?

I deliberately put this in a box because it is the most important point in this book. If you remember this and nothing else, you will comfortably have had your money's worth. Every time the bid comes round to you, this should be uppermost in your mind, noting that you may want to make a bid (typically lead-directing) in the belief that the final contract will be played by the opponents. To emphasize the point, I shall be mentioning this consideration every time I discuss a bid and hopefully the most important aspect of bidding will become second nature.

Let us start with hand valuation. I mentioned earlier that the universally accepted method, irrespective of bidding system, is the Milton point count as follows:

Ace: 4   King: 3   Queen: 2   Jack: 1

In addition, allowance must be made for distribution, as it is clearly advantageous to have long suits, singletons and voids rather than flat hands. A typical initial allowance is:

Doubleton: 1   Singleton: 2   Void: 3

When discussing hands or explaining the meaning of bids, it is usual to give your high-card point and your distribution. Thus:

♠ A x x x
♥ K x x
♦ Q x x
♣ J x x

would be 10 points with a flat 4333 distribution. While

♠ –
♥ Q x
♦ A K J x x x x
♣ K x x

would be 13 high-card points with a 0274 distribution (when discussing a hand, always give spades first, then hearts, diamonds and clubs in that order); you would then add 3 points for the void and 1 for the doubleton and treat the hand as being worth about 17 points.

However, a few words of advice are in order here. Bidding is very much a question of judgement and once you have added up your points in this way, a number of provisos should be borne in mind.

1 The high-card point values are certainly easy to remember but are far from accurate. Suppose we take the king as standard, the scale tends to undervalue the ace and overvalue the queen and jack. A more accurate scale would be:

Ace: 4.2   King: 3   Queen: 1.8   Jack: 0.8

Thus if we compare two hands:

♠ A x x   ♠ Q J x
♡ K x x x   ♡ Q x x x
♢ A x x   ♢ Q J x
♣ x x x   ♣ Q J x

Both are 3433 in shape and 11 points in high cards, but the hand on the left is clearly more powerful. On my proposed scale, it would have 11.4 points, while that on the right would only be worth 9.6. I would value the left hand at 11½ points and the right as barely 10, a considerable difference.

2 Honours appearing together in clusters make solid or semi-solid holdings and thus have greater trick-taking potential than scattered values as we learnt earlier. Consider these two examples:

♠ x x x   ♠ A x x
♡ A K Q x   ♡ K x x x
♢ x x x   ♢ Q x x
♣ x x x   ♣ x x x

Both hands are 3433 with nine high-card points. However, on the left-hand side, we have the three heart honours together and they will surely make three tricks, particularly if they are trumps or if there are no trumps. On the right hand side, the ace of spades will also surely score but there are no guarantees for the other two honours.

3 High cards are more valuable in long suits than in short ones as they may help lower cards to make tricks, notably in no

trump contracts or as side suits in trump contracts. Let us look at three examples:

♠ A K Q J x x x	♠ K J x x x x x	♠ x x x x x x x
♡ x x x	♡ Q x x	♡ J x x
◇ x x	◇ A x	◇ A Q
♣ x	♣ x	♣ K

In all three cases, we have ten high-card points with one each of the four honours and the shape is 7321, but look at the difference! On the left, we have everything in the long spade suit and barring a most unlikely distribution, seven tricks there seem certain. In the middle, the king and jack are certainly pulling their weight but the ace will be worth one trick and no more and the queen, though adequately protected against the ace and king, is by no means guaranteed to score.

On the right, the big honours are in the short suits and the hand is very poor. A great deal of work (in knocking out the honours) will have to be done before any tricks can be made in the spade suit. In diamonds, the ace will certainly make but we shall need to find the king in partner's or the right-hand opponent's hand if the queen is to be of any use. There seems little hope for either the king of clubs, which will drop under the ace on the first round, or the jack of hearts, which is inadequately protected.

4 Intermediate cards (tens and nines) may be of value if they are in suits, notably long ones, with other lower honours. Thus J 10 9 is certainly worth more than J x x, and Q J 10 x x is worth more than Q J x x x. However, 10 x x is hardly worth more than x x x and K 9 is hardly worth more than K x. A well-located 10 or two well-located nines are worth about half a point.

5 The Milton point count, even with distributional adjustment, becomes particularly inaccurate on very distributional hands. One good alternative is the *losing trick count* (applicable to trump contracts only). Very briefly, you count the potential losers in each suit as follows:

If your suit is a void, singleton ace or doubleton ace-king, count no losers. With any singleton, A x or K x, count one loser. Any lower doubleton, count two losers. Where you have a suit containing three or more cards, count one loser for each of the top three honours missing in that suit. Obviously, we must distinguish between two-loser holdings like A x x, K x x and Q x x and one-loser holdings like A K x, A Q x and K Q x. It is, for example, recommended that Q x x is counted as three losers unless: you hold the jack as well; or the suit has been bid by partner (in which case the queen is deemed to be useful in a long suit); or it is in a long suit of your own which will be played as trumps; or you have another suit including an ace which we have counted as two losers (a stronger two-loser holding than the standard K x x).

There can never be more than three losers counted in any one suit. The principle is that, once a fit is found, the two partners add up their losers and deduct the total from 18 to give the level at which they can play. Here is an example:

West		East	
♠ K J 7	(2)	♠ 5 4 3	(3)
♡ A K 4 3	(1)	♡ J 7 6 2	(3)
◇ A 2	(1)	◇ K J 7 5 3	(2)
♣ K J 9 6	(2)	♣ A	(0)
Total	6		8

$6 + 8 = 14$ and $18 - 14 = 4$ thus East-West can play at the four-level in their best suit, hearts.

This is by no means a foolproof method but does provide a useful guide. For accuracy, certain adjustments have to be made just as they do in the point-count method. I include it here so that you will know what people are talking about when you listen in on discussions of hands.

6 As the auction progresses, you must revalue or devalue your hand accordingly. If your partner bids a suit, honours in your hand, even if you are relatively short, become more valuable. Thus, if partner bids hearts and you hold, ♡ Q x, that is nothing to be ashamed of; the queen is in a long suit *of the partnership* and is said to be *working*. Against that, if your partner bids a suit in which you are very short, you must

count that shortage as a *negative* rather than a positive asset, deducting one point for a doubleton, two for a singleton and three for a void. If opponents bid a suit, then you must adjust the value your holdings according to length and where you are sitting. Let us take some examples. Say your opponents bid spades.

a With ♠ A K there will be two certain tricks, come what may.

b With ♠ A K x x x, there will again be two certain tricks, but probably no more as there is clearly a bad split against you. Thus take no credit for the long suit.

c With ♠ A Q, you must take into account where you are sitting. If the suit is bid on your right, it will probably include the king and your holding will be worth two tricks; you can value up accordingly. However, if it is bid on your left, the king is likely to be well-placed over your queen and now the holding will probably only be worth one trick. However, if you are going to be declarer in a no-trump contract, the opponents will have to lead the suit round to you and now you can give the queen full value as a second stop.

d With semi-solid holdings like K Q 10, it again depends on where you are sitting in relation to the bid. If the bid is on your right, you can count two tricks; but if it is on your left, the defender will probably wait with A J x x over you and you will have to be content with one, except in the no-trump case explained in (c) above.

What I am really trying to get at is that, right from day one, you should get into the habit of looking at the overall impression of your hand rather than religiously counting your points and bidding parrot-fashion. Most important of all, I should like you to refrain from the train of thought which goes: 'An average hand contains one ace, one king, one queen and one jack for ten points. Anything well above that is a good hand and should be bid vigorously; anything well below that is a bad hand and should be bid as little as possible or probably passed altogether.'

It is far better to get into the habit of describing a hand as good, bad or indifferent according to the following considerations:

1 The way the auction has gone so far, and particularly *how much you have promised already*. We shall thus learn that there are hands of 24 points which are very poor and others of 2 points which are enormous. Sounds crazy, doesn't it? But it is the route to accurate bidding!

2 The likely final contract, i.e. which denomination will be played and whether you will be declaring or defending.

3 The positions of your honour cards, in the light of the bidding of the other three players, and their consequent trick-taking potential.

The Opening Bid

We shall divide our study of bidding into two phases. First, we shall assume that the opponents are silent and consider the conversation purely between two partners and then we shall look at the complications caused by the opponents' entering the auction.

During the auction, the two partners will try to impart to each other their high-card strength and distribution and decide whether their combined values warrant restricting themselves to a part-score or bidding a game, small slam or grand slam. With each bid, a player will describe his hand within ranges of points and distribution and thus the partnership will gradually establish what they have between them.

We must first add a few new words to our vocabulary:

An *opening bid* is the first bid made by one of the members of the partnership.

A *response* is the first reply made by his partner.

The *opener's rebid* is the second bid made by the opener.

The *responder's rebid* is the second bid made by the responder.

A *forcing* bid is one which demands a reply from the partner. As we go through various common sequences, we shall clarify which bids are forcing and which are not.

A *sign-off* is a bid which is the opposite of a force in that the partner is now expected to pass.

Let us work out how much we need to open the bidding. We learnt earlier that there are 40 high-card points in the pack.

Leaving aside distribution for the moment, in order to score at least seven of thirteen tricks to fulfil a contract, a partnership will need about 7/13 of 40, i.e. about 21.5 of the points between them. Assuming that a player is looking at x points, he can reasonably assume that the remaining $(40 - x)$ points are evenly divided between the other players at the table.

So we must solve the equation: $x + 1/3(40 - x) = 21.5$, which gives x as a little over 12. Therefore for a no-trump opening bid, we need at least 12 points. For a suit opening bid, 12 with a five-card suit will suffice, or 11 with a six-card or longer suit. How about upper limits? For no-trump bids, it is usual to define the range fairly strictly, while for suit bids, a wider range is permissible.

When should a suit be bid? Most beginners' books take pains to define *biddable suits* and *rebiddable suits* respectively as suits you can bid once and suits you can bid twice or more often. I refrain from doing so. There are situations where you have to bid suits consisting of two small cards and others where you should refrain from bidding suits consisting of A K Q J 10 9, so it is best that we approach the problem from a more common sense angle.

If a suit is to be trumps, it seems sensible that the partnership should have the majority of cards between them, i.e. at least seven, but preferably eight or more.

Again, assuming that a player looking at one hand can assume that the remaining cards are evenly divided between the other three, he needs x cards in the suit so that $x + 1/3(13 - x) = 7$ giving $x = 4$. In other words, an average holding of cards in a particular suit is 13/4, i.e. just over 3 and you need more than your fair share of cards to make it sensible to suggest the suit as suitable for trumps. Similarly, once your partner has bid a suit, he has worked on the assumption that you have at least three cards in the suit and therefore you need that many or more to agree the suit as trumps or *support* partner's bid.

Let us start, however, with no-trump bidding. It is important that your point range be clearly defined. In the system we are going to learn, which is based on Acol (a system named after the London club where it started) an opening bid of 1NT will show

12–14 points with one of the following shapes: 4333, 4432, 5332 with the five-card suit usually being a minor (but occasionally a poor major).

With 15–16 points and a balanced hand, we will open a four- or five-card suit at the one-level (we shall discuss any choice in a moment). If partner replies in a suit at the one-level, we rebid 1NT; if partner replies in a suit at the two-level, we rebid 2NT.

With 17–18 points and a balanced hand, we will again open with a suit at the one-level and if partner replies in a suit at the one-level, we rebid 2NT; if partner replies in a suit at the two-level, we rebid 3NT.

With 19 points and a balanced hand, the same applies but we rebid 3NT over all replies.

With 20–22 points and a balanced hand, we open 2NT.

That leaves the problem of what to do with hands of 23 points or more. This will involve the use of a conventional bid which we will discuss later.

We now must consider the choice of suit in situations where we have 15 points or more and two four-card suits. It is usually best to bid the lower-ranking of the two, giving partner a chance to bid the other at the one-level (he may not be strong enough to go to the two-level). The exception arises if your higher-ranking suit is very strong and the lower very weak. In this case, bidding the latter will mislead partner as to the whereabouts of your points. Let us look at some examples. What would you open on the following ten hands?

(1) ♠ K x x
♡ K x x x
◇ K x x
♣ K x x

(2) ♠ K x
♡ 10 x x x x
◇ A K x
♣ Q x x

(3) ♠ A Q x
♡ K x
◇ J x x x
♣ A J x x

(4) ♠ Q x
♡ A K x x x
◇ K x x
♣ K x x

(5) ♠ A K x
♡ K x x x
◇ Q J x
♣ A x x

(6) ♠ K x
♡ K x x
◇ A x x
♣ A K J 10 x

(7) ♠ Q x x   (8) ♠ A K x x x   (9) ♠ Q x x
     ♡ K Q x   ♡ Q x x   ♡ Q x x
     ◇ A K x x   ◇ K x x   ◇ A K Q x
     ♣ A J x   ♣ A K   ♣ A K J

           (10) ♠ J x x
                 ♡ A x
                 ◇ A K Q J x
                 ♣ K J x

We shall discuss the answers, bearing in mind that, when I refer
to partner's response, I mean a cheap change of suit. If he takes
more dramatic action like a jump or a less exciting answer of
1NT, we may have to bid differently, as will be seen later.

(1)   Here you have a flat 12 points and will open 1NT. 3NT is
      favourite as final contract but if partner turns up with four
      or more hearts, 4♡ is a possible alternative.

(2)   Here you have 12 points and a very poor five-card major.
      Arguably the suit will only be of any use if it is trumps, but
      if you open 1♡, you will have rebid problems. If partner
      responds 1♠, your rebid of 1NT will promise 15–16 points
      and a rebid of 2♡, as we shall learn later, will normally
      promise a six-card suit or at least a far better five-card suit
      than this one. Open 1NT, 3NT or 4♡ being the final
      contracts uppermost in your mind.

(3)   Here you have 15 points, i.e. in the 15–16 point range, and
      must first open a suit with the intention of rebidding 1NT.
      The best opening is 1♣. Partner will bid diamonds if he has
      them, while he may not be strong enough to go to the two-
      level if you open with 1◇ and he has a club suit. Opening
      the lower-ranking of the two suits gives the partnership the
      best chance of finding a fit in either. Again 3NT is favourite
      for the final contract, with 5♣ or 5◇ being outside
      chances.

(4)   With this 15-point hand, you will open 1♡ and rebid 1NT if
      partner responds with 1♠ and 2NT if he bids a new suit at
      the two level. 3NT and 4♡ are uppermost in your mind as
      final contracts.

(5) Here you have 17 points and a flat hand and you will open 1♡, intending to rebid 2NT if partner responds 1♠, or 3NT if he bids a minor at the two-level. 3NT is favourite for the final contract, with 4♡ a possibility.

(6) This time, your 18 points are accompanied by a really good club suit and the hand should be valued up to 19. Open 1♣ and rebid 3NT over partner's response. 3NT is favourite for the final contract, 5♣ being a possibility if partner turns out to have a very unbalanced hand.

(7) Here you have 19 points, balanced, and you will open 1♦ and rebid 3NT irrespective of partner's response. 3NT is almost certainly going to be your final contract if you reach game.

(8) Here you have 19 points and a reasonable five-card suit which you could well value up to 20. However, the double-ton ace-king in clubs are a disadvantage in that they cannot help lower cards to make tricks. You should open 1♠ and rebid 3NT over partner's change of suit. 3NT and 4♠ are favourites as final contract.

(9) Here you have a flat 21 points and will open 2NT, angling for 3NT.

(10) Here you have 19 high-card points but the solid diamond suit is almost certain to provide five tricks and the hand can be valued up to 20 at least. Again you should open 2NT, aiming to play in 3NT, far more likely than 5♦.

We must now clarify how we decided to divide up our bidding ranges. In order to make 3NT, we need about 25 points between the partnership (although less will suffice if it is obvious that a long suit can be brought in). In order to answer a one-level opening bid with a simple change of suit at the one-level, we need a minimum of six points (or five with a good five-card or longer suit). Note, however, that there is no upper limit as such a change of suit is forcing and the bidding must continue.

The rebid of 1NT, showing 15–16 points, gives the partnership about 21 points as required.
The rebid of 2NT, showing 17–18 points, gives the partnership about 23–24 points which are needed to make 2NT.

The rebid of 3NT, showing 19 points or more, gives the partnership 25 points or more, as required for game.

We shall consider partner's responses in more detail later, but first we must go through suit opening bids. An opening bid of one of a suit shows 11–19 points and:

1 An unbalanced hand, usually involving a five-card or longer suit or a 4441 shape;
2 A balanced hand, where the intention is to rebid no-trumps as above;
3 A balanced hand, which might qualify for a 1NT opening but where there are good reasons for preferring a suit.

In all cases, the overriding considerations are:

1 What final contract have you in mind?
2 Have you an easy rebid?

When choosing a trump suit, you should first consider the one with the largest number of cards. A suit consisting of 6 5 4 3 2 will not make any tricks unless they are trumps, while one with A K Q J will provide them whether they are trumps or not, so the former suit should be preferred. With that in mind, there should be a definite accent on the major suits, as 4♡ and 4♠ are far more likely game contracts than 5♣ and 5♢. As we have already hinted, when your hands are stronger in the minor suits, your first thoughts should be towards 3NT, sacrificing the benefit of trumps to have a chance of making game with two fewer tricks. Problems arise with hands containing two suits of four cards or more and I intend to go into this in some detail.

Let us begin with two four card suits in a 4432 shape. There are six combinations and we shall work up from the lowest ranking.

1 **Clubs and diamonds** Here you are definitely angling for 3NT.
   a With 12–14 points, open 1NT. It is, of course, unpleasant with something like

   ♠ x x x
   ♡ x x
   ♢ A K x x
   ♣ A Q x x

   when you would rather not have the lead coming round to

your very poor major-suit holdings. In this situation, there are two possible actions: open 1NT anyway, accepting that there is little else you can do; or open 1 ◊, intending to support 1 ♠ to 2 ♠ but prepared to bid 2 ♣ over 1 ♡. As we shall confirm in a moment, this would show a five-card diamond suit which you do not have. Of the two possibilities I personally prefer the latter. Misleading partner over the length of a minor suit is unlikely to do a great deal of harm as he will attempt to play at the five-level only as a last resort. In any case, you will have bid the suits in which you have your values – far more descriptive than 1NT. With that in mind, you can hardly be criticized if you open 1NT.

b With 15–16 points, open 1 ♣, intending to rebid 1NT unless your club suit is very poor, in which case you should prefer 1 ◊ as explained above.

c With 17–18, open 1 ♣ (except as above) intending to rebid 2NT.

d With 19 open 1 ♣ (except as above) intending to rebid 3NT.

2 **Clubs and hearts** Here you are also angling for 3NT, but now 4 ♡ is a likely alternative. Usually, however, you will want at least eight cards between the partnership for a trump contract at that level to be viable and so you should bid the clubs, giving partner a chance to bid hearts if he has four or more.

a With 12–14 points, open 1NT but if all the points are concentrated in the two suits, there may be an alternative. With

    ♠ x x x

    ♡ A Q x x

    ◊ x x

    ♣ A Q J x

you can open 1 ♣. If partner responds 1 ◊, you can bid 1 ♡ and if he responds 1 ♠, you can raise to 2 ♠. Ideally, you would like to have an honour in the spade suit but it is certainly better to bid this way than open 1NT with two very poor suits which will be led round to you in 3NT.

A more difficult problem arises with

♠ x x
♡ A Q x x
◊ x x x
♣ A Q J x

Now you have no rebid after 1♣ if partner responds 1♠. If you open 1♡, you will have to rebid 2♣ over 1♠, promising a five-card heart suit; or raise 2◊ to 3◊ on very minimal trump support. As it is more dangerous to mislead partner about a major-suit length, opening 1♡ is not recommended and you have to choose between opening 1NT and opening with 1♣ and rebidding 2♣, which I prefer, but the majority of top bridge players do not. Again, you cannot be criticized for opening 1NT.

b With 15–16 points, you can open 1♣ unless your hearts are very good and clubs are very poor. If partner responds 1◊, rebid 1♡ – there is no need to rush to 1NT just to show your point-count; the first priority is to find the right denomination in which to play. Partner will ask about your strength later if he so wishes. If partner responds 1♠, you will rebid 1NT to show your point-count as usual. Partner will now almost certainly not have four hearts, so there is no need to bid yours. If he indeed does have a heart suit, he will have bid a five-card spade suit and will show you his hearts on the next round at the two-level. With four hearts and four spades, he will bid the hearts first to give you as much room as possible to describe your hand.

c With 17–18 points, you will again open 1♣ (except as above), again intending to rebid 1♡ over 1◊ (once again there is no need to rush to show the point-count; you can bid 2NT on the next round should the need arise) and 2NT over partner's 1♠.

d With 19 points, you will again open 1♣ but this time, you will force with 2♡ over 1◊ as you know you almost certainly have enough for game, or rebid 3NT over partner's 1♠.

3 **Club and spades** This is the easiest combination.

a With 12–14 points, much depends on the distribution of the points. If you have cover in both red suits, you can open 1NT, but with something like

♠ A Q x x
♥ x x x
♦ x x
♣ A Q J x

it is obviously better to open 1♣ and rebid 1♠. Note that you can still play in 1NT if partner so chooses but it will be better played from his side of the table. If you start with 1NT, it may be more difficult to find a club or spade contract.

b With 15–16, you again will open 1♣ and rebid 1♠. Note, as before, there is no rush to bid 1NT to show your point-count. Where your spades are very good and clubs very poor, you can open 1♠ and rebid 2NT over a two-level suit bid by partner.

c With 17–18, the same applies; except with good spades and poor clubs, you will open 1♠ and rebid 3NT over a two-level suit bid.

d With 19, open 1♣ and rebid 2♠ or, with poor clubs, open 1♠ and rebid 3NT.

4 Diamonds and hearts

a With 12–14, you will normally open 1NT. Problems arise with

(1) ♠ x x x
    ♥ A K x x
    ♦ A Q x x
    ♣ x x

(2) ♠ x x
    ♥ A K x x
    ♦ A Q x x
    ♣ x x x

Again, you cannot be criticized for opening 1NT on either of these. But there is the alternative of opening 1♦ intending: on (1) to rebid 2♠ over 1♠ or 2♦ over 2♣; on (2) to rebid 2♦ over 1♠ or 3♣ over 2♣. I prefer the alternatives to opening 1NT but it has to be said that most top players do not. The important issue is to understand the considerations involved. I take the view that, with this kind of shape, 3NT is hot favourite for the final contract and I do not want it played from my side of the table. Others, as we shall see later, take the view that 1NT should be preferred as it is now more difficult for the opponents to compete – they will have to start at the two-level.

5 **Diamonds and spades** This is handled similarly to clubs and hearts.

6 **Hearts and spades**
   a With 12–14, you should open 1NT in all cases rather than suggest a five-card major which you do not hold. Now there is less worry about playing 3NT from the wrong hand as this is now no longer hot favourite as your final contract – 4♡ or 4♠ are more likely. If partner does insist on 3NT, he will probably have plenty in the minors and little fear of a lead coming through him.
   b With 15–16, you should open 1♡. Partner will bid spades if he has them; if he bids two of a minor, you can rebid 2NT.
   c With 17–18 or 19, you should again open 1♡, this time intending to rebid 3NT over two of a minor.

We now turn to hands with a 4441 shape and will take each singleton in turn.

1 **Singleton club** Where you have 12–14, this presents a very awkward problem and opinions differ on the best way to handle it. Some people make a blanket rule of bidding the suit below the singleton on all 4441 shapes: spades with a singleton club; clubs with a singleton diamond; diamonds with a singleton heart; hearts with a singleton spade. This certainly has the advantage of being easy to remember, and if partner bids the suit with the singleton, you can bid the next suit up with the minimum loss of bidding space. But let us be a little more careful, particularly in the following case.

   If we open 1♠, intending to bid 2♡ over 2♣, we have the advantage of bidding both major suits but we are promising a five-card spade suit which we do not have. Alternatively, if we bid 2♢ over 2♣, it will be very difficult to find a heart fit, as will be explained later. A good case can be made for opening 1♡, giving room for partner to bid spades at the one-level if he has them; the disadvantage occurs when partner bids 2♣, after which our 2♢ bid will promise a five-card heart suit. If we open 1♢, we shall be in difficulties after 2♣ from partner. Two of a major now would not only promise a five-card diamond suit but also, as will be explained later, a much stronger hand.

It appears, therefore, that there are disadvantages in all three possible openings and my recommendation is that if you have a predominance of points in one particular major suit, treat it as a five-card and open that suit. So, with

   ♠ A K Q x
   ♡ K x x x
   ♢ J x x x
   ♣ x

open 1♠ and rebid 2♡ over 2♣; at least you will have shown where your strength is. With

   ♠ Q x x x
   ♡ A K J x
   ♢ Q x x x
   ♣ x

open 1♡ and rebid 2♢ over 2♣.

On all other hands, I recommend opening 1♢ and rebidding 2♢ over 2♣. In no circumstances will a major-suit fit be missed and I stress again that it is better to mislead partner about the length of a minor suit than that of a major on final-contract considerations. With 15 or more points, there is no problem. Simply open 1♢ (or 1♡ if your diamonds are very poor) and then rebid no-trumps over 2♣ at the appropriate level.

2 **Singleton diamond** This presents no problem. With 12–14 points, open 1♣ and rebid 1♡ over 1♢, giving room for partner to bid 1♠ if he has the suit. With 15 or more points, you have the option to open 1♡ if the clubs are very poor, intending to rebid no-trumps at the appropriate level over partner's 2♢. Personally, I prefer to open 1♣ even on a poor suit. Hands of this shape do not usually play well and it is best to leave maximum space to discuss the final contract.

3 **Singleton heart** Again, this presents no problem. Up to and including 19 points, you will open 1♣ (unless your clubs are

very poor, in which case you will prefer 1 ◊) and rebid 1 ♠ .
Note that you need at least 20 points to rebid 2 ♠ , as your hand
is devalued if partner bids the suit in which you have a
singleton. It is now well on the cards that you have no good
trump suit and no-trumps will be awkward to play as there
will be no long suit to develop. Hands like this are referred to
as *misfits*.

4 **Singleton spade** Here there is a problem in the 12–14 range.
My suggestion is that you open 1 ◊ and rebid 2 ♣ over 1 ♠ .
This promises a five-card diamond suit but seems the least
damaging distortion. With strong clubs and very poor diamonds, you might open 1 ♣ and rebid 2 ♣ ; we shall see later
that there is little danger of a red-suit fit being missed. With 15
or more points, you are in a position to rebid no-trumps at an
appropriate level and it is now a question of which suit to start
with. My suggestion is 1 ♣ (or 1 ◊ if the clubs are very poor) to
give maximum bidding space.

We now turn to hands with one five-card and one four-card suit.
Here you should always start with the five-card suit as that is the
favourite for your choice of trumps. Your rebid, however,
depends on two important factors: your strength and whether
the long suit is of higher or lower rank than the short.

When we bid two suits, we are offering alternatives to partner
and are asking him to give preference. If he has three or more
cards in one or other, there will be no problem, but it may well be
that he has the other two suits and will have to give preference
with two doubletons. It is for that reason that we have to have at
least five cards in the first of our suits to ensure a trump majority.
Admittedly, I have given examples of exceptions above but these
should be kept to a minimum.

I think it will be best to go through all twelve combinations if
only to ensure that we understand the principles. It will not take
too long because many require similar handling.

1 **Clubs and diamonds** If the diamonds are longer, there is little
problem. Simply open 1 ◊ and rebid 2 ♣ over one of a major.
Partner can then give preference to 2 ◊ cheaply at the two-
level. This applies up to about 17 points. With 18 or more

(bearing in mind that you should revalue or devalue, according to how much you like partner's bid major), you may force by rebidding 3♣. Where the clubs are longer, it is not so easy. You will open 1♣ but when partner responds one of a major, you may not be able to rebid 2◇. If you do and partner prefers clubs, he will have to give preference at the three-level without any extra strength and you will be responsible. For that, you need extra strength, about 17 points (again noting your attitude to partner's bid major). This sequence, bidding a long suit followed by a higher-ranking short suit which forces partner to the three or higher level is called a *reverse*. If you do not have reversing strength, you must simply repeat your clubs; partner can still bid diamonds if he has them so it is unlikely that much will be lost.

2 **Clubs and hearts** If the hearts are longer, open 1♡. If partner responds 1♠, you simply rebid 2♣ without difficulty. If he responds 2◇, you will need reversing values to go to 3♣. If you do not have them, you simply repeat your hearts. Where the clubs are longer, you open 1♣. Now, if partner responds 1◇, you simply rebid 1♡. Note that, if partner wishes to give preference to clubs, he may do so at the two-level and that this is therefore *not* a reverse. If partner, however, responds 1♠, a bid of 2♡ will drive partner to the three-level to give preference for clubs and requires reversing strength. If you are not that strong, you must quietly repeat your clubs; partner can still bid hearts if he has them.

3 **Clubs and spades** If the spades are longer, you will open 1♠ but will only be able to show the clubs without reversing if partner responds 1NT. Any two-level red-suit response by partner will mean you will need reversing values to go to 3♣. Otherwise, you simply repeat your spades. If the clubs are longer, you open 1♣ and rebid 1♠ (again note that this is not a reverse) over a red-suit response. With about 18 points (bearing in mind your attitude towards the red suit), you can force with 2♠.

4 **Diamonds and hearts** If the hearts are longer, you can open 1♡ and rebid diamonds cheaply at the two-level after a black-

suit response. If partner bids 1♠, you will need about 18 points to force with 3♢; if he bids 2♣, his raise to the two-level promises a stronger hand and about 16 will be enough. Where the diamonds are longer, you will start with 1♢. If you do not have reversing values, you will have to repeat the diamonds over a black-suit response. However, the question arises of how much you need to reverse when partner has responded at the two-level. Again your attitude to clubs must be taken into account, but about 15 points will suffice. You will still need 17 to reverse after a 1♠ response.

5 **Diamonds and spades** You should have got the idea by now. Open the longer suit and bid the shorter if strength or level permit. Note again the sequence 1♢ 1♡ is not a reverse but

$$\begin{array}{cc} & 1♠ \\ 1♢ \ 2♣ \text{ and } 1♠ \ 2♡ \text{ are both reversing sequences.} \\ 2♠ & 3♢ \end{array}$$

6 **Hearts and spades** Again you will open the longer suit, and should it be hearts, you will need about 15 points to reverse into spades as partner's minor-suit bid will invariably be at the two-level. Note that, if partner responds 1NT over 1♡, he denies four spades and therefore there is no need to bid them. If he bids 1NT over 1♠, you can bid 2♡ without reversing as the preference for 2♠ will be at the two-level.

We must now consider opening bids on hands with two five-card suits as well as one-suited and two-suited hands involving longer suits. The usual considerations apply. The final contract anticipated is at the top of the list as always but in addition, as it will usually take three bids to express such hands, strength and suit quality must be taken into account. Very often, it will be convenient to treat a very poor five-card suit, say Q 8 x x x or worse, as a four-card suit and bid according to the last chapter. Let us start with 5–5 hands.

1 **Clubs and diamonds** Here you will open 1♢ and then, if the situation warrants, bid clubs twice, allowing partner the opportunity to give preference cheaply at 3♢.

2 **Clubs and hearts** This is more complicated and strength is crucial. If you do not have reversing values, it is probably best to open 1♡ and rebid 2♡ over 2◇. This is preferable to opening 1♣ and then being unable to bid a five-card major over 1♠ for lack of strength; you are primarily looking for 4♡. If you have reversing values, then the relative strengths of the two suits become important. Normally you should open 1♡ and rebid 2♣ or 3♣ according to your strength and partner's response. However, if your clubs are markedly better than your hearts, it is better to open 1♣. Now, if partner answers 1◇, you can bid 1♡ (or 2♡ if strength and attitude to diamonds permit) and then bid hearts a second time if partner asks for more information on your hand. Strictly, this would show six clubs and five hearts. However, with this approach, you will give a more accurate description of your hand than you would if you started with hearts and bid clubs twice afterwards.

3 **Clubs and spades** Normally, to conserve bidding space, you should open 1♣, prepared to bid spades twice later if necessary. The exception arises if you have reversing values and very much stronger spades than clubs, when it is important to emphasize the spades as your prime suit. Now open 1♠ and rebid clubs at the appropriate level (twice if necessary) later.

4 **Diamonds and hearts** This is handled similarly to clubs and diamonds.

5 **Diamonds and spades** As with clubs and hearts, rebid considerations are dominant.

6 **Hearts and spades** This is similar to 1 and 4 above.

The general rule is: with touching suits (♣◇, ◇♡, ♡♠), bid the higher first and then the lower twice afterwards; with non-touching suits (♣♡, ◇♠, ♣♠) plan the auction according to suit quality, strength and partner's possible responses in your short suits.

With one-suited hands containing a six-card suit or longer, you will simply open the suit at the one-level and rebid it at the following levels (always remembering to revalue or devalue according to your attitude to partner's bid suit). If partner responds at the one-level, rebid at the two-level up to 14 points, at the three-level from 15–17 points. With 18–20, you should open the suit at the two-level (except, as we shall learn in a moment, in clubs). If partner responds at the two-level, you should repeat your suit at that level with 11–13 points but at the three-level with 14–16 points. With 17, there is something of a problem and much depends on whether your suit is a major or minor, its quality and (where it is a minor) how many honours you have in the side-suits as *stops* for no-trumps. We shall discuss this in more detail later.

We must now look at two-level openings in more detail. In Acol, the definition tends to refer to *playing tricks* rather than point-count. In other words, if your hand looks as though it can make eight tricks playing on its own, it qualifies. Something like:

♠ K Q J x x x
♥ A x x
♦ A x
♣ A x

would probably give you five tricks in spades plus the three aces to total eight. This hand contains 18 points but the system allows a two-opener on weaker hands provided the eight-playing-trick requirement is satisfied:

♠ x
♥ A K Q J 10 9 7
♦ K Q x
♣ x x

Again, the seven tricks in hearts plus a certain one in diamonds will give eight tricks despite only fifteen points. I have to say that I am not in favour of opening these hands at the two-level, taking the view that it is almost certain that you will want to play this hand in 4♥ and should therefore bid it direct. The big disadvantage of this type of hand is that, if an opponent is very short of hearts as is likely, it offers very little defensive hope against a black-suit contract and therefore should be bid at a high level to make it as difficult as possible for the opponents to enter the auction. We shall discuss this in more detail under *preemptive bidding* in a moment.

We must now consider hands where you have six cards in one suit and four in the other. Now much depends on the respective ranks – hands with a six-card major suit and four-card minor will be considered differently from their converse, as four of a major is a much more likely final contract than five of a minor. With a long minor suit, your first thoughts, even on an unbalanced hand, should be towards 3NT. Let us go through the various combinations.

1 **Clubs and diamonds** Where the diamonds are longer, bid them twice and then the clubs. The basic guide is that 6–4 hands almost invariably play better in the six-card suit. The only exception might arise if the diamonds are very poor and the clubs very strong, when you might decide to treat it as a 5–4 hand, opening 1♢ and rebidding 2♣, only mentioning the diamonds a second time if you are forced to make a third bid. Where the clubs are longer, you should open 1♣. When partner responds one of a major, you will need reversing values to bid 2♢, intending to bid the clubs again afterwards. If you do not have reversing values, simply rebid the clubs; partner can still bid a diamond suit if he has it.

2 **Clubs and hearts** Where the hearts are longer, you will almost invariably bid and rebid them before even thinking about mentioning the clubs. Only in the case of a very poor heart suit and a very strong club suit, might you treat it as 5–4. Even then, over 1♡ 2♢, you will need reversing values to bid 3♣. Where the clubs are longer, you should be thinking of bidding clubs, hearts and then clubs again if strength permits. Otherwise, you may have to bid the clubs twice. Open 1♣; now if partner responds 1♢, you can bid 1♡ (or 2♡ if you are very strong) intending to rebid clubs next time. However, if he responds 1♠, you will need reversing values to bid 2♡ and will otherwise have to rebid 2♣. Note that, by bidding 1♠, partner is already suggesting that he does not have a four-card heart suit. If he has, he will have five spades and may well bid hearts next time, so nothing will be lost.

3 **Clubs and spades** Where the spades are longer, you should treat it in a similar manner to clubs and hearts. Where the clubs are longer, you will always open 1♣ and rebid 1♠ (or 2♠ if you are very strong) without having to reverse. Your third bid will be in clubs.

4 **Diamonds and hearts** Where the hearts are longer, treat as hearts and clubs but note that a reversing situation does not arise. Where the diamonds are longer, open 1◇ and note that, over a black-suit response, 2♡ will always be a reverse. Repeat the diamonds if you lack the necessary strength.

5 **Diamonds and spades** Where the spades are longer, treat as clubs and hearts. Where the diamonds are longer, open 1◇. Now, if partner responds 1♡, you can bid 1♠ without difficulty, intending to repeat the diamonds next time. If he responds 2♣, you will need reversing values to bid 2♠; in their absence repeat the diamonds. Note that partner's 2♣ bid almost certainly denies a four-card spade suit. If he has one, he must have five clubs and at least enough points (a minimum of about 11) to bid his spades next round after your 2◇ bid and again nothing will be lost.

6 **Hearts and spades** Where the spades are longer, this situation is debatable. After opening 1♠ and hearing two of a minor from partner, a case could be made for repeating the spades or mentioning the hearts. My suggestion is that, unless your spades are very good and hearts very bad, you should bid the hearts, giving the partnership maximum chance of finding a major-suit fit. This involves accepting the risk of finishing in the wrong part-score should partner be longer in hearts than spades; a 6–1 trump fit usually plays better than a 4–3. We shall discuss giving preference in more detail later. Where the hearts are longer, you should start with 1♡. If partner fails to bid 1♠, he almost certainly does not hold four spades so, in the absence of reversing values, you can repeat your hearts without risk. If he has four spades, he will have to be strong enough to bid them on the second round if he has bid two of a minor first.

With hands of 6–5 shape, you must again plan your auction according to rank and strength and on occasions, it may be wise to break the rules and open the shorter suit first. We will go through the combinations again.

1 **Clubs and diamonds** Where the diamonds are longer, bid diamonds, clubs and diamonds unless the clubs are very much stronger, in which case you might decide to treat it as 5–5 and bid diamonds, clubs and clubs. Where the clubs are longer and you have reversing values, you can open 1♣, intending to bid the diamonds twice afterwards should the bidding warrant it. With weak hands, it is more debatable. With good clubs, you should open 1♣ and rebid 2♣, prepared to lose a possible 5–3 diamond fit (if partner has four diamonds, he will probably bid them). With good diamonds, it might be better to treat it as 5–5 and open 1♢, intending to bid and rebid clubs afterwards.

2 **Clubs and hearts** Where the hearts are longer, always open 1♡. If partner responds 1♠, you can rebid 2♣, intending to repeat hearts later. If partner responds 2♢, you will need reversing values to rebid 3♣, otherwise rebid 2♡. Where the clubs are longer, you should always open 1♣. If partner responds 1♢, you can bid and rebid hearts. If he responds 1♠, you will need reversing values to rebid 2♡, otherwise rebid 2♣, prepared to forgo a 5–3 heart fit. This is likely to be preferable to opening 1♡ and rebidding 2♡ over 2♢, which is a much more serious distortion of the hand.

3 **Clubs and spades** Where the spades are longer, you should always open 1♠, prepared to rebid 2♠ if you cannot reverse. If you can, you will rebid 3♣ after partner's two of a red suit and rebid the spades later. Where the clubs are longer, you should always open 1♣ as you will be able to bid your spades at the one-level. Should partner respond 1NT, you may reverse even without reversing strength as partner (as we shall learn in the next chapter) will be promising 8–10 points and at least good tolerance for clubs.

4 **Diamonds and hearts** Here similar considerations apply to the treatment of diamonds and clubs.

5 **Diamonds and spades** Where the spades are longer, you should always open 1♠, prepared to repeat the suit over 2♡ if you lack reversing values. Where the diamonds are longer, you should always open 1♢, prepared to repeat the suit over 2♣ if you lack reversing values.

6 **Hearts and spades** Similar considerations apply to 1 and 4 above. Hands with two six-card suits are considered in the same way as those with 5–5. Those with a 7–6 shape (and they come up once a decade if you are lucky!), should be treated similarly to those with 6–5.

We now consider the very strong hands of 23 points and more. On these hands, a slam is a strong possibility and therefore we want to be able to exchange as much information as possible for an accurate auction. It is therefore desirable to keep the early bidding at a reasonably low level and we reserve what we call a *conventional bid* for this purpose. On all hands of 23 or more points, balanced (or you can be as low as 20 with a good long suit) you should open 2♣. All this says is: 'Partner I have a game or near-game virtually in my own hand.' It does not necessarily have anything to do with clubs. It is forcing to game (with one exception).

So what do we do with hands which qualify for an Acol two-bid in clubs? We can discuss these hands in combination with the problem hands of 17 points, mentioned earlier, when partner has bid two over one and you have no suitable rebid. One plan is to open 1♣ and reverse into a three-card suit (preferably diamonds if possible so as not to mislead about the length of a major suit) and then repeat your original suit. It is not entirely satisfactory but probably the best you can do. On some hands, however, if you have honours in all four suits and a shape something like 2236, you might open 2NT.

Finally, we turn to preemptive bidding – bids at the three- or higher level. Bids of this kind take a lot of bidding space away from the partnership but also from the opponents. They are thus intended to be obstructive and convey a clear message to partner, while making it very difficult for the opponents to conduct an informative auction. Consider this hand:

♠ x x
♡ K Q J 10 x x x
◇ x x
♣ x x

Here, if you play in hearts, you can be confident of six tricks without partner contributing anything at all. But now look at your defensive prospects. If opponents play in any of the other three suits or no-trumps, how many tricks will this hand be worth in defence? Probably none. If partner also has little, your opponents will certainly be cold for a small slam or possibly a grand. Obviously, vulnerability will be highly relevant but we are thinking in terms of losing 1000 points or more. It is therefore well worthwhile offering them a relatively modest penalty in hearts rather than allow them to discuss their slam prospects in full detail. The recommended opening bid is 3♡.

The basic guide is that it is worth about 500 to prevent game and thus you should be within three tricks of your contract, non-vulnerable, or two tricks, vulnerable – but may be a little more liberal if your opponents are vulnerable as now they are set to win the rubber and possibly more valuable slam bonuses. You should have at least a seven-card suit (a lot of people do it with six and some even with five but I do not recommend it) with the bulk of what few points you have concentrated in that suit. Do not preempt on:

♠ 10 x x x x x x
♡ A x
◇ K x
♣ J x

With the high cards in the short suits, the hand has plenty of defence and a very poor suit so you should prefer not to bid for the moment. If the spades are badly distributed, a preempt could cost a great deal and there is no guarantee that the opponents can even make a game.

Preemptive bids only apply if partner has not already bid. If he has opened the bidding, he will probably have plenty of defence, so all you are doing is making life difficult for him! The time to preempt arises when it is likely that the opponents are holding the bulk of the cards.

Preemptive bids apply at the three- or higher level. When you bid at the four- or higher level, you should obviously be that much stronger as the penalty will be heavier. If you are bidding game yourself, typically four of a major, allow a considerably stronger hand – although I have to say that many experts prefer to open at the one-level for fear of missing a slam.

A few paragraphs back I mentioned:

♠ x
♡ A K Q J 10 9 7
◇ K Q x
♣ x x

Many would take the view that fifteen points is much too strong for a preempt. Some would open 2♡, others would open 1♡ intending to rebid 4♡, but as I asked then and repeat now: 'How much defence have you got in this hand?' My suggestion is that you should not stand on ceremony – just bid the contract you intend to play. You may occasionally miss a slam yourselves as partner may only credit you with something like:

♠ x x
♡ A Q J x x x x
◇ x x
♣ x

but the damage you will do to the opposition will comfortably outweigh this. I have lost count of the number of times I have preempted on strongish hands and been confidently doubled, only to make my contract in comfort, sometimes with humiliating overtricks! One famous player of the past used to say: 'A preempt which is known to be weak is a blunt weapon.'

That will be enough on opening bids and it is time for a revision quiz. What would you open on the following hands, how do you plan your rebids if partner bids a suit in which you are short, and what final contracts have you got in mind? Start your stop-watch.

(1) ♠ Q x x x
     ♡ x x
     ◊ A K J x x
     ♣ K x

(2) ♠ A x
     ♡ K Q x x
     ◊ K Q J x x
     ♣ x x

(3) ♠ A K x x x
     ♡ Q x x x x
     ◊ A x
     ♣ x

(4) ♠ x x x x x
     ♡ x x
     ◊ A K Q J x
     ♣ A

(5) ♠ K x x
     ♡ A K x x x x
     ◊ Q x
     ♣ x

(6) ♠ K J x x
     ♡ K x
     ◊ x
     ♣ A K Q J x x

(7) ♠ A K x x x
     ♡ K Q x x x x
     ◊ x
     ♣ x

(8) ♠ x
     ♡ K Q J x x x x
     ◊ J x x x
     ♣ x

(9) ♠ A K Q x x
     ♡ A K Q x x
     ◊ A x x
     ♣ –

(10) ♠ x
     ♡ K x x x
     ◊ A K x x
     ♣ K x x x

(11) ♠ A Q x x
     ♡ x
     ◊ A K x x
     ♣ x x x x

(12) ♠ A K
     ♡ A K x
     ◊ x x x x x x x
     ♣ A K

We will now discuss the answers:

(1) On this 13-point hand, you do not have reversing values
     and should therefore open 1◊, prepared to repeat the suit
     over 2♣. If partner responds 1♡, you will, of course, be
     able to show your spades at the one-level as no reverse is
     involved. At the moment, you are angling for 5◊ or 4♠,
     possibly 3NT.

(2) On this much better 15-point hand, you have the values for
     a reverse if partner bids two over one, but not if he responds
     at the one-level. Thus open 1◊, prepared to bid 2♡ over
     2♣ but 2◊ over 1♠. 4♡, 3NT and 5◊ are your candidate
     contracts.

(3) Here you open the higher of the two touching suits,
     intending to bid the hearts (perhaps twice) later. You are
     obviously angling for 4♠ or 4♡.

(4) Here your 14 points are insufficient for a reverse and it is
     wise to treat the very poor spades as a four-card suit. Open
     1◊; if partner responds 1♡, you can show your spades.
     Over 2♣, likely to deny a four-card spades suit anyway,

you should be prepared to repeat the diamonds. 4♠ is still favourite as final contract but 3NT is more likely than 5♦.

(5) With only 12 points, you cannot reverse so you must open 1♡ and rebid 2♡. Note that, if partner fails to bid 1♠, he will probably not have four spades or will have enough strength to bid 2♠ over 2♡ so that the spade fit will never be lost. 4♡ is the most likely game with 4♠ a possible alternative.

(6) Here you will open 1♣ and if partner responds 1♦, you can bid 1♠, probably intending to jump in clubs later. However, if your partner responds 1♡, the hand will have improved sufficiently to justify a jump to 2♠, after which you can repeat your clubs if necessary. Despite the shape, 3NT is your most likely game with 4♠ and 5♣ being the alternatives.

(7) On this 12-point hand, you cannot reverse and it is therefore wise to treat the hand as 5–5, opening 1♠ and bidding the hearts twice afterwards. You are obviously angling for 4♡ or 4♠.

(8) Here you have a good seven-card suit and little or no defence outside and you should therefore preempt with 3♡. Note that, once you have done so, you should not bid again unless partner makes a force. He knows what you have but you have little or no idea of his hand and thus he, rather than you, must be responsible for the decision on the final contract. At the moment, the final contract you are aiming for is 3♡ only. Partner will raise you to 4♡ if he is strong enough.

(9) With this 22-point hand and two excellent suits, you can virtually guarantee game on your own and should force with 2♣. Note that your void of clubs is beside the point. You will reach at least 4♡ or 4♠ but will be disappointed if there is no slam.

(10) On this awkward hand, your best opening, in my opinion, is 1♦, intending to rebid 2♣. At least your distortion (the promise of a five-card diamond suit) will only be in respect of a minor. You are primarily aiming for 4♡, with 5♣ and 5♦ being outside chances. It should be stressed again that it

usually pays to show restraint on 4441 hands; the lack of a long suit makes it difficult to take many tricks.

(11) With the singleton heart, you have an easy rebid in spades if you open in either minor. With the diamonds so much better, it is preferable to open 1 ◊. You can always support clubs if partner bids them but it is unhelpful to suggest the suit as trumps yourself when it is unnecessary to do so. You are primarily looking for 4♠ with 5◊ and 5♣ being outside chances.

(12) This is a very awkward hand and with the long suit being a minor, you are best advised to treat it as a five-card suit and open 2NT. 2 ◊ would suggest a much better suit and you are primarily angling for 3NT rather than 5 ◊. Were the suit a major, the position is much less clear. All your cards outside are aces and kings, described as *quick tricks*, which suggests a trump contract is preferable (as opposed to queens and jacks, which are referred to as *slow tricks* and are more appropriate to no-trump contracts). Four of the major would now be favourite and it might therefore be preferable to open with two of the major, contrary to definition. Expert opinion varies on such questions.

You should have taken under eight minutes to answer these questions, with a view to getting your time down to three or less. Eventually you should be proficient enough to take one look at a hand, assess its worth and plan your auction in a matter of a few seconds. The most important thing, when considering your bid, is to pay particular attention to the way the auction is likely to develop and where it will end. We shall continue these themes in the next chapter.

Partner's First Response

We are now going to consider partner's responses, starting with those where the opening bid was one of a suit. They can be conveniently divided into three categories:

1 A bid of no-trumps, which again strictly limits the strength of the hand (and albeit to a lesser degree, the shape) and is therefore non-forcing.
2 Support of partner's suit, which also limits the strength of the hand and is therefore non-forcing.
3 A change of suit, which does not limit either the shape or strength and is therefore forcing.

We shall consider each in turn.

A response of no-trumps

This shows a point-count according to level and an inability to make an informative suit bid. The response of 1NT shows: 6–8 points if partner has opened 1 ♦, 1 ♥, or 1 ♠ (although it must be said that many recognized authorities allow 6–9 – I consider this too wide a range and would like to be able to pass as opener with 16 points, confident that game is most unlikely); 8–10 points if he has opened 1 ♣.

The possible shape of the hand varies considerably with the opening bid. Over 1 ♦, it denies a four-card major (you should bid one if you have it irrespective of quality – again some authorities demand at least Q x x x). If you have four or more diamonds, you should support the suit, particularly if you have a useless doubleton in another suit. Let us understand why. In hands in which minor suits are dominant, your first thoughts should be towards 3NT. If you bid 1NT now, you will eventually be declarer with a hand of 17 points or more going down on dummy and the lead coming round to that useless doubleton when it is clearly preferable that partner should play the hand, giving much less visible information away to opponents and ensuring that the lead comes round to the strong hand which may well include a tenace position in spades which needs to be protected. Thus with

♠ x x
♡ Q x x
◇ K x x x
♣ J x x x

you should prefer 2◇ to 1NT. With long clubs, however, as in:

♠ x x x
♡ Q x x
◇ x x
♣ K J x x x

you have no choice but to bid 1NT; a change of suit at the two-level would promise 9 points minimum and would be forcing.

With something like:

♠ x x
♡ Q x x
◇ K x x
♣ J x x x x

it is more debatable; personally I still prefer 2◇, but many would bid 1NT which is not so unreasonable with the minimal diamond support. Note that 1NT in response does not necessarily promise a balanced hand as does the opening bid. You would still have to bid it with:

♠ x x x
♡ Q x x
◇ x
♣ K J x x x x

hardly ideal, but you have little other choice.

Over 1♡, 1NT denies a four-card spade suit and is likely to

show two or fewer hearts unless the hand is very flat or you have
three poor hearts and a doubleton honour. Thus you should bid
1NT with:

	♠ K x x	or	♠ Q x
	♡ x x		♡ x x x
	◇ K x x x		◇ K x x x
	♣ Q x x x		♣ J x x x

or	♠ x x x	or	♠ x x
	♡ x x x		♡ x
	◇ K x x		◇ K x x x x
	♣ K x x x		♣ K x x x x

Over 1♠, there is an even wider range of hands and in all cases,
you could have a six-card or longer lower-ranking suit. If you do
not have nine points, you should not force at the two-level. You
would even have to bid it on:

♠ –
♡ Q x x
◇ K x x x x x
♣ J x x x

At least you are warning partner that you are not very excited
about the hand! A jump to 2NT shows 11–12 points and now the
shape is much more clearly defined as you had the opportunity
and strength to bid a suit at the two-level.

Over 1♣, it denies a four-card major and indeed a diamond
suit should almost always be bid unless you have honour
holdings in all non-club suits and want the likely 3NT to be
played from your side. So bid 2NT on:

♠ Q 10 x	or even	♠ K x
♡ Q 10 x		♡ Q x x
◇ K x x x		◇ J x x x x
♣ A x x		♣ A J x

but not on

♠ x x x
♡ Q x x
◇ A K x x
♣ K x x

when 1◇ should be preferred.

Over 1◇, again 2NT denies a four-card major and similar considerations apply in terms of mentioning a club suit. By all means bid it on:

♠ K x x	but not on:	♠ x x
♡ Q 10 x		♡ Q x x
◇ x x		◇ K x x x
♣ A Q x x x		♣ A Q x x

when 2♣ should be preferred. You can always support diamonds later if you think 5◇ is a candidate game contract but at the moment, 3NT is still favourite and you should, at least for the time being, try to avoid playing that contract from your side of the table with that poor spade holding.

Notice again how hot I am on this final contract consideration. It is my experience from teaching that ignoring this point is the cause of a large proportion of bidding mistakes and it therefore cannot be emphasized too often – and it isn't only beginners that are at fault; intermediates and even many so-called 'experts' are sometimes the worst offenders!

Over 1♡, 2NT denies a four-card spade suit and the same considerations apply again when considering whether to bid two of a minor or 2NT. Bid 2NT

on	♠ K x x	or	♠ K 10 x
	♡ Q x		♡ Q x x
	◇ K x x x		◇ K x x
	♣ K x x x		♣ K x x x

but prefer 2♣ with

	♠ x x	or	♠ x x x
	♡ Q x x		♡ K x
	◇ K x x x		◇ K Q x x
	♣ A Q x x		♣ K x x x

Notice that, where you do prefer the suit bid, there is still room to bid no-trumps later should the subsequent auction commend it. But bidding no-trumps immediately involves the loss of a great deal of bidding space and it will be much more difficult to find a minor-suit fit cheaply.

Over 1♠, you need a five-card suit to bid 2♡. With a poor four-card suit, you may bid 2NT if you want 3NT to be played from your side (partner can still bid 3♡) but otherwise, you are entitled to bid a three-card minor suit. Do not worry that it will mislead partner because you will invariably have three cards in spades and will be able to correct partner's support of your assumed minor suit back to spades. Thus bid 2NT with:

	or	
♠ x x		♠ x x x
♡ Q x x x		♡ K x x
◇ K J x		◇ K x x x
♣ A Q x x		♣ A Q x

but prefer 2♣ with:

	or	
♠ x x		♠ x x x
♡ A Q x x		♡ A Q x x
◇ x x x		◇ x x x
♣ A J x x		♣ K Q x

As we shall learn in a moment, partner is likely to have four-card support if he raises your minor, which means he must have five spades (otherwise he would have opened with one of the minor!). Therefore there is no danger.

A response of 3NT direct shows 13–15 points and it is strongly recommended that it should show a 3334 or 3343 shape and no other with stops (at least Q x x or J x x x) in all suits other than that bid by partner. Some players tend to bid it on hands with a good long minor, hoping to run home before the opponents find their best line of defence and in fairness, it must be said that such tactics very often work. However, it makes life very difficult for partner if he has a big and/or distributional hand with slam ambitions.

Supporting partner's suit

Here again, the final contract anticipated is important and therefore a critical distinction arises between the majors and the minors. When supporting a major, four of that suit is hot favourite as the final contract; with a minor, 3NT is still far more likely and five of the minor is an outsider unless one or both partners are very distributional and/or a side suit is wide open, ruling out a no-trump contract.

We saw earlier that three cards are needed to support partner's bid suit. Ideally, they should be headed by an honour but there are times when you have to do it on x x x for lack of another bid. The next question is how to value long trumps and side suit shortages. The following is a reasonable guide based on four-card trump support:

Doubleton: 1 point, but do not count that point if it includes an honour as that honour is reduced in value, i.e. count Q x as two points and no more;

Singleton: 3 points with the same proviso;

Void: 5 points.

The values of these shortages increase if you have plenty of trumps and I suggest you add half a point to the above scale for every trump in excess of four but reduce to 2 points for a singleton and 3 points for a void if you only have three trumps. Thus:

♠ x
♡ K x x x
♢ Q x x x x
♣ x x x

would be worth 8 points in support of hearts while:

♠ Q x
♡ K x x x x
♢ Q x x x x x
♣ –

would be worth 12 points in support of hearts.

According to your supporting points, you may raise one of a major as follows:

6–10: to the two-level;

11–12: to the three-level – a wide range is undesirable here as partner has to take a decision whether to go to game or not. The wider range at the two-level is acceptable because partner has room to ask for a more detailed description of your hand within the range as we shall learn later under *trial bids*. Note that to raise to the three- or higher level, you must have at least four trumps as you are categorically setting the denomination. With only three, change suit first and wait until you are confident that partner's major is five-card or longer. If it is only

four, no-trumps may be preferable, so keep the
bidding low to allow maximum discussion.
13 upwards: to game.

The general principle is that, unless there is a terrible misfit, two
hands of opening-bid strength should always bid a game, which
usually requires around 25 points combined. These figures are all
very approximate and in trump contracts particularly, you
should remember to value up aces and value down queens and
jacks, quick tricks being favourable in trump contracts. It should
also be emphasized that a direct raise in partner's suit gives him
very little information about your hand apart from your agreement of the trump suit. As we shall see, it often pays, particularly
if you have a good suit, to bid that suit, before giving the trump
raise to help partner decide whether to proceed further, viz. from
part-score to game or from game to slam.

When raising a minor, you should normally have four cards in
the trump suit, unless, as explained earlier, you cannot find a
more sensible bid. Unless you are highly distributional, you
should avoid raising to the four or higher level on hands of
appropriate strength as 3NT may well be the best game contract.
Thus with:

♠ Q x x
♡ x x
◇ A Q x x x
♣ A Q x

you should bid 2♣ over 1 ◇. Don't worry that partner will think
you have a club suit; you can always correct to diamonds if he
supports the clubs. It is more difficult with:

♠ x x x	or, even worse,	♠ x x x
♡ K x		♡ K x x
◇ x x x		◇ x x
♣ A K Q J x		♣ A K Q J x

What should you bid if partner opens 1♣? To tell the truth, the
bridge world has yet to find a satisfactory answer. It is currently
accepted that 1 ◇ seems the best (although some recommend
bidding a good three-card major), intending to go back to clubs if
you are supported and the partnership cannot bid no-trumps.

Partner will have to realize what is happening and refrain from going back to diamonds despite his very poor clubs.

Change of suit

At the one-level, this shows at least 6 points (or 5 with a good five-card or longer suit). At the two-level, it shows at least 9 points (or 8 with a good five-card or longer suit) and is forcing for at least one round.

Once partner has opened the bidding, you know that he has between 11–19 points and at least four cards in the suit that he has bid. The aim will be to narrow down the point-range and find out more about his distribution by exchanging as much information as possible to decide whether to play a part-score, game or slam and in which denomination. This may require several rounds of bidding and therefore we want to use as little bidding space as possible – hence the insistence on keeping the bidding open even with apparently modest bids.

As soon as you hear partner's opening bid, your first thought should be (as if it needed repeating!) 'What final contract?' (assuming, for the moment, that you are heading for game). Probably the most convenient way to work is to consider partner's possible opening bids in turn:

1♣: You should start by bidding your longest suit at the one-level; if you have two four-card suits, bid the lower-ranking first, giving partner a chance to bid the other cheaply if he has it. On the other hand, if you have two five-card suits, bid the higher-ranking first. You will bid the other on the next round, enabling partner to give preference at the same level cheaply. This distinction has already been mentioned when we discussed opening bids and it is important to make sure that you understand the difference. With four-card suits, if you bid the lower-ranking first and partner fails to bid the other, there will be no eight-card fit and the suit is unlikely to be the best choice for trumps. There will therefore be no need for you to bid the higher-ranking suit at all. With five-card suits, three will be enough in partner's hand and you will want to bid both of them in the most economical order.

1◊: Similar rules apply but if your longest suit is clubs, you will need at least 9 points to go on to the two-level. If you have 6–10, a four-card major takes precedence as you will need 11 points to bid both suits. With two five-card majors, you will obviously bid spades first; with two five-card suits including clubs, you will obviously bid the major first.

1♡: Here you should always bid a four-card or longer spade suit unless you have at least 11 points, when you can bid a longer minor first and spades afterwards. If your only biddable suit is a minor, you must have at least 9 points to bid it at the two-level.

1♠: Here you will bid a four-card or longer minor at the two-level with 9 points or more but you must have at least a five-card suit to bid 2♡. If you have nothing apart from a four-card heart suit, you are allowed to bid a three-card minor suit, giving partner a chance to bid a four-card heart suit if he has it. If not, you will probably play in spades as explained earlier.

I mentioned above that it is often wise to change suit before raising partner's trump suit to give him more information. Let us take an example. Suppose you hold:

♠ x x
♡ Q x x x
◊ x x
♣ A Q J x x

It is your lucky day and partner opens 1♡. You have 12 points in support of hearts and are fully justified in raising to the three-level with a four-card trump support. But why not tell partner more about your hand first? Bid 2♣ and (unless partner shows a strong hand by reversing or jumping, in which case you can insist on game) you can then bid 3♡. Partner is now much better placed to take a decision on whether to go further. He can upvalue the ♣K (which you want) or devalue a shortage in the suit (which you do not want). Similarly, low honours in spades and diamonds can be devalued as they will be of little worth facing your useless doubletons.

Also with:

♠ K x x x
♡ x x
◇ K Q J 10 x
♣ K x

you are easily worth a raise to game when partner opens 1♠, but why not bid 2◇ first and then 4♠ on the next round? If partner has a good hand, there could be a slam on and he will be much better placed to judge whether to continue bidding if he knows you have a good diamond suit. This form of bidding is referred to as a *delayed game raise*. You could even do it on:

♠ A Q x x
♡ x x x
◇ x x x
♣ A K Q

You know that you will play in at least 4♠ but by bidding 2♣ first, you put partner in a much more informed position to value his hand. A void or singleton in a red suit would be priceless, while a shortage in clubs would make a good warning sign to stop in game; 5♠, never mind the slam, might be in danger. For that reason, a direct raise of partner's suit to the three or higher level should indicate a strong trump holding and/or scattered values elsewhere. With:

♠ A K x x
♡ Q x
◇ x x x x x
♣ x x

you should bid 3♠ direct. It is worse than useless to bid those diamonds first. You have no intention of playing the hand with that suit as trumps; the discussion is as to whether to play three or more spades? Again the consideration of final contract is paramount. So far, we have considered simple changes of suit, but there are rare situations in which you should jump in a new suit. Remember, this will cost you a round of bidding (although the damage varies from 1♣ 2◇, which still leaves a fair amount of space, to 1♠ 3♡, which often forces the opener to the four-level immediately) and should therefore convey a very clear message to partner. Three conditions should be satisfied:

1 You must have a one-suited hand. Never jump with two suits, irrespective of strength, as there is too much to discuss.
2 The suit should be of very good quality. Expert opinion varies on how good – the test I recommend is to ask yourself: 'Would I be happy to have this suit as trumps with a useless doubleton in partner's hand?' I suggest K Q J 10 x or any six-card or longer suit with three of the top four honours should be minimum and the bigger the loss of bidding space, the stricter you should be in this respect.
3 You should be strong enough to have serious slam ambitions.

A jump in a new suit is obviously forcing to game and would be justified with hands like:

♠ A K Q 10 x	♠ x
♡ A K x	♡ K Q J 10 x x
◇ J x x	◇ A K Q
♣ x x	♣ x x x
♠ A x	♠ A K Q
♡ K x	♡ x
◇ A Q J x x x	◇ x
♣ K x	♣ A K J x x x x

but not with hands like:

♠ K Q 10 x	♠ x
♡ A K x	♡ Q J x x x x
◇ J x x	◇ A Q x
♣ A x x	♣ K J x
♠ A x x x	♠ A K Q
♡ K x	♡ A K x
◇ A Q J 10 x	◇ x
♣ K x	♣ J x x x x x

The first is a balanced hand. In the second, you are not really strong enough to suggest a slam and to jump to the three-level over 1♠ takes away too much bidding space and the suit is not quite good enough. In the third, you have two suits and much to discuss – it is not clear that you will want to play in diamonds. In the fourth, the suit is very poor and you have little idea where to play with only one piece of information from partner so far.

Sticking to the rules I have suggested makes life much easier for partner. He can support happily with a doubleton honour and need not show a poor second suit which he already knows is of no interest to you.

We now turn to responding to an opening bid of 1NT. Here you already know a great deal about partner's hand – 12–14 points with no singleton, void or good five-card major suit. Against that, partner knows nothing about yours, so *you* must take charge of the auction and decide the final contract.

If you have a poor balanced hand of 10 points or less, no game is in prospect and you should be happy to pass 1NT. With weak distributional hands, you should realize that your long suit will be of no use unless it is trumps and therefore should bid it at the two-level as a sign-off. So with:

♠ x x x x x	♠ x	♠ x x x
♡ x x x	♡ Q J x x x x	♡ x x
◇ x x x	◇ A x x x	◇ J x x x x x
♣ x x	♣ x x	♣ A K

bid respectively 2♠, 2♡ and 2◇, which the opener must pass. The club suit has been left out in the cold for the moment for reasons which will be explained below.

With 11–12 and any 4333 shape or a 4432 or 5332 shape without a four-card or longer major, raise to 2NT. Note again the close range one level below game; partner has to take a final decision with no more room for further investigation.

Where you have a 4432 shape including one or both four-card majors, 4♡ and 4♠ become candidates for the final contract so that, if you have 11 points or more, i.e. enough to raise to 2NT (although, as we shall see later, you can do it on weaker and/or more distributional hands), you may set about investigating whether a 4–4 major suit fit is available. For that, we use a conventional bid named after a famous American player, Samuel Stayman and known as the *Stayman convention*.

The conventional bid is 2♣, which is obviously forcing and the 1NT opener replies as follows (see overleaf):

2 ◇ : no major suit;

2 ♡ : definitely a four-card suit and possibly a four-card spade suit as well;

2 ♠ : a four-card spade suit but no four-card heart suit.

Over 2♡, the responder, with four spades, may bid as follows:

1 With 11–12 points 2NT, after which the opener, if he has four spades in addition to his four hearts, can pass or bid 3♠ or 4♠, intending to play there; if he hasn't, he will bid 2NT or 3NT according to his strength, again intending to play there.

2 With 13 points or more, bid 3NT, which partner will correct to 4♠ if he has a four-card suit.

The Stayman convention can also be used for hands where you have a long club suit and (debarred from making a sign-off bid in 2♣) are prepared to play in 3♣ rather than leave partner in a hopeless 1NT. So with:

♠ K x
♡ x x x
◇ x x
♣ Q J x x x x

you can bid 2♣ and whatever partner replies, your bid of 3♣ will be a sign-off for the final contract. However, with weaker hands like:

♠ x x
♡ x x x
◇ x x x
♣ x x x x x

it is best to pass 1NT. Opponents, with at least 26 points between them, are almost certain to double (if not, the penalty will compare favourably against the value of the game they are almost certain to make) and now you can remove to 2♣ and note that, if 1NT is doubled, 2♣ is a natural sign-off and no longer Stayman.

With hands like:

♠ x
♡ Q x x x
◇ A Q J x x x
♣ x x

you can bid 2♣ and if partner fails to show a heart suit, your bid of 3 ◇ will be invitational to game in 3NT, but non-forcing. This applies to all sequences involving Stayman. Hands with about 10–12 points and a five-card major suit crop up frequently. With something like:

♠ A K x x x
♡ x x x
◇ K x x
♣ J x

bid 2♣ and unless partner bids 2♠ (which you will raise to game) your next bid will be 2♠ on 10–11 points and 3♠ on 12. This describes this type of hand and partner can pass, bid 2NT or 3NT, or raise to game according to his strength and attitude to spades.

A direct jump in a new suit, viz. 1NT 3♣, 1NT 3 ◇, 1NT 3♡, 1NT 3♠, are all forcing to game and may be bid on hands with slam ambitions. Because of the two-level sign-offs and the limitations of Stayman to invitational non-forcing hands, the restrictions applicable to jumps in a new suit over an opening bid of one of a suit set out earlier do not apply. However, you must have a five-card suit.

With a balanced hand you may raise to 4NT (non-forcing) on about 19–20 points, which partner will raise to 6NT with a good 13–14 points. He may also bid a good four-card or five-card suit at the five-level on the way – it costs nothing – and you can still stop in 5NT or end in 6NT or six of a suit.

With 21–22 points, balanced, you may confidently raise to 6NT (a sign-off).

With 23–24 points, you may invite a grand slam with 5NT. This is forcing at least to 6NT, but note again that the opener can still show a good four-card or five-card suit at the six-level, giving the options of a small or grand slam in the suit or in no-trumps. With 25–28 points, you can confidently bid 7NT. At the very worst, it will depend on a finesse against a king.

We now turn to responding to two-level opening suit bids (other than 2♣, which we shall discuss later). Partner will normally have shown you a good six-card suit and if that is a major, it is very likely to be the chosen trump suit. If it is a minor,

3NT is still likely to be favourite, but five of the minor is now a more serious possibility.

Your partner's bid is forcing for one round and as a slam is a possibility, your first duty is to show your general strength, in particular your top controls. The usual form is to draw the dividing line between a *positive* and *negative* response. If you have at least an ace and a king, or three kings, or ten points, in high cards in a hand lacking these controls, reply positively; if you have less than the above, reply negatively.

The first thing we have to sort out is the negative bid. There are two schools of thought on this. The old-fashioned way is simply to bid 2NT in response to all two-level suit openers – certainly easy to remember, but there are two disadvantages. First, and this applies particularly if partner has opened 2◊, the most likely final contract, 3NT, will be played from the wrong side. Second, again notably relevant in the 2◊ case, there may be an awkward loss of bidding space.

The alternative, modern method, which by no means solves the above problems but is certainly an improvement, is referred to as the *Herbert* negative. This involves bidding the next suit up:

2♡ over a 2◊ opener;
2♠ over 2♡;
either 2NT or 3♣ (opinions vary but I recommend 3♣) over 2♠.

This is something on which a partnership must agree. Once they have done so, they can use all other bids as positive responses. Distinction must be made between answering 2◊ and two of a major for final contract considerations. You can bid your longest suit over either at the cheapest level available or no-trumps on a balanced hand (bearing in mind that this will make you declarer in 3NT) but the distinction arises when you wish to support partner.

Over 2◊, always bid 3◊, irrespective of strength. A positive response to a two-opener is obviously forcing to game and this way you do not rule out 3NT. Over 2♡ or 2♠, it is usual to bid three of the major with one or more aces and (unless you are very strong – say eleven points up) four of the major with no ace. The rationale behind this is that, if you have no ace, game is likely to be the limit; but if you have one or more, a slam might be on and you therefore want more room for discussion. We shall learn more about the use of this space under slam bidding later.

Responses to an opening 2NT bid have slight differences to those opposite 1NT in that bidding space considerations rule out the weak-take out in diamonds, hearts and spades. 3♣ is Stayman as before, with similar responses, but three of any other suit is game-forcing and thus shows enough to make game opposite a minimum of 20 points, balanced. With very weak hands, you should pass 2NT.

When raising 2NT with balanced hands, the point ranges are as follows:

5–10: 3NT (sign-off);
11–12: 4NT non-forcing, invitation to 6NT (opener can bid suits on the way if he so wishes, as over 1NT 4NT);
13–14: 6NT (sign-off);
15–16: 5NT forcing at least to 6NT, invitation to 7NT (again opener can bid suits as before);
17 up: 7NT.

When responding to a game-forcing 2♣, the universally recognized negative is 2♦, any other bid being positive, a suit showing a five-card unless your shape is 4441. So, if you wish to respond positively in diamonds, you should bid 3♦.

We turn now to responding to preemptive bids. In this situation, it should be emphasized that partner has shown you his hand within fairly strict limits and it is now up to you to control the auction. You should credit partner with a seven-card suit, the strength of which will vary with the vulnerability, and very little outside, probably not more than one big honour. You should either be able to decide the final contract immediately and – unless you are very strong and/or have considerable support for partner's suit – that will usually mean passing the opening bid, or you will have to make further investigations.

A direct game bid by you is a sign-off and must be passed. It is alarming that so many people, including many 'good' players,

carry on repeating their preempt suit '. . . because I had seven of
them, partner!' Partner heard that the first time. A change of suit
below game is natural and forcing. Now the preempter, especially if he has opened in three of a minor, may bid a major to
show an honour card with a view to 3NT (remember that the
preempt has shown a single-suited hand). He may support your
suit, or repeat his own to show that he has nothing further to add
to his initial preempt.

That will be enough for the time being. Let us do some
practice. In the following quiz, I should like you to respond to the
given opening bids and indicate what final contract(s) you have
in mind. Start your stop-watch.

(1) Partner opens 1♣. You hold:

(a) ♠ K Q x x
     ♡ x x
     ♢ K x x x
     ♣ x x x

(b) ♠ x x x
     ♡ x x x
     ♢ J x x
     ♣ K Q x x

(c) ♠ K x x x x
     ♡ A x x x x
     ♢ J x x
     ♣ −

(d) ♠ K Q x
     ♡ x x x
     ♢ K Q x x
     ♣ J 10 x

(2) Partner opens 1♢. You hold:

(a) ♠ J x x x
     ♡ x x
     ♢ x x
     ♣ K Q x x x

(b) ♠ K Q x
     ♡ K Q x
     ♢ x x x
     ♣ K x x x

(c) ♠ Q x x
     ♡ Q x x
     ♢ x x x
     ♣ J x x x

(d) ♠ A x
     ♡ K x
     ♢ x x x
     ♣ A K Q x x x

(3) Partner opens 1♡. You hold:

(a) ♠ J x x x   (b) ♠ x x
    ♡ K Q x x   ♡ A x x x
    ◇ x x   ◇ x x x
    ♣ x x x   ♣ K Q J x

(c) ♠ x x x   (d) ♠ Q x x
    ♡ A K Q x   ♡ x x
    ◇ Q x   ◇ K Q x x
    ♣ x x x x   ♣ K J x x

(4) Partner opens 1♠. You hold:

(a) ♠ x x   (b) ♠ x x
    ♡ A Q x x x   ♡ Q J x x
    ◇ x x x   ◇ K x x
    ♣ x x x   ♣ A x x x

(c) ♠ A K Q x x   (d) ♠ Q x x
    ♡ Q x   ♡ x x
    ◇ x x x   ◇ Q x x x
    ♣ Q x x   ♣ Q x x x

(5) Partner opens 1NT. You hold:

(a) ♠ x x   (b) ♠ K Q J x x x
    ♡ x x x   ♡ A x
    ◇ Q x x   ◇ A K x
    ♣ J x x x x   ♣ K x

(c) ♠ x   (d) ♠ A K x
    ♡ K x   ♡ A K x
    ◇ x x x   ◇ A x x
    ♣ J 10 x x x x x   ♣ Q x x x

(6) Partner opens 2♣. You hold:

(a) ♠ x x x x   (b) ♠ Q x
    ♡ x x x x x   ♡ K Q x x x
    ◇ –   ◇ x x x
    ♣ x x x x   ♣ x x x

(c) ♠ A K x
   ♡ J x x x x
   ◇ x x x x
   ♣ x

(d) ♠ A K x
   ♡ x x x
   ◇ J x x x x
   ♣ x x

(7) Partner opens 2◇. You hold:

(a) ♠ x x x
   ♡ x x x
   ◇ A x x x
   ♣ x x x

(b) ♠ x x x
   ♡ J x
   ◇ A Q x x
   ♣ K x x x

(c) ♠ x x
   ♡ K Q x x x
   ◇ A x
   ♣ x x x x

(d) ♠ x x
   ♡ x x x x
   ◇ x x x
   ♣ A K Q x

(8) Partner opens 2♡. You hold:

(a) ♠ K Q x
   ♡ x x
   ◇ x x x x
   ♣ J 10 x x

(b) ♠ A K Q x x
   ♡ x x
   ◇ x x
   ♣ J x x x

(c) ♠ K x x
   ♡ Q x x
   ◇ K x x x
   ♣ K x x

(d) ♠ Q x x x x
   ♡ x
   ◇ K x
   ♣ A Q J x x

(9) Partner opens 2♠. You hold:

(a) ♠ K Q x x
   ♡ K Q J x x
   ◇ x x
   ♣ x x

(b) ♠ K J x x
   ♡ x x
   ◇ x x x x x
   ♣ K Q

(c) ♠ A J x
   ♡ x x
   ◇ K x x x
   ♣ J x x x

(d) ♠ x x
   ♡ x x
   ◇ A K J x x x x
   ♣ x x

(10) Partner opens 2NT. You hold:

(a) ♠ x x x
    ♡ J x x x
    ◇ x x x
    ♣ x x x

(b) ♠ K Q x x
    ♡ x
    ◇ J x x x
    ♣ x x x x

(c) ♠ A K x
    ♡ x x x
    ◇ A x x
    ♣ J x x x

(d) ♠ K x x
    ♡ x x x
    ◇ Q J x x x
    ♣ x x

(11) Partner opens 3♣. You hold:

(a) ♠ K Q x x
    ♡ K Q x x
    ◇ J x x x x
    ♣ –

(b) ♠ x x x
    ♡ –
    ◇ x x x x x
    ♣ K x x x x

(c) ♠ x x x
    ♡ A K x
    ◇ K Q x x x
    ♣ A x

(d) ♠ A K Q
    ♡ K x x
    ◇ A K x
    ♣ A x x x

(12) Partner opens 3◇. You hold:

(a) ♠ A K x x
    ♡ K Q x x
    ◇ –
    ♣ K x x x x

(b) ♠ K x
    ♡ K x
    ◇ x x
    ♣ A K Q x x x x

(c) ♠ Q x x
    ♡ A x
    ◇ –
    ♣ A K Q J x x x x

(d) ♠ J x
    ♡ J x
    ◇ Q
    ♣ Q J 10 x x x x x

(13) Partner opens 3♡. You hold:

(a) ♠ K x x x
    ♡ x
    ◇ K x x x
    ♣ K x x x

(b) ♠ K x
    ♡ A J x
    ◇ Q J x
    ♣ A K x x x

(c) ♠ –
     ♡ A Q x
     ◇ A x x
     ♣ A K x x x x x

(d) ♠ K x x
     ♡ –
     ◇ K x x
     ♣ K Q J 10 x x x

(14) Partner opens 3♠. You hold:

(a) ♠ x
     ♡ A K Q J x x x
     ◇ A K
     ♣ x x x

(b) ♠ K Q x
     ♡ K x x
     ◇ A K Q J x x x
     ♣ –

(c) ♠ –
     ♡ A Q x
     ◇ x x
     ♣ K Q J x x x x x

(d) ♠ –
     ♡ –
     ◇ K Q J x x
     ♣ K Q J x x x x

There were 56 questions and it should have taken you less than quarter of an hour to answer them. As you improve, you should be aiming to bring your time down to about a third of that. Let us go through the answers – but allow me to stress again the importance of the way to think about a bid.

(1)(a) Here you bid 1◇, the lower of your two four-card suits. Partner will bid spades if he has four or more, otherwise it is unlikely that you will want to play in that suit. At the moment, your candidate contracts are 3NT and 4♠, with 5♣ and 5◇ being outside chances.

(b) Here your best bid is 2♣. With this very balanced hand, 3NT must be favourite as final contract but partner will need at least 18 points and you certainly will not want to play it from your side of the table. This is a limit bid and, unlike the change of suit, is non-forcing. Note that 1NT over 1♣ promises 8–10 points; you only have 6.

(c) With two five-card suits, you will want to bid both with a view to 4♡ or 4♠. The most economical way to bid them is the higher-ranking first so that after your 2♡ bid on the second round, partner can, if necessary, give preference to spades at the two-level. So you should bid a forcing 1♠.

(d) This hand is balanced and is in the point range qualifying for a limit non-forcing bid of 2NT. However, you should bid a forcing 1 ◇. I should not need to tell you why. You certainly are angling for 3NT but you will not be wanting the lead to come round to that poor heart holding. You can always bid 2NT later if partner bids 1 ♡ over 1 ◇.

(2)(a) Here you should bid 1 ♠. The clubs are admittedly longer but you do not have the 9 points necessary to go on to the two-level. You are primarily looking for 3NT or 4 ♠, with 5 ♣ being a very outside chance.

(b) Here you have an balanced opening bid and two opening bids facing each other should make game, except in the case of a bad misfit. Here you have no other interest but 3NT and you should bid it direct, non-forcing. Partner will realize that you have this type of hand and can remove to another contract should his hand warrant it.

(c) This hand has only 5 points and although the honours are well protected, they are two isolated queens and a jack and with game being most unlikely, you should pass, content to play in 1 ◇.

(d) Here you will be insisting on a game at least and again a slam is well on the cards. This time, rather than making a low-level bid, you can give a clear message to partner by bidding 3 ♣ direct. This is game-forcing and shows a good, long club suit. Let him take things from there.

(3)(a) In this hand, you are almost certainly going to play with hearts as trumps and are angling for 4 ♡. With this in mind, it will be of little help to partner to tell him about that very poor spade suit. Just raise to 2 ♡ direct, a non-forcing limit-bid.

(b) As in (a), you will almost certainly be playing with hearts as trumps and are angling for 4 ♡. This hand is worth a raise to 3 ♡ but it is far better to tell partner something about your hand to help him decide whether to raise to game or even look for a slam. Simply force with 2 ♣ and then raise to 3 ♡, giving partner a far more accurate picture of your hand.

(c) You have the strength for a raise to 3♡ and are aiming for 4♡, but this time you should give it immediately as a non-forcing limit bid. You have nothing significant in the side suits to tell partner about to help him in deciding whether to proceed further.

(d) This hand qualifies for a limit-bid of 2NT and as you have cover in all the non-heart suits, you may bid it direct. 3NT is favourite for the final contract but five of a minor may be on. However, you will not be interested in those minors unless partner bids one of them himself.

(4)(a) Here you have a good five-card heart suit and you are probably aiming for 4♡. However, you need at least 9 points to bid it at the two-level and despite not wanting the lead in 3NT (certainly a candidate) to come round to those poor minor trebletons, a non-forcing 1NT is all you can bid to limit your hand.

(b) Here you are strong enough to go to the two-level and should bid your lower-ranking four-card suit, 2♣ being forcing. Partner will bid 2♡ if he has four or more of them, otherwise you will be angling for 3NT with 5♣ being an outside chance.

(c) In complete contrast, you have no interest in discussing anything else except 4♠ and should bid it direct. You have nothing outside about which to tell your partner beforehand.

(d) Here you are worth no more than a non-forcing, limit-raise to 2♠. You are primarily angling for 4♠ but as your hand is balanced and all queens (slow tricks) it may well play better in 3NT. In that event, you will want partner with his strong hand to be declarer to avoid the lead coming round to those two small hearts. With three small spades and Q x in hearts, 1NT is preferable because now you do want to be declarer in 3NT if partner has A x x or K x x in hearts. You can always support spades later should the auction warrant it.

(5)(a) In this and all problems involving a reply to 1NT, partner has already limited his hand in both shape and strength and it is therefore up to you to take command on the basis that you know far more about his hand than he about yours. The same principle will apply when replying to preempts later on. This first hand is of little use to partner and you know that you are already too high! You realize that your hand is of more use if those clubs are trumps but you cannot make a weak take-out sign-off in that suit as 2♣ is Stayman and forcing. It is certainly not worth going to the three-level to play in clubs in preference to no-trumps. You must therefore pass and be prepared to accept a likely but modest penalty. If 1NT is doubled, you may then remove to 2♣, which reverts back to being a natural weak take-out. Your two possible final contracts are therefore 1NT or 2♣.

(b) With 20 points and a good six-card suit, you will almost certainly be insisting on a small slam and a grand is a strong possibility. The first move is to jump in your good suit, i.e. bid 3♠ to force to game. You will then proceed to game, small slam or grand slam according to partner's reaction. Currently, you are angling for 6♠ or 7♠.

(c) This is not dissimilar to (a), but now the clubs are so long that it is worth going to the three-level to ensure that they are trumps. Start with a forcing Stayman 2♣ and irrespective of partner's reply, sign-off in 3♣, the only final contract in which you are interested.

(d) With 20 points, completely flat, you will almost certainly want to play in no-trumps and you know that the combined point-count is 32–34. 33 is enough for a small slam and the way to find out your partner's strength is to invite with 4NT. This is non-forcing and partner is expected to pass with 12 points only, bid 6NT with 14 points and possibly 5NT or a four- or five-card suit at the five-level with 13. You can thus still stop in 5NT. At the moment, you are aiming for 4NT or 6NT.

(6)(a) In replying to a game-forcing (with one exception) 2♣ opener, the first message refers to your general strength, Here, you could hardly be worse and must therefore give the negative response of 2♢. Note that, just as your partner's opener had nothing to do with clubs, your reply has nothing to do with diamonds; the void is totally irrelevant. You have little idea of final contract at this stage but will obviously be hoping for 4♡, 4♠ or possibly 5♣.

(b) You need, in principle, an ace and a king or three kings to respond positively. So for the moment, you must give the negative response of 2♢. You will bid your hearts later, 4♡ and 3NT being the most likely final contracts.

(c) Here you have enough for a positive response and should simply bid your five-card suit with 2♡. At present 4♡ or 3NT are favourites as final contract but if partner is more than minimum for his opener, a slam is very likely.

(d) Another positive response but what you should do here is a little more debatable. If you bid those diamonds, it will have to be at the three- level and with the suit being fairly poor, you might arguably treat the hand as balanced and prefer 2NT. However, as you are likely to finish in 3NT, you will prefer partner to be declarer and I prefer 3♢ for that reason.

(7)(a) This is not worth a positive response and you should give the negative of 2♡. Note this has nothing to do with hearts. You can support diamonds later, hoping to finish in 3NT or 5♢.

(b) This is easily strong enough for a positive response and your best bid is 3♢, showing one ace. You will be looking to finish in 3NT, preferably played by your partner, or 5♢ or 6♢.

(c) For the positive response this time, you will have to bid 3♡ as 2♡ would be negative and bear no relation to hearts. With the good suit, you have no reason to do anything else, angling for 4♡ or 3NT.

(d) Another positive response, but with all your points concentrated in one suit, you should refrain from bidding 2NT as you will want the most likely final contract of 3NT to be played from your partner's side. Even though, strictly speaking, it shows a five-card suit, the most illustrative bid on your hand is 3♣. You will not want to play in hearts unless partner can bid them and a direct 3♢, showing a positive response with one ace, will put partner in difficulties with his poor clubs. 3NT is the most likely final contract, but 5♢ is a possibility.

(8)(a) Here you are well short of a positive response and should bid a negative 2♠. Note that your spade holding is irrelevant. 3NT and 4♡ are the most likely final contracts.

   (b) This is easily a positive response but as you are debarred from bidding 2♠, which would be a negative bid and nothing to do with the suit, you should bid 3♠ on this excellent suit, prepared to play in four or more of either major.

   (c) Here you have a balanced hand with heart support. You could show an aceless raise by bidding 4♡ direct but it is better to bid a positive 2NT first and support hearts later to show scattered values and a balanced hand outside – far more descriptive. You are looking for 4♡ or 6♡ or possibly 6NT, which may well have to be played from your side.

   (d) Here you have another big hand but with a misfit. You certainly must respond positively to insist on game, but bidding a direct 3♠ will use a lot of bidding space, the last thing you want as it may well be that 3NT is your best contract. As the clubs are so much better than the spades, it is probably best to treat the hand as 5–4 rather than 5–5 and start with 3♣, intending to bid spades at the three-level below 3NT. Game in any denomination apart from diamonds is possible but a slam is only likely if partner has some support for clubs.

(9)(a) Here you have a positive response and tremendous trump support but an aceless raise to 4♠ is inappropriate. It costs nothing to show that excellent heart suit first by bidding 3♡, intending to support spades later to end in 4♠ or 6♠.

(b) This is a positive response and you have little reason to bid anything other than an aceless raise to 4♠, intending to play there or in 6♠. Bidding that poor diamond suit is unlikely to be of any help to partner and you could only show your club values at the four-level (3♣ being negative). This would give the impression of a suit rather than a doubleton.

(c) This is also a positive response and as you do not have values concentrated in a side suit, you should simply give a one-ace raise to 3♠, intending to play 4♠ or (admittedly unlikely) 6♠.

(d) This is a positive response and you should simply bid 3♦. 6♦ could be on but you may well have to settle for 4♠ or 5♦ dependent on partner's spades and top controls. Your doubletons in the other suits are a bad feature.

(10)(a) Partner has promised 20–22 points balanced, but remember that this opening bid is limited and therefore non-forcing. You need 25 points combined for 3NT to be a reasonable contract and even the fact that the vast majority of the points are in one hand is a very distinct disadvantage. You will not be able to lead from weakness towards strength very often. Here there is no hope of game and you should pass, intending to play 2NT which partner will be lucky to make, playing virtually on his own.

(b) With 6 points, you have enough for game and it is a question of whether to play 3NT or 4♠. (There are hands in which the only makable game would be five of a minor but it is very difficult to establish this.) You should therefore bid a Stayman 3♣, forcing partner to bid a major if he has one. If he replies 3♦, you will settle for 3NT; if he bids 3♥, he may have both majors, so you will then bid 3♠, after which he will raise you to 4♠ or settle for 3NT.

(c) With this 12-point, balanced hand, you will almost certainly want to play in no-trumps but the combined point-count is 32–34 so a slam (requiring 33) is possible. Invite with a non-forcing 4NT and partner will bid in a similar manner to the sequence 1NT 4NT discussed earlier. You are thus aiming for 4NT or 6NT.

(d) With 6 points, you have enough for game as mentioned before but this time you have a five-card suit. However, refrain from bidding it as a slam is most unlikely and given that you are going to play in game, 3NT is far more likely than 5♦, particularly as your other three suits lack a singleton or void. Simply sign off in 3NT.

(11)(a) In this and all problems concerned with answering preemptive openings, you should credit partner with a seven-card (it may be longer but this is very rare) suit to two or more of the top four honours (may be less when non-vulnerable against vulnerable) and enough tricks to fail in his contract by two tricks (vulnerable) or three (non-vulnerable). Then mentally put that hand opposite yours and decide what contract you can make. This first hand is a classic illustration of a situation in which even 'experienced' players go wrong. One temptation you must resist before even going near a bridge table is the idea that: 'Partner has got clubs; I have the other three suits, therefore let us play no-trumps.' If you bid 3NT, how are you going to make it? Where are your nine tricks coming from? You probably will not be able to get to your partner's hand to make use of his clubs which do not have to be solid anyway. Similarly, he is unlikely to have much to help your hand. In practice, you will probably be held to four or five tricks if you are lucky! What you have to realize is that, if partner preempts in clubs, the hand is a disastrous misfit and the best contract is unquestionably 3♣! You should therefore pass and hope the penalty will not be too heavy. If the contract is doubled, you must still pass; you know that anything else is surely going to be a lot worse!

(b) Here you have a fabulous fit and no defence whatsoever. In this kind of situation, the first point to realize is that the opponents will almost certainly make 6♡ and quite possibly 7♡. At the moment, partner has opened 3♣ and the next hand has passed, which means that the hand behind you must be huge. You should therefore bounce the bidding as high as you can to make it as difficult as possible for the opponents to find their best contract. (You know what it is but they may not). How high do you go? Let us work it out at various vulnerabilities.

At love all, 7♡ will cost you 210+1000 for the grand slam +300 for the value of a non-vulnerable game: about 1500 in all and you will not be able to outbid that contract in clubs. 6♡ will similarly be worth about 1000. In clubs, you can afford to concede a penalty of at least 900 to show a profit. That is five down doubled at this vulnerability. If partner is short in diamonds (as is likely) you will probably make at least eight tricks in clubs and it is worth bidding 7♣ immediately. This should put the big hand behind you to a very unpleasant guess as to whether to accept what might be a fairly modest penalty or bid a grand slam blind which may not be made. Non-vulnerable against vulnerable, you should certainly bid 7♣ at once; the grand slam to the opponents is now worth about 2200 and the small about 1400.

At game all, it is less clear-cut. Five down doubled is now 1400 which is still respectable against the small slam and shows a big profit against the grand. 7♣ is therefore still reasonable but you should certainly bid at least 6♣.

Vulnerable against not, it may be too expensive to offer the opponents a likely 1100 and possible 1400 and now 6♣ is probably enough.

All these bids are very much a question of judgment and top-class players have varying opinions on how high to go. The important thing is to understand how the prospects are worked out.

(c) Here 3NT is a possibility but the spades are wide open and you certainly cannot bid it outright. You need to know more about partner's hand, in particular whether he can offer a spade stop, the ace, K x, Q x x or better.

Start by making a forcing bid of 3◊. The final contract you have in mind is 3NT and partner should work on that assumption, at least for the time being. He is expected to show a major-suit stop if he has it by bidding 3♡ or 3♠, returning to 4♣ if he does not have one. You will then decide whether to play 3NT or 4♣. Remember a change of suit below game opposite a preempt is natural and forcing.

(d) Here you have an almost certain slam but there is a danger in that heart holding and you will want to be declarer. For that reason, rather than support the clubs, you should bid 6NT as your final contract.

(12)(a) Here you are stronger than you were in a similar situation in (11a) but still nowhere near strong enough to improve on the present contract and should pass, prepared to play 3◊.

(b) Here partner needs little more than the ace of diamonds to make 3NT a good contract and you should bid it as a sign-off. Opponents are likely to attack one of the majors, after which you hopefully will be able to run nine tricks.

(c) This is similar to (b) and it is even more likely that you will be able to make 3NT on your own unless the opponents can run five tricks in spades. Note that 5♣ is most unlikely to be made.

(d) It is probable that your clubs are longer than your partner's diamonds but where are you hoping to finish? Even if 4♣ were non-forcing, you would already be a level higher. You are sadly short of top cards and should pass and let the opponents have their major-suit game. Your singleton diamond might mean that your partner has enough defence against a possible major-suit slam.

(13)(a) Here you have a misfit and no improvement on the current contract; pass, intending to play 3♡.

(b) This shows the corollary to the last hand. If you play 4♡ this time, you may well lose two tricks each in diamonds and spades if the ace of spades is sitting on your left. In 3NT, however, partner's hearts will still make tricks and the opponents will have to find a diamond lead and spade switch with the ace again being offside to have any chance of defeating you. 3NT as a sign-off should be your bid. Strange game, isn't it? I first suggested that you accept partner's suit on a singleton and now I am advising against it on A J x. This is a perfect illustration of the importance of considering the final contract and the still greater importance of understanding what you are doing rather than bidding or playing like a parrot.

(c) Here you are almost certainly going to be able to set up long tricks in clubs and as you have no losers, you can bid 7♡ confidently. You will be very unlucky to fail.

(d) This looks a powerful hand but you are short of aces and unlikely to make game in any denomination; you should therefore pass and settle for 3♡.

(14)(a) Here you will want to play 4♡ but note that a case can be made for 3NT in which opponents will probably have to find five quick club tricks to beat you.

(b) This time you have the choice of two slams, 6♠ and 6◇. The diamond slam will be safe if the ace of hearts is on your left when a heart lead may defeat the spade slam. This is a much bigger danger than the spade ruff or bad diamond split you might sustain in 6◇. You should thus sign off in 6◇.

(c) Here 5♣ could be on but it is unlikely and you should pass and settle to play in 3♠.

(d) This time, barring a bad split in either minor, you can make 5♣ in your own hand so you should bid it as a sign-off.

Well, how did you get on? It is a good idea to go over these examples again and again until you get them consistently right and are completely familiar with the reasoning behind them. Once you attain that position, you will be fully prepared for the heat of the battle. We now move on to the opener's rebid and subsequent development of the auction.

The Opener's Rebid

Let us review what we have done so far. One player has opened the bidding and his partner has replied. So the ball is now back in the opener's court and he must ask himself the following questions:

1 Is partner's response forcing?
  If it is, I will have to make a bid.
  If not, I may still bid but have the option to pass.
  If it is a sign-off, I shall be expected to pass.
2 Into what point range has he placed his hand?
3 What has he said so far about his distribution?
4 Has his response improved my hand, worsened it, or made little difference? In other words, how do I feel about the denomination he has chosen?
5 In the light of what has happened so far, what final contracts are now candidates?
6 How good is my hand in the light of what I have promised so far?

It is this last point that, in my experience, causes the largest number of errors in that even famous names insist on bidding their hands twice or even three times when once would suffice. In fact, some of the better players are very often the worst offenders and you should not be frightened to double them. The principal cause of the trouble lies in the manner in which players define 'good', 'bad' and 'average' hands.

Early in the course in our study of the pack, we noted that

there are 40 high-card points to be divided among the four players at the table and thus 10 points would be average, anything more would be good and anything less would be bad. I have already indicated that it is most inadvisable to look at it in this way. The recommended approach is to consider how good your hand is *within the range you have suggested by your bidding so far*. The best way to illustrate this is to look at a couple of examples.

♠ K Q x
♡ K x x x
♢ J x x x
♣ Q J

Here you have a balanced 12 points but as 12-point hands go, it is very poor in that it is aceless, your five spade points are in a trebleton and worse still, the club honours are doubleton and therefore do not carry their full weight. On top of that, the red-suit honours are isolated. So should you open 1NT or not? Personally I would not, but many good players would. Let us consider each action. If you do decide to open, you are putting your hand in the 12–14 point category: in that bracket, it could scarcely be worse. On the other hand, if you decide to pass, you are putting the hand in the 0–11 category, and in that bracket, it is huge – it could hardly be bigger! See the point? In two sentences, I have described the same hand as very poor and very good. The same principle applies when you make a bid and partner answers. Let us now look at this:

♠ x
♡ A K x x x
♢ Q J x x
♣ A x x

With this 14-point hand, you correctly open 1♡. You have put your hand into the 12–19 point range and it is towards the poorer end of the bracket, but nonetheless perfectly respectable.

Now, if partner responds 1♠, this hand becomes very poor as he has bid the one suit you did not want to hear. The response is forcing and you will rebid 2♢ but will have no reason to get very excited about future prospects. If partner responds 2♣, that is a lot better as you now have a reasonable trump holding and the singleton spade becomes an asset. You will still rebid 2♦ but will feel entitled to support clubs later on. If partner responds 2♦, that is better still as you now have four trumps and can raise to 3♦, (the hand is nearly good enough for 4♦) being prepared to go to game at the slightest provocation.

See the idea? The same hand can be good, bad or indifferent according to what is happening around it. So try to treat absolute point-count and distribution as merely an initial guide and no more. The principle applies with even greater force when the opponents enter the auction, as we shall learn later.

7 Is the rebid I am going to make forcing and in any event, am I prepared for partner's likely responses? How do I visualize the rest of the auction proceeding?

We have so far discussed 14 possible opening bids and to each one there are several possible replies. That would give over a hundred possible first-round bidding sequences and at least ten times as many continuations and so far, we haven't allowed the opposition to say one word! If I were to cover all possibilities, a book of encyclopaedic proportions would result which is obviously impractical. So rather than going through long lists of rules, I am going to throw you in at the deep end by giving you examples to do which will, at least, cover a reasonable cross-section. What I should like you to do in each case is to answer the seven questions above to illustrate that, not only can you find the correct bid, but (far more important!) that you fully understand why you have done so. Start your stop-watch.

(1) On each of the following hands you open 1♦ and partner responds 1♠. What do you rebid now on:

(a) ♠ x x
♡ J x
♦ A K x x x
♣ A J x x

(b) ♠ K x x
♡ A K x x
♦ A J x x x
♣ x

(c) ♠ J x x
♡ Q x x
♦ A K Q x
♣ K x x

(d) ♠ J x
♡ K Q x
♦ A K Q x x
♣ Q J x

(e) ♠ Q x x x
♡ x x
♦ K Q J x x
♣ K J

(f) ♠ Q J x x
♡ A x
♦ K Q x x x
♣ K x

(2) On each of the following hands, you open 1♡ and partner responds 1NT. What is your rebid now?

(a) ♠ K x x   (b) ♠ K x   (c) ♠ K x
    ♡ K Q x x x   ♡ K Q x x x   ♡ A K x x x x
    ◇ K x x   ◇ x x   ◇ A x
    ♣ Q x   ♣ K Q x x   ♣ J x x

(3) On each of the following, you open 1♠ and partner responds 2◇. What is your rebid now?

(a) ♠ A K J x x   (b) ♠ K Q x x x x   (c) ♠ A K J x x
    ♡ J x x x   ♡ A x   ♡ x x
    ◇ Q x   ◇ A x   ◇ A x x x
    ♣ Q x   ♣ Q x x   ♣ x x

(4) On each of the following, you open 1♡ and partner responds 2NT. What is your rebid now?

(a) ♠ A K J x   (b) ♠ K x x   (c) ♠ A K
    ♡ Q x x x x   ♡ Q J x x x   ♡ Q J x x x
    ◇ Q x   ◇ A K Q   ◇ A K Q x x
    ♣ x x   ♣ K x   ♣ x

(5) On each of the following hands, you open 1♣ and partner responds 2♡. What is your rebid now?

(a) ♠ A K x x   (b) ♠ x x x x   (c) ♠ K J x
    ♡ x   ♡ K J x   ♡ K x
    ◇ Q x x x   ◇ x   ◇ Q J x
    ♣ A Q x x   ♣ A K Q x x   ♣ A K x x x

(6) On each of the following hands, you open 1♡ and partner responds 3NT. What is your rebid now?

(a) ♠ A x x   (b) ♠ x   (c) ♠ –
    ♡ Q J x x x   ♡ A K J x x   ♡ K Q x x x x
    ◇ K x x   ◇ A K J x x   ◇ A x x
    ♣ A Q   ♣ Q x   ♣ Q x x x

(7) On each of the following hands, you open 1♠ and partner responds 2♠. What is your rebid now?

(a) ♠ A K x x x   (b) ♠ A K x x x x   (c) ♠ A Q J x x
    ♡ x x x   ♡ K J x   ♡ K x
    ◇ Q J x   ◇ A x   ◇ Q x x x
    ♣ K x   ♣ Q x   ♣ K x

(8) On each of the following hands, you open 1◇ and partner responds 3◇. What is your rebid now?

(a) ♠ K Q x   (b) ♠ K x   (c) ♠ K J x
    ♡ x x   ♡ Q x x   ♡ K J x
    ◇ A K x x x   ◇ J x x x x x   ◇ A Q x x x
    ♣ A J x   ♣ A Q   ♣ A x

(9) On the following hand ♠ K x x   you open 1NT.
                    ♡ A x x x
                    ◇ K Q x x
                    ♣ Q x

What is your rebid if partner responds: (a) 2♣; (b) 2◇; (c) 2♡; (d) 2♠; (e) 2NT; (f) 3♣; (g) 3◇; (h) 3♡; (i) 3♠; (j) 3NT; (k) 4NT; (l) 5NT; (m) 6NT?

Would any of your answers be altered if the queen of diamonds were a low one instead?

(10) On each of the following hands, you open 2♣ and partner responds 2◇. What is your rebid now?

(a) ♠ A K x   (b) ♠ A K x x   (c) ♠ K Q J x x x
    ♡ A K x   ♡ K Q x   ♡ A K x x
    ◇ K x x x   ◇ A K Q   ◇ A K Q
    ♣ A Q J   ♣ K Q x   ♣ –

(11) On each of the following hands, you open 2♣ and partner responds 2♡. What is your rebid now?

(a) ♠ A Q x   (b) ♠ A K   (c) ♠ A K x
    ♡ J x   ♡ A Q x x   ♡ –
    ◇ A K Q J   ◇ K Q J x x   ◇ A K Q x x
    ♣ A K Q J   ♣ A x   ♣ A K x x x

(12) On the following hand ♠ K J   you open 2♡.
                        ♡ A K Q J x x
                        ◊ A x
                        ♣ Q x x

What is your rebid if partner responds: (a) 2♠; (b) 2NT; (c) 3♣ (d) 3♡; (e) 4♡?

(13) On the following hand ♠ K x x   you open 3◊.
                        ♡ x
                        ◊ K Q J x x x x
                        ♣ x x

What is your rebid if partner responds: (a) 3♡; (b) 3♠; (c) 3NT; (d) 4◊; (e) 4♡; (f) 5♣; (g) 6♡?

There are about sixty questions and you should be able to write down complete answers with correct explanations in under half an hour, aiming later on towards ten minutes. Let us go through the answers.

(1)(a) Partner's bid is forcing with 6 points minimum and at least four spades, but it certainly does not improve this hand. You can, however, rebid 2♣, prepared to be put back to 2◊ if necessary. It looks as though 3NT is favourite if you get to game.

(b) This time the spade bid has improved the hand considerably. You have respectable trump support and the singleton club is an asset. This time, although a point or two under strength, you can justify reversing into hearts which is forcing for one round. 4♠ seems favourite for the final contract but you may end in five or more diamonds. Note the heart bid guarantees a five-card or longer diamond suit.

(c) Here the spade bid does no harm but you are very flat and 3NT is still favourite. You have a rebid of 1NT on your 15 points (limited and therefore non-forcing) and having explained that you are balanced in the 15–16 point range, you can give delayed support for spades later should partner demand to know more about your hand.

(d) The spade bid does not improve your hand, but with 18 points, a really good diamond suit and the other suits covered, you are entitled to bid 3NT (again limited and non-forcing) which is where you want to play. Partner will go higher if his hand warrants it.

(e) With only 12 points, you have a very limited opening bid but the spade bid has improved your hand and, forced to bid, you are happy to raise to 2♠ with a view to 4♠, the only possible game now.

(f) The spade bid has improved your hand markedly and you are worth a limited non-forcing raise to 3♠, inviting 4♠. Partner will only pass with an absolute minimum.

(2)(a) A response of 1NT over one of anything but clubs promises 6–8 points, balanced, is obviously non-forcing and, notably over a major, suggests lack of enthusiasm in opener's suit. It rarely improves opener's hand unless he too is balanced. That implies that opener will have to be either very distributional and/or just short of a two-bid if game is to be attempted. Most of the time it is a question of looking for the best part-score. In this case, you barely have your opening bid and no reason to bid again. You should refrain from repeating your hearts 'because I had five, partner'; all you would do is to raise the level for little benefit as partner may well have a singleton or, on rare occasions, a void. You can see again why I am not very keen on the ideas of 'biddable' and 'rebiddable' suits which are regularly drummed into beginners.

(b) With two good suits and a more distributional hand, you will normally prefer a trump contract and should bid 2♣. This is non-forcing and partner will normally pass or correct to 2♡ as we shall discuss later. These are your two candidate contracts; you are nowhere near game.

(c) The point-count is only 15 but you have a good six-card heart suit and will want to be in game if partner is maximum. The way to invite is to bid 3♡. Unlike the previous example, this is a limit-bid and therefore non-forcing and partner is likely to pass, bid 3NT or raise to 4♡ according to his strength, presence of quick or slow tricks and attitude to hearts.

(3)(a) Here we have a similar situation to the problems in (1) but the forcing change of suit has been at the two-level and therefore a minimum of 9 points as opposed to 6 has been promised. In this first example, you have a minimum 13 points and although the queen of diamonds is likely to be useful, the queen of clubs is devalued in the doubleton. Here you should show your second suit, hearts. Many players, including a number who might be described as 'good', would rebid 2♠ on the grounds that the spades are so good and the hearts very poor. However, by bidding 2♡, you are already promising five spades and it is better to offer two options than one. 2♡ is non-forcing (although you should be advised that some ultra-modern theorists prefer to play it as forcing). Currently you are looking for 4♠, 4♡ or 3NT.

(b) With fifteen points and a reasonable six-card suit, you are almost entitled to insist on game and you should bid a highly invitational 3♠. Some players play this as forcing and, even if it isn't, partner will very rarely pass, usually raising to 4♠ or bidding 3NT, your two candidate contracts.

(c) Here you have a limited opening bid but the diamond bid is most encouraging. Raise to 3♢ (limited and non-forcing) to show almost certainly four-card diamond support and therefore five spades. 4♠ and 5♢ are your candidate contracts but partner may be able to bid 3NT if he can cover the other two suits.

(4)(a) Here partner has shown 11–12 points balanced and has denied interest in either major. It is now up to you to direct operations. On this hand, you have only 12 points and have been told that partner does not have four spades. You have little hope of game, particularly as the hearts are very poor and unlikely to produce many tricks. You should pass 2NT, prepared to play there.

(b) Here you have 18 points but have been told that the partnership limit is 30. There is little hope of a slam, which would require 33 and you should settle for a sign-off in 3NT.

(c) This time, there is every chance of a slam as you have such excellent distribution and only three obvious losers. Your first move should be to find the best denomination by bidding 3◊. This new suit on the three-level is forcing for one round. Partner will realize that you are distributional (otherwise why disturb no-trumps?) and either support the diamonds, give preference to hearts or repeat no-trumps if his values are concentrated in the black suits. You can proceed from there, looking for 4♡, 5◊, or a slam in either suit.

(5)(a) Here partner has forced to game and you can afford to go slowly, irrespective of strength. The heart bid has devalued your hand and 3NT is now very likely to be your final contract. However, partner is unlimited and should be allowed to describe his hand further. Thus all you need do for the moment is to quietly bid as you would have done at the one level, i.e. 2♠.

(b) Now, at the one-level, you would have bid 1♠ but you should refrain from bidding 2♠ here. Partner has, in principle, shown a one-suited hand and you should simply support him with 3♡. Those four low spades will be of no interest to him and indeed you would want him to upvalue rather than devalue a shortage in that suit. You will reach at least 4♡ and possibly a slam in that suit.

(c) With 17 points and good tolerance for the hearts, you will almost certainly be insisting on a slam but, as you are in a game-forcing situation, there is no need to hurry below game-level. Simply describe the balanced nature of your hand with 2NT and await further information. You are likely to finish in 6NT, 6♣ or 6♡ or a grand slam in one of those denominations. Note that jumping to 3NT in this situation does not exist; it simply wastes bidding space. Neither player has the right to do that, least of all the partner of a big and unlimited hand!

(6)(a) This time, partner has shown you 13–15 balanced and has again denied interest in both majors. As you are in game already, the bid is non-forcing despite its strength. On this 16-point hand, you know that you will not have enough for a slam so you should pass and settle for 3NT.

(b) Here there is every chance of a slam, all depending on whether partner has quick or slow tricks and you will probably want to play in one of your suits rather than no-trumps. Bid your second suit, 4◇, forcing as the partnership is committed to game, and see how partner reacts. You will probably finish in six of one of your suits or 6NT.

(c) Here you have a very minimum opening bid and you have been told that opponents have ten or eleven spades between them. You therefore will prefer to play in 4♡, which you should bid as a sign-off.

(7)(a) Partner's simple raise is limited and therefore non-forcing. In this example, you have a respectable opening bid but no more and have no reason to look for game opposite a partner who is unlikely to produce much more than 8 points and a three-card spade support. You should therefore pass and be happy to play in 2♠.

(b) Here with 17 points and a six-card trump suit which has been supported, you have enough for game and should bid 4♠ as a sign-off.

(c) Here with 15 points and only five spades, game is less certain but it is worthwhile investigating. You could simply invite with 3♠, asking partner to bid game if he is maximum for his raise or pass otherwise. However there is a better bid, referred to as a *long-suit trial*, which is used after one of a major has been raised to two. With this kind of hand, the ability to make game will probably depend on the diamond situation. You have a poor suit with possibly up to four losers in it and the question is:

'Can partner help?' You will need to find him with either honours in the suit or a shortage (a doubleton or, better still, a singleton or void) with plenty of trumps. To find this out, you make the long-suit trial bid of 3 ◇. Note that spades has been agreed as the trump suit so that this bid is forcing and the partnership is debating whether the hand will be played in 3♠ or 4♠. To sum up, what you are saying to partner is: 'I am about half-way between giving up in 2♠ and bidding game outright. How do you feel, paying particular reference to the diamond position?' You will be ending in 3♠ or 4♠.

(8)(a) After a minor suit has been raised to the three-level, five of that minor is a good bet for a game contract, but your first thoughts should be towards 3NT. The problem here is that you are wide open in hearts and will probably want partner to be declarer to protect his heart holding if he has one. Now, when partner raised you to 3 ◇, he denied a four-card major suit so you know that he does not have a spade suit and therefore 4♠ is not being considered as a final contract. You can thus bid 3♠ to tell partner that you have the spades covered and to ask him whether he can stop hearts. If he can, he will bid 3NT; if not, he will return to diamonds, at the four- or five-level, according to his strength within the range he has promised and taking into account your likely heart holding.

(b) Here you have only 12 points and, although the support of diamonds has improved the trick-taking power of your long suit, you are not strong enough to suggest 3NT or to contemplate 5 ◇. You should pass, content to play in 3 ◇.

(c) With 18 points and all the suits stopped, you have enough to bid 3NT yourself as a sign-off.

(9)(a) In all cases, you have defined your hand fairly accurately and partner is in charge of the auction. He will ask for an even more accurate description and then decide the final contract. Thus all you have to do is to answer his questions where appropriate. In the first case, he has

asked you for a four-card major and you can oblige with
2♡. This is non-forcing and any further move is up to
partner. He will decide the final contract – perhaps 3NT
or 4♡.

(b), (c), (d) In all these cases, partner is saying: 'I have heard
what you have got; we shall play in two of my long suit.'
You should pass, accepting his decision, right or wrong.

(e)   Here partner is asking you a question – whether you are
minimum or maximum. In other words, he is saying
that, if you are maximum, he wishes to play in 3NT;
otherwise the partnership must settle for 2NT. Thus with
this maximum hand, you are happy to bid the game. If
the ◇Q is replaced by a low one, you should pass, being
minimum for your original opener.

(f), (g), (h), (i) In all these cases, partner has forced to game
and your first duty, irrespective of strength, is to give
your reaction to the proposed trump suit as he is likely to
be looking for a slam and will probably have an unbalanced hand. Over 3♣, you are not all that keen and
should settle for 3NT. If partner makes another move, for
example, raising to 4NT (invitational but non-forcing),
you will go for a slam with the maximum hand, having
warned partner that you may only have a doubleton
club. In the other three cases, you should support
partner's suit to the four-level. In diamonds, your bid is
forcing as the partnership is committed to game. However, in the majors, partner may pass if he is minimum for
his game force.

(j)   This is a sign-off and you should pass, irrespective of
shape or strength.

(k)   This is an invitational but non-forcing limit raise. You
should accept 6NT with the maximum hand but pass
with the minimum. With 13 points, you have the option
to bid 5◇, giving the partnership a chance to finish in
6◇ or 6♡.

(l)   This is an invitational and forcing raise, committing the
partnership to at least 6NT. With the maximum hand,
you should accept 7NT; with the minimum hand, you

should settle for 6NT. With 13 points, you might bid 6♦ to give the partnership a chance to finish in 7♦ or 7♥.

(m) This is a sign-off and you should pass, irrespective of strength. Had partner wanted to know your exact point-count, he could have found out with 5NT. Accept his decision.

(10)(a) Here you are minimum for your opener and should bid 2NT to show 23–24 points, balanced. Note that this is the only sequence following a 2♣ opener which is non-forcing. If partner is balanced and very weak, he may pass. Bearing in mind the inconvenience of playing with all the strength in one hand, he should have about 3 or more points to go to game.

(b) With 26 points, you should have a chance in 3NT even if partner has nothing, so you should bid it. This limits your hand in both size and shape and is therefore non-forcing. It is up to partner to make any further move if he is strong within the limits of a negative response.

(c) Here you can almost certainly make 4♠ on your own but there is no need to bid it immediately. Partner may have length in hearts and/or diamonds, enabling a slam to be reached in one of those two suits. For the moment, just quietly bid 2♠ (game-forcing) and see how partner reacts. You can always finish in 4♠ but it costs nothing to look for more on this two-loser hand.

(11)(a) This time, partner has responded positively and the partnership is immediately committed to game with a slam likely. For that reason, with partner unlimited, the longer the conversation, the better. Here, with 27 points, you know that you will reach the small slam level at least and a grand slam is very likely. For the moment, however, all you need do is show the balanced nature of your hand by bidding 2NT and wait for partner to describe his hand further. You are looking for 7♣, 7♦ or 7NT, but may have to settle for 6NT.

(b) Here you were nearly minimum for your opener but the response has improved your hand very considerably.

You will certainly be insisting on at least 6♡ and be looking for 7♡. The best move is to quietly agree hearts with a bid of 3♡ and thereby invite partner to show other features of his hand in the manner we shall describe later under 'slam bidding'.

(c) The positive response is certainly good news but the choice of hearts is not. Nevertheless, even giving partner all his values in hearts, a small slam in either minor will be on if partner has three cards in the suit. You should thus bid both suits, observing the usual rule of bidding the higher-ranking of five-card suits first. You will thus bid 3♢ now and 4♣ later if the diamonds are not supported. You are looking for 6♢ or 6♣ but may have to settle for 4NT.

(12)(a) Here partner has given you a negative response and remember that the bid has nothing whatsoever to do with spades. By opening 2♡, you have already indicated a good long suit, so there is no need to repeat it. There is no harm now in showing the balanced nature of the remainder of your hand by bidding 2NT, particularly as you have some feature in every other suit and will want to play 3NT from your side of the table. This is likely to be your favourite game contract, 4♡ being the alternative. As 2♡ is a limit-bid, this is not forcing but it is most unlikely that partner will pass. Even with nothing, he is likely to prefer 3♡, which you can then pass.

(b) Here partner has responded positively, committing the partnership at least to game with a slam a strong possibility as partner is unlimited. Again you can show the balanced nature of the hand by bidding 3NT (non-forcing) but you could also bid 4♡. This sounds like breaking my recommended rules of keeping the conversation going as long as possible by using up as little space as necessary. Yes, indeed, and therefore a jump like that must carry a very specific message, here a *solid* suit, defined as A K Q x x x or better. This may well help partner to decide whether a slam is on, notably if he is short of hearts. If there is no slam, neither 3NT nor 4♡ are likely to be in any danger, so the choice will probably not matter.

(c) Again partner has responded positively and is sure to have a five-card suit, which you should support with 4♣. You are looking for at least a small slam in that suit or hearts with a grand being a strong possibility.

(d) Here partner has shown a raise with exactly one ace and a slam may be on. The approach will be discussed in detail under slam-bidding later but in principle, when a suit is agreed in a potential slam situation, the partners are called upon to bid their *controls* (aces, or voids outside trumps) and you will bid 4◇, looking for 6♡ but prepared to settle for 4♡ – more about that in the next chapter.

(e) Here partner has denied an ace and as you know that, with two aces missing, a slam cannot be on, you are happy to pass and play in 4♡.

(13)(a) Partner has made a change of suit which is natural and forcing so you cannot pass. The heart bid is, of course, bad news with a singleton in your hand and you are entitled to repeat your diamonds to tell partner that you cannot help. Note that, as you were forced to bid, this promises nothing extra, viz. partner is not entitled to expect eight diamonds in your hand rather than seven. 4◇ is therefore perfectly reasonable but I am wondering if you considered anything else.

Let us look at the position from partner's point of view. His 3♡ bid was undoubtedly looking for 4♡ but he bid in the knowledge that you have a weak hand with little interest outside diamonds. The fact that he has bid at all implies either that he has an enormous hand or that he has some diamonds with you and will be prepared to play in four or even more of that suit. But if he has a big hand with diamond support, how about 3NT? It may well be that your spade king will help stop the suit and enable that contract to be made by running the diamonds. Also knowledge of the fact that you hold a spade honour may help partner decide how high to go in diamonds or hearts. In any event, it cannot cost to tell partner more about your hand by bidding 3♠. Note that by preempting, you have already denied a four-card major (because your bid showed a one-suited hand) and therefore 3♠ shows purely what we call a *feature* in the suit. Again the consideration of final contract was crucial to finding the best bid.

(b) Here partner's natural forcing bid has improved your hand and you are happy to raise to game in 4♠. Any further move is up to partner.

(c) This time, partner has signed off with a direct game bid and you have no reason to argue with his decision.

(d) A raise of a preemptive bid merely extends the preempt to make life still more difficult for opponents. You have no reason to bid again and should pass, content to play 4♦.

(e) Same applies as (c). You do not like it but your opener did not promise any hearts. You are even entitled to think that you have one more heart than you might have done! Pass and settle for 4♡.

(f) Same applies as (c).

(g) Same applies as (c). If partner had wanted to know more about your hand, he could have started with 3♡, enabling you to make your famous 3♠ bid. As it is, he has taken a decision on his own, so you must accept it, right or wrong.

Well, how did you get on? I strongly advise you to go over these examples again and again until you get them right in the recommended time. It is far better to make mistakes now, at no cost, than later at the table when the expense could be considerable. Above all, the important point is to understand the way to think about your bid. You should already be well aware that bridge is a game of understanding rather than pure memorizing.

The Responder's Second Bid

In this section, we shall look at the responder's rebid with a view to subsequent rounds of bidding, give a few hints on slam bidding and consider what differences, if any, apply if the first member of the partnership entitled to bid, actually passes. Up to now, we have assumed that he has opened the bidding.

Under the responder's rebid, there are two important items. First is the concept of preference, applying after partner has bid two suits in sequences like:

1♡	1♠,	1♠	2♣	or	1♡	1NT
2◇	?	2♡	?		2♣	?

The responder is not forced to speak unless the second bid has been a jump or reverse and we shall consider that position later. On the above sequences, the responder has six options:

1 Go back to the first suit, knowing that it is at least as long or longer than the second;
2 Repeat his own suit;
3 Bid no-trumps;
4 Support the second suit.

Each of these will be done at a level appropriate to his strength, and will be a limit-bid and almost always non-forcing.

5 Pass and accept the second suit;
6 (And this is our second important item) bid the fourth suit.

It may well be that the hand is a misfit as neither partner has supported the other so far and if this seems likely, two very important points should be remembered. First, in the conversation, you should be talking *to* your partner rather than *at* him – a very important difference. I have lost count of the number of substantial penalties I have collected and serious arguments I have been embarrassed to listen to following people's inability to handle misfit hands. Second, as has already been indicated and is well worth repeating countless times, you should avoid rushing into no-trumps as soon as you see that the hand is a misfit. Such hands are difficult to play and you will need extra high-card strength to have any reasonable chance of success.

To give a concrete example, it was earlier indicated that a partnership needs about 25 high-card points combined to make 3NT but that applies to average conditions. Given a long suit which will run and easy communications, you will very often make it on 23 or even less. Against that, with no running suit and poor communications, you could well fail on 28 or even more. Similarly, when considering a trump contract, the poorer the fit, the more trumps you need between you for success and vice versa.

How do we decide on the above options? Normally, when partner has bid two suits, he guarantees no more than four in each if you are still on the one-level but (subject to rare exceptions indicated earlier) at least five in the first suit if the second bid is at the two-level.

The following guides (but note they are no more than that) are appropriate:

1 The second suit is very likely to be of four cards only; therefore try to avoid supporting it unless you also have four cards.
2 If you are longer in the first suit or your holdings in the two suits are equal, you should prefer the first suit to the second.
3 If your holding in the second suit is two cards longer than that of the first, you should prefer the second suit.
4 If your holding in the second suit is one card longer than that in the first, prefer the second suit if you have four cards in it and three in the first. But if you have three cards in the second and two in the first, then the choice is more debatable:

a If you are still on the one-level, you should not go back to the first suit on a doubleton which involves pushing up to the two-level and possibly playing there in a 4–2 fit. However, if you have two doubletons, you should think about no-trumps (remember it will be only at the one-level) or repeating your own suit.

b If you are now on the two-level, you are in the position where partner has five cards in the first suit (except in rare 4441 hands – do not worry about those) and four or five cards in the second. If he has five cards in both suits, you will obviously prefer the second, but if he has five and four and you have two and three, a five-two fit usually plays a lot better than a 4–3 fit and you should therefore prefer the first, giving what is known as *false preference*.

So which is it to be? In practice, 5–4 hands come up far more often than 5–5 hands and false preference usually pays off in the long term and should therefore be given.

5 If you dislike both partner's suits, you will be considering repeating your own but should be reluctant to do so unless you are prepared to play it opposite a singleton (and partner might well turn up with a void). This normally means a six-card suit or very good (two of the top three honours or three of the top five) five-card suit.

6 You should not bid no-trumps at the two- or higher level unless you have the appropriate strength and a good stop in the fourth suit. What that means is open to debate, but any certain or potential double stop (A Q, K J x, Q 10 x x) is certainly good enough; holdings like A J, K J and Q 10 x are in the grey area.

7 If you have a strong hand and need more information from partner before you can take a decision on the final contract, that is the time to bid the fourth suit. It is reasonable to assume that, if three suits are bid, it is most unlikely that the fourth will be selected as trumps. For that reason, we introduce the universally played concept of *fourth-suit-forcing*, i.e. a bid of the fourth suit does not necessarily guarantee a biddable suit but simply asks partner for more information about his hand,

notably with a view to help in that fourth suit for no-trumps.
This even applies in the sequence 1♣   1♢
                                   1♡   1♠

but the opener, if he is 4414, may support the spades on the
assumption that it is a suit so that a spade fit is not lost; the
responder will correct to no-trumps if his spade bid is not
genuine.

In all these considerations, need I remind you of what must be
uppermost in your mind – yes, the final contract. So let us start
the stop-watch and do some examples. Now that three bids have
already been made, you ought to be able to make a fairly accurate
assessment of what is happening. Write down your bid with full
justification, indicating the likely final contract(s).

(1) The bidding goes 1♣   1♡
                        1♠   ?

What do you bid now on:

(a) ♠ Q x x x   (b) ♠ K x x
     ♡ Q x x x   ♡ J x x x
     ♢ Q x x   ♢ Q J x
     ♣ x x   ♣ x x x

(c) ♠ Q x x x   (d) ♠ K x x
     ♡ K Q x x   ♡ K x x x
     ♢ x   ♢ K Q x
     ♣ x x x x   ♣ J x x

(2) The bidding goes 1♡   1♠
                        2♢   ?

What do you bid now on:

(a) ♠ K x x x   (b) ♠ K x x x
     ♡ x x   ♡ J x
     ♢ x x   ♢ Q x x
     ♣ Q J x x x   ♣ Q x x x

(c) ♠ K Q J x x x   (d) ♠ K x x x x
     ♡ x x   ♡ A x
     ♢ x   ♢ A x x
     ♣ Q x x x   ♣ J x x

The eight questions should have taken you under five minutes and you should be aiming to get under three. Let us work through the answers.

(1)(a) Here you have a minimum six points for your initial response and although the spade bid has improved your hand markedly, you must accept that neither of your two red queens is likely to be of any use. There is little prospect of game and you should therefore pass, content with 1♠.

(b) This hand is very flat and although you could play in spades or clubs, that might involve a 4–3 fit and you have no ruffing potential. With a respectable diamond stop, you can bid 1NT. Certainly 3NT is the most likely game if partner produces 18 or more points.

(c) Here you have some support for both partner's suits and a good ruffing value in the singleton diamond. Which suit do you choose? As always, the choice rests on your consideration of final contract. If you are going to get to game, it is far more likely to be in 4♠ than 5♣, and you should therefore support to 2♠.

(d) With 12 points, you have enough for 2NT and your diamond stop is certainly adequate. This is a limited, non-forcing bid. The most likely final contract is 3NT.

(2)(a) With all your points outside partner's suits and a minimum count anyway, this hand is very discouraging and you should aim to put the brakes on as soon as possible. With equal length in partner's suits, you should prefer the first (a five-card being guaranteed in principle) and correct to 2♥, hoping to play there. Remember this does not promise a three-card support implied by a direct raise over 1♥. It is no more than grudging (possibly false) preference.

(b) This time, you are up to 8 points but again most of them are in the black suits where they are of relatively little use. This is the time to prefer the likely 5–2 fit in hearts in preference to the 4–3 fit in diamonds. You should bid 2♥, hoping to play there.

(c) This time, that much better spade suit will be of no use unless it is trumps, whatever partner's holding. Here you should persist with 2♠ hoping to play there and partner should respect that, having heard his offers in the red suits, you have wisely opted for yours. The only possible game is 4♠, which may be reached if partner has spade support.

(d) With 12 points and a five-card suit and two aces where they will be most useful, you are certainly entitled to insist on game, but in which denomination? Here you need more information on partner's hand and should ask with a fourth-suit-forcing bid of 3♣. This offers the options of 3NT, 4♠ or even 4♡ on a 5–2 fit.

We now consider replying to a reverse or jump in a new suit. These bids are forcing and you are deprived of the option of passing if you are weak and prefer the second suit. In these situations, bidding the fourth suit, to inform partner that you do not know what to do, is very often the answer. However, you should try to avoid bidding it on the four-level as 3NT may well be the best final contract. Bidding the fourth suit is also important even if you have an adequate stop in it for no-trumps when your first response was in a five-card major. Partner may have three-card support and you should give him a chance to show it. Another use of the fourth suit arises when you have a very strong hand with support for one of partner's suits and you want to suggest a slam. Bidding the fourth suit first and then supporting partner is recognised as stronger than an immediate support.

Start your stop-watch again and try these examples.

(1) The bidding goes 1♣   1♠
                    2♡   ?

What do you bid now on:

(a) ♠ K Q x x x x   (b) ♠ Q x x x x
    ♡ J x   ♡ x x x
    ◇ x x x   ◇ K Q x
    ♣ x x   ♣ x x

(c) ♠ A K x x   (d) ♠ Q x x x
    ♡ x x   ♡ x x x
    ◇ Q x   ◇ A K J
    ♣ A K x x x   ♣ x x x

(2) The bidding goes 1♠   2◇
                    3♣   ?

What do you bid now on:

(a) ♠ x x x   (b) ♠ x x
    ♡ x x x   ♡ x
    ◇ A K Q x   ◇ Q J x x x
    ♣ x x x   ♣ A Q x x x

(c) ♠ K x x   (d) ♠ K x ،
    ♡ x x   ♡ J x x x
    ◇ A Q x x x   ◇ A J x x x
    ♣ J x x   ♣ x x

Another eight questions and you should have been working to the same time limit as before. Let us work through the answers.

(1)(a) Partner has shown a strong hand but you are not encouraged. As in previous examples, you must inform partner that you have no interest in anything else but spades by repeating the suit cheaply at 2♠, hoping to play there unless partner can go higher in that suit. 4♠ is the only likely game contract.

  (b) This is not much better but you can show your good diamond stop by bidding 2NT – limited and non-forcing. Partner still has the option to support your spades if he wishes (and 3♠ from him would be forcing, asking you to choose between 3NT and 4♠).

  (c) Here you have a very big hand and will almost certainly be insisting on a small slam in clubs with the grand a strong possibility. The way to initiate an investigation is to bid a fourth-suit-forcing 3◇ and then support clubs at the four-level afterwards. This is a game-forcing sequence and we shall discuss the procedure under slam bidding later.

  (d) Here you have the bulk of your points in diamonds and no interest in a spade game. You should make the position clear to partner by a direct 3NT, which you want to play. Partner should understand your message and is unlikely to go further unless he has a singleton or void in spades, when a slam may be on in one of his suits.

(2)(a) With a minimum hand for your 2♦ bid, you have no right to do more than give simple preference to 3♠. Partner will not pass this as he has forced to game but he must take charge of the remainder of the auction. He will probably elect to play in 3NT or 4♠.

(b) Here it may be that 3NT is still the best contract but five or six clubs are far more likely and you should make the position clear by supporting the clubs immediately to 4♣. Partner can initiate a slam investigation if he so wishes.

(c) Here you are near minimum for your 2♦ bid and clearly will want to play in spades. Partner has set up a game-forcing situation and if you bid 4♠ immediately instead of a simple preference to 3♠ you are telling partner that this is the limit of your hand. To show a stronger hand, you had the option to bid the fourth suit first. Note that, in this game-forcing situation, 3♠ is a stronger bid than 4♠

(d) Here you are minimum for your 2♦ bid and have no enthusiasm for either of partner's suits. You cannot bid 3NT outright because your hearts are not good enough, so you must ask for help by bidding a fourth-suit-forcing 3♡.

We now turn to situations where the opener has repeated his own suit. Important distinctions must be made between: majors and minors; simple and jump rebids; and whether your first response was at the one- or two-level. The rebid of the opener's suit is always a limit-bid and never forcing, so you have the option to pass. The importance of the distinction between majors and minors has already been indicated. With a major, you are primarily aiming to play in four of that major; while with a minor, you are primarily aiming for 3NT with five of the minor being a markedly less likely chance. The bidding will be orientated accordingly.

Let us start with an opening bid of 1♣. If the reply is 1♦, then 2♣ indicates a six-card (that means six or longer) suit. Can you see why? If you had a four-card major, you would bid it; if you had a four-card diamond suit, you would support your partner; and if you were 5332, you would either have opened 1NT or be in a position to bid it now according to your strength.

After a one-over-one bid, a repeat at the three-level guarantees a six-card suit in all cases. Again you can see why. You have the option to jump or reverse into a second suit and if you do not have one, you will be able to support partner or bid no-trumps.

Thus it is particularly important to note that, if an opener bids and jump repeats in a minor, he denies a four-card major – if he had one, he could always have bid it as he would have had the strength to reverse.

If the reply to 1♣ is one of a major or 1NT, then 2♣ need only guarantee a five-card suit. The opener might have a second suit in diamonds or hearts and not be strong enough to reverse. From that, we can work out a little guide which will apply to the other suits. If partner bids one over one in the next suit up, a repeat of the opener's suit indicates a six-card suit; otherwise it guarantees no more than five.

After a two-over-one bid, a repeat of the opener's suit at the two-level always guarantees a minimum of five cards, but a jump to the three-level always guarantees at least a six-card suit.

The difference in strength between simple and jump repetition of opener's suit has already been discussed and depends on whether responder has bid one-over-one or two-over-one, i.e. promised respectively a minimum of 6 or 9 points.

Remember that a simple repetition promises nothing in addition to the initial opening bid as the opener was forced by responder's bid to speak.

When replying to an opener who has bid and repeated his suit, a new suit on the three-level or a responder's reverse (i.e. second suit ranking higher than the first) at the two-level are both forcing, but a new suit below the rank of the first at that level we shall play as non-forcing (note, as mentioned before, some partnerships play it as forcing).

With that in mind, I should like you to try the examples given overleaf. Start your stop-watch.

The twenty questions should take you under ten minutes, and you should be aiming to cut it down to less than half that time.

(1) The bidding goes: 1 ◇   1 ♠
                        2 ◇   ?

What do you bid now on:

(a) ♠ K J x x   (b) ♠ K Q x x
     ♡ x x x   ♡ x x x
     ◇ x x   ◇ –
     ♣ Q x x x   ♣ J x x x x x

(c) ♠ A K x x x   (d) ♠ A K Q x x
     ♡ x x   ♡ K Q x x
     ◇ x x   ◇ J x
     ♣ A Q x   ♣ x x

(2) The bidding goes: 1 ♡   1 ♠
                        2 ♡   ?

What do you bid now on:

(a) ♠ K J x x x x   (b) ♠ A K x x
     ♡ x x   ♡ x
     ◇ x x   ◇ K x x x
     ♣ Q x x   ♣ K x x x

(c) ♠ A K x x x   (d) ♠ K Q x x
     ♡ A K x   ♡ x
     ◇ x x   ◇ x x x x x x
     ♣ x x x   ♣ K x

(3) The bidding goes: 1 ◇   1 ♠
                        3 ◇   ?

What do you bid now on:

(a) ♠ K J x x   (b) ♠ A K x x
     ♡ K x x   ♡ x x
     ◇ x x   ◇ Q x x
     ♣ Q x x x   ♣ x x x x

(c) ♠ A K x x x   (d) ♠ K J x x x x
     ♡ x x   ♡ x x x
     ◇ A Q   ◇ x
     ♣ x x x x   ♣ Q x x

(4) The bidding goes: 1 ♡   2 ♣
                      2 ♡   ?

What do you bid now on:

(a) ♠ A K x x   (b) ♠ K Q x x
     ♡ x x   ♡ K x x
     ◊ x x   ◊ x
     ♣ A Q x x x   ♣ K Q x x x

(c) ♠ x x x   (d) ♠ x x x
     ♡ x x   ♡ x
     ◊ K x   ◊ Q J x x
     ♣ A Q x x x x   ♣ K Q J x x

(5) The bidding goes: 1 ♡   2 ◊
                      3 ♡   ?

What do you bid now on:

(a) ♠ x x   (b) ♠ K Q x
     ♡ K x   ♡ x x
     ◊ A Q J x x   ◊ A Q x x x
     ♣ x x x x   ♣ x x x

(c) ♠ x x   (d) ♠ x x x
     ♡ x   ♡ –
     ◊ Q J x x x   ◊ A K Q x x
     ♣ A Q x x x   ♣ K Q J x x

Let us work through the answers.

(1)(a) In this sequence, the first point to remember is that
        partner, forced to speak, has promised nothing in addition
        to his opening bid except that he has confirmed a five-card
        diamond suit. In this example, having a minimum and no
        reason to bid again, you should be content with 2 ◊ and
        pass.

   (b) Here you have a minimum point-count and the hand
        appears to be a complete misfit. It is likely that you should
        actually be playing in clubs but 3 ♣ would be forcing and

show a much stronger hand, not to mention a five-card
spade suit, and therefore introducing the suit now is out of
the question. Just accept that the hand is hopeless and pass
2◇, hoping that partner has a very long suit and that the
penalty will be minimal. It is a good guide that, when you
are in a non-forcing situation and it is clear that the hand is
a misfit, the best thing to do is to stop bidding before the
opponents realize what is happening and start doubling.
In other words, try to see to it that your mishaps – there
will be plenty of them – are small ones, rather than trying
to be greedy and finishing with bigger losses.

(c) Here, with an opening bid, you are entitled to insist on
game, but as well as 3NT, 4♠, 5♣ or possibly even 5◇
might be the best contract. To find out more about
partner's hand, simply carry on bidding your hand naturally with a forcing bid of 3♣. Partner can then give
preference to spades, bid 3NT himself, or ask for help in
hearts with a fourth-suit forcing 3♡. In that case, you will
not be able to oblige and will have to repeat your spades,
after which partner can decide the final contract.

(d) With 15 points, you must insist on game and should force
with a jump to 3♡. This guarantees a five-card spade suit
(otherwise you would have bid hearts first) and leaves
options to play in 3NT, 4♡ or 4♠. If partner has really
nothing but diamonds, you may even be able to play 5◇.

(2)(a) In this sequence, partner has promised a six-card heart
suit. In this first example, you have a guaranteed 6–2 heart
fit and it is clear that you are nowhere near a game, so it is
probably best to pass and settle for 2♡. However, it could
well be argued that, as there are unlikely to be outside
entries to your hand, it will be useless unless those spades
are trumps. For that reason 2♠ may be a better contract,
even on a 6–1 fit. However, the sequence 1♡   1♠
                                          2♡   2♠

sounds very much like a misfit and I should not like to
even tempt opponents to start doubling which could be
very expensive if partner is void in spades. 2♡ has not

gone down yet and you are best advised to pass, accepting at worst a small penalty against what would have been a successful part-score.

(b) With 13 points, you have the right to think that opening bid plus opening bid equals game and insist on it by bidding an obvious 3NT. However, it is worth thinking first about how you are going to make it. Partner's principal feature is his six-card heart suit and you have only a singleton, so it will be difficult to establish for long-suit tricks. For that reason, I suggest that you devalue your hand by a point or two and invite with a non-forcing 2NT. Partner can still give you 3NT if he is above minimum for his opener. Had your hand contained a few tens and nines in the side suits, they would be useful as potential second stoppers in opponents' suits, in which case you may have been justified in bidding the game outright, despite the misfit.

(c) Here with a good fit and 14 points, you need have no hesitation in bidding game in hearts outright. You have little interest in any contract other than 4♡.

(d) This is similar to (1b) and you have no reason to bid over 2♡. Just settle for the 6–1 fit and hope that your eight points will help partner to make 2♡.

(3)(a) Here partner has promised about 15–17 points with a six-card diamond suit and with 9 points, you are entitled to insist on game in no-trumps. With the other suits covered, you can bid it yourself as a sign-off.

(b) (c) and (d) I should like to consider these three problems together because they highlight an increasing controversy in bidding theory and bridge teaching. The basic problem is: What is the meaning of the sequence 1♢   1♠
                                    3♢   3♠?

In days gone by, it used to show a weakish hand with long spades, non-forcing, like the hand in (d). Nowadays, there is greater awareness that if you play it that way, there is no satisfactory bid to express the hands in (b) and (c). It may well be that 3NT is the best contract, but you certainly cannot bid it with confidence when wide open in both the other suits and in any case, even if it is the right contract, you will want partner to be declarer. For that reason, modern theory recommends playing the 3♠ bid as forcing, inviting 3NT, 4♠ or 5◇ or even 6◇ on (c). On (d) you should give up the hand as having little prospect of game and pass, accepting that you will occasionally miss 4♠.

(4)(a) Here you have already promised 9 points by going on to the two-level and again remember that partner's rebid has taken this into account and promises no more than his opening strength apart from confirming his five-card suit. In this first example, with your opening bid and top cards in long suits, you are certainly entitled to insist on game. Your first move should be to continue to bid your hand naturally with 2♠. This is a responder's reverse (in that partner will have to go to the three-level to give preference to clubs) and therefore forcing for one round. Remember partner can still have a four-card spade suit in a hand below reversing strength, so 4♠ is a possible final contract as well as 3NT (probably favourite), but you could end in 4♡ or 5♣.

(b) The bidding has improved your hand and with a guaranteed 5–3 fit and an opening bid, you can certainly insist on 4♡. There is no harm, however, in bidding 2♠ first in case partner has a four-card spade suit and/or a respectable hand with three aces. 4–4 fits tend to play at least as well and usually better than 5–3 fits in that you have the possibility of discards on the unbalanced side suit. Also by bidding 2♠ first and then supporting hearts, you indicate the singleton diamond (having promised at least five clubs, four spades and three hearts), which might be crucial if a slam is on.

(c) This hand gives another example of the controversy discussed in question (3). A repeat of your suit at the three-level should be considered constructive and forward-going, and therefore on this hand, you should pass and accept 2♡. 3♣ may be a better final contract but no bidding system comes near to covering all eventualities and it is better that you worry about the bid hands where mistakes could be expensive while accepting a possible small loss in the part-score zone.

(d) Here you are minimum for your 2♣ bid. With a likely bad misfit (particularly remembering that partner had the chance to bid 2◇), you are advised to stop bidding in this non-forcing sequence and hope for the best in 2♡.

(5)(a) Here you have again gone to the two-level to show a minimum 9 points and partner will have taken this into account before jumping. Thus 14 points and a good six-card suit will be sufficient and even 13 with a useful holding in your suit might be enough. This should be borne in mind when considering your next move. In this first example, you have only one point over minimum and for that reason, could justify a pass as partner's bid is non-forcing. However, there are several points in favour of this hand. First, the king of trumps is bound to be a useful card. Second, you have a doubleton spade and thus a possible ruffing value (three small spades and three small clubs would not have been as good). Third, all your side honours are in a good long suit which is likely to provide tricks. If partner is low on points for his jump, he is likely to have the king of diamonds, which gives tremendous trick-taking potential to your hand. For that reason, 4♡ is fully justifiable. This is a sign-off as partner has limited his hand.

(b) With 11 points opposite a hand with more than an opening bid, you are entitled to insist on game with 3NT and 4♡ being obvious candidates. It is not clear, however, which is better. The way to find out is to remember that partner has denied a four-card spade suit and therefore, as 4♠ is not under consideration, it is safe for you to bid 3♠ yourself to show good values in that suit and indicating to partner that he will need good clubs to be sure of 3NT. Remember we had a similar situation earlier and this problem was included to see if you recognized it. 3♠ is, of course, forcing and partner should be able to take a decision from there.

(c) Here you have two good five-card suits but if you are to make game, it will have to be at the five-level, which is unlikely with partner having a limited hand and your dislike of hearts. You could try 3NT, but as explained in the last example, there will be considerable danger from spades and you certainly do not want to play it from your side. For these reasons, it is probably best to accept that it is unlikely to be game on the hand and pass 3♡, prepared to play there. It may well be that the hand plays better in four of one your suits, but it will be impractical to stop there. 4♣ shows a much stronger hand.

(d) This time, with 15 points in two strong suits, you should try for game despite the misfit. Arguably, you could try 3NT on the grounds that partner is likely to have spade values as he is known to have little in the minors. However, a slam in either minor is possible and you can bid 4♣, prepared to accept 4♡, if partner has no interest in either of your suits.

We now turn to the position where partner's rebid has been in no-trumps. In all cases, he has limited his hand strictly in point-count and has indicated a balanced shape, although occasionally he may have reluctantly had to bid it with a singleton in your suit. You must now decide whether, in the light of the known combined point-count, game is on and whether the shape of your hand warrants suggesting a suit in preference to no-trumps. Partner's bid, irrespective of level, is non-forcing. If you bid at the two-level over 1NT, your bid will also be non-forcing unless you reverse. If you bid on the three-level over 1NT, your bid will be forcing if you mention a new suit, but not if you repeat your own or support partner's. If you bid at the three-level over 2NT, your bid is always forcing except when you repeat your own suit, and in that case, it is a sign-off. This is only likely to occur when 2NT has followed a one-over-one bid and you have an absolute minimum 5 or 6 points with a poor six-card suit.

Try these examples, with the usual prime consideration uppermost in your mind! Start your stop-watch:

(1) The bidding goes: 1 ◊   1 ♠
                       1NT   ?

What do you bid now on:

(a) ♠ K x x x   (b) ♠ K Q x x
    ♡ K x   ♡ A x x
    ◊ x x x   ◊ A J x
    ♣ x x x x   ♣ J x x

(c) ♠ A K x x   (d) ♠ K x x x x
    ♡ x   ♡ Q J x x x
    ◊ Q x x x   ◊ x
    ♣ x x x x   ♣ x x

(2) The bidding goes: 1 ♣   1 ♡
                       2NT   ?

What do you bid now on:

(a) ♠ x x   (b) ♠ x x
    ♡ K x x x   ♡ A K x x x
    ◊ J x x   ◊ Q x x x
    ♣ Q x x x   ♣ x x

(c) ♠ x x x   (d) ♠ x x x
    ♡ J x x x   ♡ K Q J x x x
    ◊ Q x x   ◊ Q x x
    ♣ A J x   ♣ x

(3) The bidding goes: 1 ♡   2 ◊
                       2NT   ?

What do you bid now on:

(a) ♠ x x   (b) ♠ K Q x x x
    ♡ x x   ♡ x
    ◊ A Q J x x   ◊ A Q J x x x
    ♣ K x x x   ♣ x

(c) ♠ x x x   (d) ♠ A J x
    ♡ K x x x   ♡ K x
    ◊ A Q J x   ◊ A Q x x x
    ♣ x x   ♣ K Q x

The twelve questions should have taken you not much more than five minutes and you should be aiming to get down to just over three. Let us work through the answers.

(1)(a) Partner has promised 15–16 points and with only six in your hand, you can see that game is out of the question; you should therefore pass and be content with 1NT.

  (b) This time, with 16 points, you can insist on game with a lot to spare but notice that 31 is the maximum combined point-count the partnership can have and you should not invite a slam. Simply sign off in a safe 3NT.

  (c) Here you have enough points to suggest a game, 3NT and 5♦ being the candidates. This time, you should jump to 3♦, which is very invitational but non-forcing, so that partner can look for game if he is maximum or pass otherwise.

  (d) Here you have only 6 points and the singleton in partner's suit is a further setback. However, you will much prefer to play in a major than 1NT and you should now offer the choice by bidding 2♡. This is non-forcing and weak. Partner is expected to pass or give preference to spades. On this occasion, the likely false preference is just bad luck!

(2)(a) This time, partner has shown 17–18 points, balanced. You have only 6 points and therefore no reason to go on. It is possible that 3♣ would be a better part-score contract, but this bid would be forcing and forward-going so you could never stop there. Pass and settle for 2NT.

  (b) With 9 points, you again have enough for game, but with all your points concentrated in two suits and the five-card major, you should offer the alternative contract of 4♡. Simply bid a forcing 3♦, which promises five hearts (otherwise you would have bid diamonds first) and let partner choose. He will try to avoid supporting the diamonds unless he is wide open in spades and if he is short of hearts as well, you might have to play 5♦. More often than not in this sequence, you will finish in 3NT.

  (c) With 8 points balanced, you have enough for 3NT, even opposite a minimum 17, and have no reason to bid anything else. 3NT is a sign-off.

(d) Here you have enough to insist on game and you have no interest in any other contract than 4♡. You should bid it direct as a sign-off.

(3)(a) Partner has, in principle, promised exactly 15 points and with 10 in your hand, game should be on. There are two possible approaches. One is to accept that it will probably be 3NT or nothing and simply bid it as direct sign-off rather than give opponents clues about what to lead. The other (which I personally prefer, but it is certainly not clear-cut) is to bid a forcing 3♣, pin-pointing the spade weakness and thereby giving the partnership the opportunity of staying out of game by stopping in 3♢, or playing the alternative contracts of 5♢, 5♣ or possibly even 4♡, if partner has a good five-card suit. Remember that partner has not promised a spade stop by bidding 2NT and you would look silly to lose the first five or more tricks in 3NT when another game is available. I should add that, however you bid, it is likely that you would get a spade lead anyway.

My style of bidding is very much orientated towards enjoying options when choosing the final contract. Others take the view that quick auctions (known in bridge jargon as 'bashing' or 'punting') with the minimum of discussion pays in the long run. It is a question of balancing the loss of bidding accuracy against the gain from a lower standard of opening lead and defence against you. The debate continues!

(b) This time no-trumps is not for you as you will want to play in one of your long suits at anything up to slam-level. Simply force with 3♠ now, intending to bid 4♠ over 3NT. You will probably end there or in 5♢ if you do not reach a slam.

(c) Here you have no interest in a slam so you should sign off in 4♡. Note the contrast between this and the last problem. In this situation, 3♡ is a stronger bid than 4♡.

(d) Here, with 19 points, you have no interest in anything other than 6NT and should sign off by bidding it direct.

We have discussed the first two complete rounds of bidding and although this could continue for hours, that is as far as I intend to go. The work we have done so far is enough to give you the general idea of what constructive bidding is all about.

Slam bidding

We now turn to slam bidding and once it has been established that a partnership has enough combined strength to consider a slam – we had a number of examples in previous chapters – the players should be able to check whether they have adequate controls, i.e. aces and kings, voids and singletons, to ensure that they do not lose two tricks off the top.

The most commonly played convention in respect of slam bidding is known as 'Blackwood' after its inventor of that name, Easley Blackwood, who came from Indiana. I include this with great reluctance as it is probably the most misunderstood and misused convention in the game. However, even if you do not use it yourself, and I advise you to avoid it in most situations, it is important that you are aware of it if only to be able to understand what your opponents are doing. You will meet it fairly often as it is universally used, particularly among weaker players.

The conventional bid is 4NT. Now it was mentioned earlier that if you raise 1NT or 2NT to 4NT, that shows a point-count and is a non-forcing invitation to a slam. This still holds even if you are playing Blackwood. The convention primarily applies to trump contracts. If a suit is agreed or if a partner suddenly jumps to 4NT after a suit has been bid opposite him, then the bid is Blackwood and should be answered as follows, showing the number of aces in your hand:

  5♣: 0 or 4 aces
(it will normally be obvious which it is, although the Italian world champions once had a famous disaster in this respect – they are still laughing about it!)
  5♢: 1 ace
  5♡: 2 aces
  5♠: 3 aces

Once you have had your reply and realize that your partnership has all the aces, and you wish to investigate a grand slam, then 5NT asks for kings, answered in a similar manner at the six-level, although, with four kings, you bid 6NT. Before using the convention, you must be sure of the following points:

1 If you bid 4NT, you are taking charge of the auction and must be ready to select the final contract irrespective of partner's reply. Furthermore, partner must not overrule you. It is very disturbing to see players with a few points hearing their partner's two-level opener and going rushing into Blackwood with little idea of what is opposite them. Normally, if at all, the big hand should ask questions of the little hand, so that the former can take a more informed decision.

2 You should not ask for aces if you have a void yourself or are likely to find partner with a void. Some players allow normal Blackwood replies to be pushed up to the six-level with a void, e.g. 4NT 6♡ would show two aces plus a void, but in which suit the void is may be unclear and the questioner, already on the six-level, may not only be too high already but also ignorant of what to do.

3 Blackwood is only appropriate when you have plenty of first and second round controls. Do not use it when you have two losers in one suit as the information on aces alone will be insufficient.

4 The use of Blackwood commits the partnership at least to the five-level. You must carefully take account of which suit you have agreed before bidding 4NT. For example, if clubs is the agreed suit, one ace from partner will be shown by 5♢ and that will commit you to 6♣. If a major is agreed and partner does not produce enough aces for a slam to be viable, can you be confident of eleven tricks? With a major suit agreed, note that if you go one off in 5♠ or 5♡, you have thrown away a game. Does the chance of a slam make this investment worthwhile? In practice, you should be confident that the slam will have a 50 per cent chance *at worst* before looking for it. Always bear in mind that the prime purpose of the convention is to keep you out of bad slams rather than to propel you into good ones.

5 It is inadvisable to go into Blackwood when the combined trump holding may be weak. For that reason, some partnerships play what is known as 'five-ace Blackwood' where the king of trumps is considered a fifth 'ace'. Now 5♣ promises 0 to 4 'aces', 5◊ promises 1 or 5, 5♡ and 5♠ respectively being 2 and 3 as before.

See if you can put these points into practice with some examples. Start your stop-watch. I shall expect you to give good reasons for using or refusing to use the Blackwood convention.

(1) Partner opens 1♣. Is Blackwood appropriate on:

(a) ♠ x
     ♡ K Q J x x x
     ◊ x
     ♣ A K Q J x

(b) ♠ x x
     ♡ K Q J x
     ◊ A K Q
     ♣ A J x x

(c) ♠ A x x
     ♡ A x
     ◊ A x x x
     ♣ A K x x

(2) Partner opens 1♠. Is Blackwood appropriate on:

(a) ♠ J x x x
     ♡ K Q J x x x
     ◊ A K
     ♣ A

(b) ♠ K J x x x
     ♡ A K J x x
     ◊ A
     ♣ Q x

(c) ♠ A Q x x x
     ♡ Q x x
     ◊ A K x
     ♣ Q x

(3) You open 1♡ and partner responds 3♡. Is Blackwood appropriate on:

(a) ♠ A x
     ♡ K J x x x x
     ◊ −
     ♣ A K Q x x

(b) ♠ A K
     ♡ Q J x x x x
     ◊ A x x x
     ♣ A

(c) ♠ x
     ♡ A K x x x x
     ◊ A K J x
     ♣ K x

The nine questions should have taken you under four minutes and you should be aiming to achieve well under two. Let us work through the answers.

(1)(a) Here you have 16 points and only three obvious losers so you are well in the slam zone. However, partner can easily have an opening bid with only one ace and a 5◊ reply to your Blackwood enquiry would commit you to 6♣, which you know will be defeated. In fact, although it would be very unlucky, partner could turn up with: ♠ K Q J x ♡ x ◇ K Q J ♣ 10 9 x x x, in which case not even 5♣ will be made. You should therefore bid your hearts and let partner describe his hand further. 3NT and 4♡ are not ruled out yet. Force to game with 2♡.

(b) Here again you will be disappointed if a slam is not on but if partner shows one ace, he could still be missing the ace and king of spades. Furthermore, if he shows two aces, how will you find about the trump position for a grand slam? You can bid 5NT and take a sensible decision if partner shows no king or two kings but if he shows one king, you are committed to the grand slam and may be missing the king of trumps, not to mention the queen. Again you should bid your hearts first. You can always try Blackwood later anyway.

(c) Here I have insulted you. What is the purpose of asking for aces when you already know the answer? With 19 points in top controls, you are certainly in the slam zone but the right contract will depend on partner's strength and shape, so the longer the conversation, the better. Start by bidding your diamonds, then the fourth suit if partner bids a major and you should get some idea of what he has before deciding the final contract. Thus a quiet but forcing 1◇ is sufficient for the moment.

(2)(a) Here you have 18 points with a good fit and are again in the slam zone, but as well as aces, you are very concerned about the strength of the trumps. In fact, if partner is strong in clubs, e.g. K Q J x, it could well be that you can discard your poor spades on those clubs and make a grand slam in hearts, while 6♠ is a failure. You will certainly not gather enough information with Blackwood and indeed you only need give partner ♠ Q x x x x x ♡ x ◇ Q J x ♣ K Q J and 5♠ will go down. Describe your hand first, forcing to game with 3♡.

(b) Again with 18 points and a fabulous fit, you are in the slam zone but if you ask for aces and hear exactly one, how do know that there aren't two quick club losers? On top of that, if partner shows two aces, a decision on a grand slam will depend on the major suit queens at least as much as the number of kings in partner's hand. Again, you should start by forcing to game with 3♡.

(c) With 17 points, you are again in the slam zone but there is still room for the partnership to be missing the ace and king in either of two suits. Also, without knowing your partner's shape, it is difficult to judge how many tricks you are going to be able to make, even given the required number of controls. Again, you should proceed slowly to find out your partner's strength and shape. Start with a quiet but forcing 2◊.

(3)(a) Partner has promised a four-card heart suit and if you find him with two aces, you can confidently bid the grand slam. Similarly, if he has no ace, you will be very unlucky to go down in 6♡. But what happens if he shows exactly one ace? If it is the heart, 7♡ will be almost certain; if he has the diamond, it has no chance. Thus you will not be able to take a decision and should not use Blackwood at this stage.

(b) Partner almost certainly has at least one of the top two hearts but the success of a heart slam will depend on his diamond length and strength. Blackwood will not give you that information, so is inappropriate at this stage.

(c) This is a little bit nearer the mark. With at least second round control in all suits and no worry about trumps, the prime interest is in those two black aces. You will be most unlikely to go down in 5♡ if partner fails to produce either as he surely will be able to cover a possible diamond or second club loser.

So in the nine hands I have given you, in only one is an immediate Blackwood enquiry appropriate. Yet in my teaching and playing experience, I have, on countless occasions, seen very 'experienced' players use it on totally inappropriate hands.

The recommended approach is a little advanced for the beginner's stage and must be studied in a later volume for intermediate players. The purpose of this section is to make you aware of the Blackwood convention and its pitfalls and realize that it is almost invariably better to change suit and bid the fourth suit if necessary to get a picture of partner's strength and shape before taking a decision on a slam.

The passed hand

To conclude the section on bidding against silent opposition, we have to consider the differences, if any, that arise if the first member of the partnership passes. That means that, in principle, he will have limited his hand to 11 points or less. For that reason, any response to a one-opener is non-forcing except a jump in a new suit, which indicates values for a raise to the three-level in the opener's suit and a reasonable holding in the suit actually bid. Thus with ♠ K x x x
 ♡ x x
 ◇ x x
 ♣ A K x x x

if partner opens 1♠, you can reply 3♣, but should be content with 2♣ over 1♡ or 1◇. Notice that your hand is strong within the 0–11 range indicated by your initial pass and has improved dramatically if partner has opened 1♠ but not otherwise. The bid of 3♣ is much more informative to partner than a simple raise to 3♠. With ♠ K x x x
 ♡ A x
 ◇ K x
 ♣ x x x x x

you should bid 3♠ direct as those five small clubs are no help to partner in deciding whether to proceed to game or slam.

Once partner has passed as dealer, he could be very weak and if you do not have much yourself, you have to think in terms of defending rather than declaring, or possibly sacrificing if the vulnerability makes it worthwhile. For that reason, plus the fact that you will not be required to find a rebid over a change of suit, most experts recommend that it is worthwhile opening in the third position (i.e. when partner has dealt and passed and the next hand has also passed) despite being understrength. There are a number of possible advantages:

1 In indicating a lead to partner, as it seems likely that the hand behind you is strong and will probably be declarer, putting your partner on lead.

2 In taking bidding space away from opponents, particularly if you can open one of a major, especially spades, or can preempt, which many people do on six-card suits, some even on five, in this position.

For these reasons, the light third-hand opening is generally accepted in the higher echelons of bridge and is a recognized part of most American systems. I do not recommend it and never indulge in it myself for several reasons:

1 In basic Acol, an opening bid puts your hand in the 12–19 point range, which is inconveniently wide already. If you open light, you are widening the range even further, making life extremely difficult for partner, especially if he is strong within the pass (0–11) point range.

2 If you open with a broken suit e.g. A Q x x x, you enable an opponent to devalue or revalue his king according to where he is sitting, so that, instead of forcing your opponents to bid less accurately because of the bidding space deprived from them, you are positively helping them.

3 Even if you open with a solid suit, e.g. K Q J x x, which is certainly much safer, the opponents can still revalue or devalue lengths and shortages in that suit, again to their advantage.

4 As we shall learn very shortly, a third-hand opening can be positively helpful to the opposition if the player in fourth position holds a three-suited hand.

My advice therefore is: do not think you are being clever or 'up-market' by opening light third-in-hand. At best, you will lose as much as you gain and that does not take into account the loss of partnership confidence. However, you must be aware that other people are liable to do it.

Competitive Bidding

We are now going to allow the opponents to join in the auction and in this respect, we must consider the following:

The simple overcall;
The jump overcall;
The take-out double and the redouble;
The cue-bid, i.e. the bid of the opponents' suit;
The no-trump overcall;
The jump no-trump overcall, i.e. the *unusual no-trump*;
The penalty double and redouble.

The simple overcall

Once the opponents have opened the bidding, one of them has demonstrated that he has at least 12 points and may well have more, so the chances that they have the balance of the points in the pack and will be declaring are increased markedly. That does not mean that you are debarred from bidding and there are a number of purposes in making in overcall. Despite at least one opening bid being advertised against your partnership, you might still find a fit and buy the contract in your own long suit. Even if you do not, you may be able to push the opponents too high; in any event, you may take important bidding space away from them, reducing the accuracy of their bidding. Finally, even if you fail to buy the contract, you may gain advantage in having indicated a good opening lead to partner should the opponent on your left become declarer.

However, you must take special care that you avoid a big penalty when entering the auction, particularly as opponents need not necessarily have a game on and you might be giving away a lot of points for nothing. For this reason, your prime consideration is not so much your point-count but the length and quality of the suit you are bidding. Heavy penalties at a low level are only likely to materialize if you run into a bad split in your proposed trump suit and that must be your prime concern.

Thus before making an overcall, you must consider whether you are calling one-over-one, i.e. when an opponent has opened with a lower-ranking suit than yours; or two-over-one, when he has opened a higher-ranking suit than yours, when you will obviously need to be that much stronger. In both cases, you must take both your own and your opponents' vulnerability into account because your overcall is primarily orientated towards a sacrifice and there is little point in suggesting a sacrifice when it is likely to be too expensive.

Another factor that I recommend taking into account is the number of cards you hold in the suit bid against you. The shorter you are, the less likely it is that the opponents have a misfit and will want to defend at a low level, and therefore the safer it is for you to enter the auction. I ought to mention that many good players take a different view on this, arguing that if you have length in the opponents' suit, then your partner is likely to be short and will be well placed to ruff your losers.

In any event, in all cases you should not overcall without a six-card suit to one top honour or a five-card suit to two of the top three or three of the top five, and you should have about 3–4 playing tricks, non-vulnerable, or 4–5 vulnerable if you are bidding one-over-one, and one more in each case if you are bidding two-over-one. If in doubt, take your opponents' vulnerability into account (being more conservative if they are non-vulnerable) and the length of the suit bid against you, as explained above.

I refrain from being dogmatic on the next examples because in general, many expert players tend to bid on lighter hands than I do and therefore, rather than have a stop-watch test, I will give a few examples of hands to illustrate where I draw the line.

Let us first consider a simple one-over-one. The opponent on my right opens 1♡. I would overcall 1♠, non-vulnerable, on:

♠ K Q 10 x x	♠ A K J x x	♠ K J x x x x	♠ Q J 10 x x
♡ x x	♡ x x x	♡ Q x x	♡ x x
◇ K J x	◇ Q x x	◇ K x x	◇ A K x
♣ x x x	♣ x x	♣ x	♣ x x x

or stronger hands.

Vulnerable, I should like to be a little stronger:

♠ A K 10 x x	♠ A K J 10 x	♠ K J x x x x	♠ A J 10 x x
♡ x x	♡ x x x	♡ A x x	♡ x x
◇ K J x	◇ K x x	◇ K x x	◇ A Q x
♣ x x x	♣ x x	♣ x	♣ x x x

or stronger hands. Note the insistence on a stronger suit in five-card examples.

For a two-over-one, I shall normally be looking for a six-card or very strong five-card suit, but a good five-card-suit is all right non-vulnerable. After the same 1♡ opener, I would overcall 2♣ non-vulnerable on:

♠ A x x	♠ x x	♠ Q x x	♠ x x x
♡ x x	♡ x x	♡ J x	♡ x x
◇ Q x x	◇ J x x	◇ K x x	◇ A K x
♣ K Q 10 x x	♣ A K J x x x	♣ K Q J x x	♣ Q J 10 x x

or stronger hands. Vulnerable, I should like to be a little stronger:

♠ A x x	♠ x x	♠ A x x	♠ x x x
♡ x x	♡ x x	♡ J x	♡ x x
◇ K x x	◇ K x x	◇ J x x	◇ A K x
♣ K Q J x x	♣ A K J x x x	♣ K Q J 10 x	♣ A Q 10 x x

or stronger hands. But I should refrain from doing so, vulnerable, on:

♠ x x	♠ A J	♠ A x x	♠ x x x
♡ A Q 10 x	♡ x x x	♡ J x	♡ x x
◇ Q x	◇ J x x	◇ K x x	◇ A Q x
♣ K J 10 x x	♣ K J x x x	♣ Q J x x x	♣ Q J 10 x x

or weaker hands.

In the first hand, the hearts are such that I should be happy to defend, and in the other three, I would not consider the clubs long enough or strong enough to make a two-over-one overcall worth the risk.

Up to now, we have considered the case where you are sitting immediately over the opener. Where an opponent opens on your left and this is followed by two passes, you know that the hand on the right is very weak (0–5 points) and that it may well be that your partner was unable to find a suitable bid despite, as we shall see in a moment, holding up to 14 points. For that reason, you can be a little weaker in what is called the *protective position*. Bear in mind that, if you decide to pass, you are allowing the one-level contract bid against you to be played, so again your attitude towards the trump suit is highly relevant.

I still recommend the need for a five-card suit in principle but you need not be quite so strict about quality and sometimes you have little alternative but to bid a good four-card suit. You should have a minimum of 8 high-card points when non-vulnerable or 10 when vulnerable (after devaluing any badly-placed honours in the suit opened on your left).

The jump overcall

Still discussing one-suited hands, the question arises about what you should do if you are very much stronger than the minimum for the overcall. There are various styles of playing here, ranging from those who insist on a six-card suit but play the jump overcall as weak, say up to 9 points, with the prime purpose of taking bidding space away from opponents. However, this is really only suitable for tournament bridge where big losses on a single hand do not hurt too much. At the other extreme, there are those who insist on a near two-opener for a jump overcall, particularly in a lower-ranking suit, which involves going to the three-level.

The most popular method nowadays is the *intermediate jump overcall* which requires a good opening bid in high cards with a six-card suit, or a queen stronger than that with a very good five-card suit, but bear in mind again that suit quality and whether your bid is two-over-one or three-over-one must be taken into account. So too must the vulnerability, although this is less relevant now as you are striving to play the hand rather than sacrifice.

I would recommend 2♠ over 1♡ on hands like the following:

♠ A K Q 10 x x	♠ A K J x x	♠ A K x x x x	♠ Q J 10 x x x
♡ x x	♡ x x x	♡ x x	♡ x x
◇ K J x	◇ A Q x	◇ A Q x x	◇ A Q x
♣ x x	♣ Q x	♣ x	♣ A x

or stronger hands.

When bidding three of a minor, you are primarily looking towards 3NT, intending to make it by running the suit and so the weaker the suit, the stronger in points you must be to justify the jump. I would recommend 3◇ over 1♡ on:

♠ 10 x	♠ A K	♠ Q x	♠ A Q J
♡ x x	♡ x x x	♡ x x	♡ x x
◇ A K J x x x	◇ K J x x x x	◇ A K Q J x	◇ A K x x x x
♣ A K x	♣ A Q	♣ A x x x	♣ x x

or stronger hands.

In the protective position, the jump overcall may be about a queen weaker.

The take-out double

We now turn to two-suited and three-suited hands. When we studied the scoresheet, we introduced the double as a bid which meant that you wished to defend the contract bid against you for 'double' the stakes, although we learned that the term was something of a misnomer as the penalty scale usually gave bigger than double rewards according to vulnerability. In practice, it is rare that you will want to double a low-level contract for penalties and it is therefore universally accepted in all bidding systems that it is more useful to reserve the double for other hands. Let us look at an example:

You hold: ♠ A x x x   and 1♡ is opened on your right.
♡ x
◇ A x x x
♣ A J x x

You have an opening bid and the singleton in opponents' suit is certainly an advantage, putting you in a position to ruff the opponents' high cards in hearts after the first round. But what are you to bid? You could play in any of three suits but you do not know which to choose. None of them are long enough or strong enough to overcall so you appear to be stuck. The solution lies in what is called a *take-out double*. After the 1 ♡ bid, you double. This does not mean 'I want to defend 1 ♡ because I think I can defeat it for a considerable penalty.' It means precisely the opposite, suggesting shortage in hearts and a willingness to play in another suit. In the first place, you are offering all three unbid suits to your partner, but if you only have two, i.e. less than three cards in the missing side-suit, you will correct partner's choice of your other short suit to the cheapest available. Let us take some examples:

(a) ♠ K Q 10 x   (b) ♠ A K x x
     ♡ x x   ♡ x x
     ◊ K J x x x   ◊ Q x
     ♣ A x   ♣ A K J x x

(c) ♠ x x   (d) ♠ x x
     ♡ A Q J x   ♡ A K x x
     ◊ K x x x x   ◊ x x
     ♣ K x   ♣ A Q x x x

With a two-suited hand, it is important to note that it is generally accepted that, except on very strong hands, a take-out double of one of a major suit is primarily oriented towards finding a fit in the other and you should therefore have four cards or at least a strong trebleton in it.

On hand (a), if 1 ♡ is opened against you, you can double and correct 2♣ from partner to 2 ◊, offering spades and diamonds. If 1♣ is opened against you, you can again double, intending to correct 1 ♡ to 1♠, again offering spades and diamonds. It is, of course, preferable to bid your longer suit first, but this is a kind of 'reverse' situation where you are forcing the bidding up to the two-level and you need to be about a king stronger than this hand to be able to bid the diamonds in front of the spades.

On hand (b), you are that much stronger. If 1◇ is opened against you, you can double and correct partner's 1♡ to 2♣, offering clubs and spades, with clubs the longer suit. If 1♡ is opened against you, it is slightly more debatable whether you are strong enough to double and then correct 2◇ to 3♣. Strictly speaking, you should have about a queen more, but the alternative, a direct bid of 3♣ (the hand being too good for a simple overcall of 2♣) is less descriptive and just as high.

On hand (c), you can double an opening bid of one of either black suit and correct the reply to 2◇ to offer diamonds and hearts.

On hand (d), however, while you can double 1◇, intending to correct 1♠ to 2♣, offering clubs and hearts, you are not strong enough to double 1♠ as you cannot force the bidding up to the three-level if partner responds 2◇. You should simply overcall 2♣ and hope you have a chance to bid your hearts later.

Note also that, if you are sitting in the fourth position and the opponents bid two suits before you have a chance to bid, a take-out double promises at least four cards in each of the other two suits. However, before bidding in this position, you should remember that opponents have suggested at least 18 points between them and you will usually be able to work out that your partner is very weak. It is usually wise, therefore, not to enter the auction unless, despite this knowledge, you have serious aspirations of playing the hand. This will normally imply rather more distribution than 4–4 in the suits you are offering and – much more important – you must have all or nearly all of your points in the suits you are offering so that any penalty will be relatively light.

When replying to a take-out double, the first point to realize is the meaning of the bid. You have been asked to choose a suit and when you do so, you promise no points at all; partner is responsible for your bid and if you have 7 points or less (and you should devalue by at least two points any honours in the opener's suit, which will probably be of no value to partner), you should simply bid your longest suit subject to the following provisos:

1 If partner has made a take-out double of a major, you should prefer a four-card suit in the other major at the one level, viz. spades after a double of 1♡, to a five-card minor at the two-level, particularly if you are very weak. When both suits are at the same level, you should prefer the long suit, again especially if you are weak.

2 If you have two four-card majors, answering a take-out double of a minor, you should bid hearts first, allowing partner to correct to spades as cheaply as possible.

3 If partner has doubled 1♣ and you hold two four-card suits in diamonds and a major, then your bid depends on your strength. With five points or less, I recommend keeping the bidding low by bidding diamonds. Partner can still bid a major at the one-level. If you have 6 or 7 points, you can bid the major. If partner has the other major, you are happy to play diamonds at a higher level.

4 If you have two five-card suits, then just with opening bids, you should bid the higher-ranking first, intending to bid the lower next to allow partner to give preference to the higher cheaply.

5 If your longest suit happens to be the opener's, you should not pass the double, which would convert the take-out into a penalty double unless your trumps are long and solid, e.g. K Q J x x. Remember your partner has announced shortage in opener's suit (ideally a void) and therefore a pass in this situation is a strong bid! If you have to bid a three-card suit, so be it – partner is responsible.

All this covers hands with 7 points or less (again remember to devalue honours in the opener's suit). Once you have 8 or more, you can consider jumping in your long suit or, if you are strong in the opener's suit, bidding no-trumps. A couple of considerations should be borne in mind:

1 The final contract: you need to be stronger to jump if you are angling for five of a minor than four of a major.

2 Where you are strong in opener's suit, the hand will be something of a misfit and you will probably need rather more than the usual 25 points to make 3NT. However, this is at least

partially mitigated by the fact that, should you reach that contract, you will know where all the enemy points are and will be able to play that much more accurately. Also, if the opener wants to attack his suit, he will have to lead away from his honours round to your holding.

So you need about 8–10 points and a potential double stop in the opener's suit to respond 1NT to a take-out double, 11–13 for 2NT, 14 up for 3NT. To jump in a suit, you should have 8–10 points in a major, 9–10 in a minor, but you can add a point for every card over the fourth in the bid suit.

Where you have 11 points or more and are unsuitable for a direct bid of no-trumps, you should make what is called a *cue-bid*, i.e. bid the opponent's suit. This establishes a forcing situation and bidding must continue at least until one of the partners limits his hand with a non-forcing no-trump bid or until a suit is agreed. The partnership can thus discuss their final contract in the knowledge that they are at least near the game zone.

Let us try some examples against the stop-watch. Write down what you would bid and the final contract you have in mind. In each case, you are the fourth person to speak.

(1) The bidding goes (X means double): 1♣ X Pass ?
What do you bid now on:

(a)   ♠ x x x x   (b)   ♠ x x x
       ♡ x x x   ♡ x x x
       ♢ x x x   ♢ x x x
       ♣ x x x   ♣ K x x x

(c)   ♠ x x x   (d)   ♠ x x x x
       ♡ x x x x x   ♡ A Q J x
       ♢ x x   ♢ A x x
       ♣ A Q J   ♣ J x

(2) The bidding goes: 1♠ X Pass ?
What do you bid now on:

(a)   ♠ K Q J 10 x   (b)   ♠ x x
       ♡ x x x   ♡ Q x x x
       ♢ x x x   ♢ J x x x x
       ♣ x x   ♣ x x

(c) ♠ K J x   (d) ♠ x x x
     ♡ K Q x x x   ♡ A Q J x
     ◇ x x   ◇ A Q J x
     ♣ x x x   ♣ J x

The eight questions should have taken you under five minutes and you should be aiming to get well under three. Let us work through the answers.

(1)(a) You could hardly be worse but partner has asked for your longest suit so 1♠ it has to be, hoping to play there. Remember that all replies to a take-out double (even jumps) except the cue-bid are non-forcing and the cheapest bids promise 0–7 useful points.

(b) Here all you have is a probably badly-placed king of clubs and no four-card suit to bid. However, your clubs are nowhere near strong enough to let the double stand (remember 'Pass' is a *strong* bid in this situation) so you must bid as cheaply as possible and treat your three-card suits as biddable (remember partner is responsible) and bid them in ascending order as before. 1◇ is your reply, hoping to play there or in one of a major.

(c) Here you have a five-card major and should bid it. It is easy to be carried away on hands like these but the position is not encouraging. All your points are in badly-placed clubs, the one suit in which your partner has said that he has no interest. Simply bid 1♡, but remember again that this puts your hand in the 0–7 point range. So given another chance, you will be entitled to bid no-trumps to show this type of hand. At the moment, all you are interested in is to play 1♡, but if partner is very strong (remembering that his double is forcing and therefore unlimited), 4♡ or 3NT may be on.

(d) Here with 11 useful points (the jack of clubs is unlikely to be worth anything) and two four-card majors, you will be looking towards game in four of a major. For the moment, all you need do is set up a forcing position with a cue-bid of 2♣. After that, you can discuss which major to play and will probably finish in 4♡ or 4♠.

(2)(a) In this case, with very strong solid spades, you are best advised to try to defeat 1♠ and should therefore pass the double, converting it into a penalty double. In this situation, partner will be expected to lead a trump, if he has one, so that you can draw declarer's trumps and prevent his making tricks with his low trumps by ruffing other suits.

(b) This is a little more debatable. The double of 1♠ strongly indicates a four-card heart suit, which suggests that you should prefer your heart suit to ensure a four–four fit. However, with this very weak hand, your prime concern is to keep out of trouble and you should prefer your long suit for the moment. If partner has four cards in both red suits, you will prefer to play in 2♦ and if he is strong with hearts, he can always bid them over 2♦.

(c) Here you are balanced in the 8–10 range, but even if you get a spade lead, you may only have one stop in the suit. Furthermore, partner has invited a heart contract and you should accept with your good five-card suit. The question is at what level to bid it. You should realize that, if hearts are trumps, spades will not be led and your honours are likely to be worthless. For the moment, therefore, you should be content with 2♡, prepared to play there but, being very strong in 0–7 point range, you will be happy to offer 3NT or 4♡ if partner makes a forward-going move.

(d) With 15 points, you will certainly want to be in game, almost certainly in 4♡, but a slam could well be on despite the opening bid, so there is no need to rush. Just establish a forcing situation with a cue-bid of 2♠ and you can always bid 4♡ later. This delayed game arrival shows partner that you have a little in reserve. He need only have: ♠ x ♡ K x x x ♦ K x x x ♣ A K x x – a mere 13 points – for the slam to be on.

Note that in all these examples, it was assumed that the partner of the opener passed. If he bids, the force of the take-out double is cancelled as your partner has another chance to speak – this applies to all forcing situations. In that event, you need about 5 working points to make what is referred to as a *free bid* at the one-level, 6 or more at the two-level.

Before considering how to bid when a take-out double has been made against you, we must clearly define when a double is for take-out and when it is for penalties. The rule is very simple. If partner has not made a bid, a double of any contract below game is for take-out and that includes preempts (unless you and your partner agree otherwise). If partner has made a bid, then he has shown his suit and now any double is for penalties. The exception lies against an opening bid of 1NT when a double, whether you are sitting over or under the bid, is for penalties and if the opponents run to a suit after being doubled in 1NT then any subsequent double is also for penalties. You can always cue-bid if you wish to discuss playing a suit-contract in preference to defending.

There are a number of schools of thought on the question of bidding after an opponent's take-out double. The modern theory is that you should redouble to show a point-count of about 10 or more and otherwise (apart from 2NT as explained below), bid naturally, completely ignoring the double. Thus simple changes of suit would be forcing as usual.

This certainly has the advantage of being easy to remember, but neglects a number of important points, and I think it is better to at least understand the position before deciding what action to take.

When partner opens the bidding and the next hand doubles, the first point to realize is that the opponents are now in a forcing situation and therefore, unless the double is left in, i.e. converted to a penalty double, which is very rare in practice, you will have another chance to bid. It is this very point that seems to be completely overlooked by most players, including the experts. You therefore have far more options than you would have had without the double.

Basically, there are a number of situations in which you might find yourself, drawing the line between weak and strong at about the 10–11 point mark:

1 You are weak with a misfit in partner's suit;
2 You are weak with a fit in partner's suit, and
   a many of your points are in partner's suit or,
   b few of your points are in partner's suit;
3 You are strong with a misfit;
4 You are strong with a fit, again with the two subdivisions as in 2.

In each case, the overriding consideration is deciding what to do is 'What final contract do you have in mind – and in particular, are you aiming to declare or defend?'

Let us go through the various positions:

1 With a weak hand and a misfit, you will be delighted to defend, the only danger being that, if you pass, the double may be left in. My recommendation is: pass, unless you are singleton or void in partner's suit and have a long suit (preferably six-cards or more) to suggest as a preferable alternative. Even then, be particularly wary of going to the two-level. Thus after 1 ◊ X, I would move to 1 ♡ with

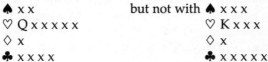

     ♠ x x   but not with ♠ x x x
     ♡ Q x x x x x   ♡ K x x x
     ◊ x   ◊ x
     ♣ x x x x   ♣ x x x x x

The 1 ♡ bid is obviously non-forcing; if anything, it is a sign-off and a warning to partner that you cannot stand his diamonds.

2 With a weak hand and a fit in partner's suit, then it is less clear-cut whether you want to play or defend. The more cards and more points that you have in partner's suit, the less defence you have to offer against a contract in another trump suit and therefore the higher you should bid – and indeed it is now worth stretching a trick to make life as difficult for the opponents as possible. Bear in mind, however, that the take-out double implies that the defender has a shortage in your partner's suit, which may mean a bad split, so that, if you are going to raise to three-level, you should have at least a four-card trump support. The usual guide is to raise to the two-

level on very little, raise to the three-level on a hand which is worth about 3 points less than a normal raise to that level, and bid 2NT on a full value raise to the three-level. If you have more than that, or are very distributional with very little defence, you may go higher still, taking the vulnerability of both sides into account.

Where you have only limited trump support, say three or four poor cards, and have most of your few points outside partner's trump suit, then you are more orientated towards defence and my recommendation is that you pass now and support partner's suit afterwards to advise him of that situation. Many experts rarely take this action, arguing that this 'lets the opponents in', but my answer to that is that, with points in their suits and an opening bid opposite me, I am hardly worried. I shall enlarge on that further when discussing 3 and 4 below.

3 If you are strong and have a misfit (doubleton or less in partner's suit), then you will definitely want to defend and in my opinion, now and only now, is the time to redouble. You should be able to double at least two of the other three suits for penalties at a low level. What you are effectively saying to partner is that you think you can make his one-level contract redoubled by sheer strength of high cards, perhaps with overtricks, and are confident that you can defeat the opponents in their contract. If you are strong with a one-suited hand and would still prefer to play rather than defend, you should still redouble and then bid your suit afterwards.

4 If you are strong with a fit, then your action will depend on how you feel about playing as opposed to defending, and now vulnerability may have to be taken into account as you will probably have a game on and the opponents may want to sacrifice. If you are keen to play rather than defend, simply bid a game outright if it is in a major, otherwise pass and next round aim for 3NT by cue-bidding opponents' bid suit if necessary; you can always go to five of the minor if it becomes clear that 3NT is not on.

If you have plenty of defence, bearing in mind that partner has promised you an opening bid, then my recommendation is to pass and see what happens. In this kind of situation, you know that three of the four hands have opening or near-opening bids and therefore that the doubler's partner will be looking at next to nothing. My recommended policy is that: 'If you have a good hand and the opponents are in a forcing situation, let them bid'. You never know what you will find out. It may well be that the fourth hand may have to bid a poor suit, possibly even of three cards, and/or that there is a really bad trump split and he will stand the double – stranger things have happened! You can always support partner afterwards or, if you have a suit of your own in addition to support for partner, you can bid the suit to indicate both features; meanwhile you may find out something unexpected. In any case, more will be known about the distribution and the hand will be easier to play. Furthermore, both your partner and the doubler have a second chance to speak and that may well give you still more information.

Let us try some examples against the stop-watch. Write down your proposed bid and the final contract you envisage.

(1) Partner deals at love all and the bidding goes: 1 ◊ X ? What do you bid now on:

(a) ♠ x x x x
    ♡ x x x
    ◊ x x x
    ♣ x x x

(b) ♠ Q x x x x x
    ♡ x x x
    ◊ –
    ♣ J x x x

(c) ♠ A Q x x
    ♡ K J x x
    ◊ x
    ♣ K J x x

(d) ♠ x x x x
    ♡ x x
    ◊ K J x x
    ♣ x x x

(e) ♠ x x
    ♡ x x x x
    ◊ x x
    ♣ Q x x x x

(f) ♠ –
    ♡ x x x
    ◊ K Q J x x x
    ♣ J x x x

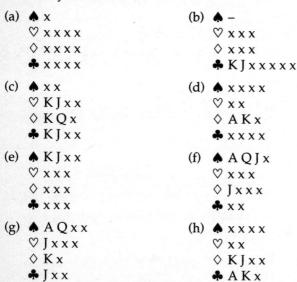

(g) ♠ Q J 10 9 x x x   (h) ♠ A Q x x x
     ♡ x x   ♡ Q x
     ◇ x   ◇ K J x x
     ♣ x x x   ♣ x x

Would a change of vulnerability make any difference to your answers?

(2) Partner deals at love all and the bidding goes: 1♠ X ?
What do you bid now on:

(a) ♠ x   (b) ♠ –
     ♡ x x x x   ♡ x x x
     ◇ x x x x   ◇ x x x
     ♣ x x x x   ♣ K J x x x x x

(c) ♠ x x   (d) ♠ x x x x
     ♡ K J x x   ♡ x x
     ◇ K Q x   ◇ A K x
     ♣ K J x x   ♣ x x x x

(e) ♠ K J x x   (f) ♠ A Q J x
     ♡ x x x   ♡ x x x
     ◇ x x x   ◇ J x x x
     ♣ x x x   ♣ x x

(g) ♠ A Q x x   (h) ♠ x x x x
     ♡ J x x x   ♡ x x
     ◇ K x   ◇ K J x x
     ♣ J x x   ♣ A K x

The sixteen questions should have taken you well under eight minutes and you should be aiming to bring your time down nearer to four. Let us work through the answers:

(1)(a) Here you have no reason to bid and with three diamonds in your hand, are happy to pass, intending to defend whatever contract the opponents choose.

   (b) Here there is the danger that the doubler's partner on your left is very long in diamonds and will stand the double and in that case, your partner may be unsure of what to do. With the worst misfit possible, you should remove to 1♠, intending to play there. Note that partner should respect your decision and refrain from repeating his diamonds unless you are doubled in 1♠. In that case, if he dislikes the suit intensely and his diamonds are so good and long that he considers that it will be cheaper to play them at the two-level, he may do so. Note again, the air of cooperation rather than argument between the two partners in a difficult situation.

(c) Here you have a similar and probably stronger hand than that of the doubler and will be delighted to defend any contract he plays for what is certain to be a huge penalty. Simple redouble, intending to double any contract the opponents bid. Note that, on hearing the redouble, the opener should move to another contract if his diamonds are poor and only four-card. It may be that the doubler has diamonds after all, as we shall learn later when we study overcalling with very strong, balanced hands. However, almost invariably, opener will pass, intending to accept his partner's decision to defend.

(d) This is a poor hand but with four diamonds including two honours, you can afford to take bidding space away from opponents by raising to 2♦, at the moment intending to play there but suggesting a possible sacrifice. Note that it is most unlikely that the opponents will be able to double 2♦ for a worthwhile penalty.

(e) This is a very poor hand and although there is a slight danger of the double being left in, you have nowhere to go. You are most unlikely to gain by bidding four small hearts and to suggest your clubs would involve going to the two-level, which is more likely to invite trouble. Pass and hope to defend whatever the opponents choose.

(f) Here you will certainly not want to defend as an enemy diamond void is likely and will reduce your defensive potential to nil. How high you should go depends on vulnerability but it is likely that the opponents can make 4♠ and I would suggest going straight to 5♦. (If I were vulnerable against not, 4♦ would probably be enough so that partner can take the final decision on whether to defend or sacrifice).

(g) This is similar to (1b), but as you have a suit that is likely to stand up for five tricks on its own, you might bid more than 1♠, this being a rare situation where it may pay to preempt despite the misfit. I would suggest 3♠ at this vulnerability but would be content with 2♠ if vulnerable. Note that partner should understand that this means that you cannot play anything but spades and should bid accordingly. Note that a jump in a new suit is non-forcing and should be considered a sign-off unless partner has a fit in that suit!

(h) Here you have enough to raise to at least 3◊, but you also have a spade suit and 4♠ is not out of the question. My recommendation is to pass now (delighted to play 1◊ doubled) and then bid spades afterwards to offer game in spades, diamonds or no trumps. At what level you bid the spades depends on how high the opponents go. If they stop in 1♡, I would jump to 2♠; otherwise bid them at the three-level.

(2)(a) This is a most unpleasant situation but although you do not like spades, any move would be to the two-level and you have no suit anywhere near worth bidding. You should pass, hoping that 1♠ doubled is not allowed to stand and that you can defend whatever contract the opponents choose.

(b) Here with a void of spades and a very long suit of your own, it is well worthwhile moving to 2♣ as you know that, with an opening bid opposite you, a double and large penalty are unlikely even if partner is short in clubs. Remember again that partner should respect your decision.

(c) Here with an opening bid and a misfit, you are delighted to defend, particularly as you know the opponents will have to go to the two-level; 1NT is clearly going to be a disaster for them. Just redouble for the time being, intending to double anything the opponents bid.

(d) This time, you have a comfortable raise to 2♠, but with two top defensive tricks outside, you do not want to suggest a sacrifice and it is for this reason that I recommend passing now and supporting spades at the two-level later (you will be prepared to go to the three-level if necessary but only in competition).

(e) Here you are weak and what little you have is in a four-card spade suit, so now is the time to bid 2♠ at once, taking bidding space away from opponents and indicating a possible sacrifice to partner as you are unable to defend.

(f) Here you are stronger but again do not wish to defend. You should now bid 3♠, being a little understrength for a normal raise to this level.

(g) Here you have a normal raise to 3♠ and should show it by bidding 2NT. Note that this is forcing at least to 3♠ and that a natural 2NT bid has become an obsolete bid, as with 11–12 points and good values outside spades, you would redouble, with a view to defending.

(h) Here you again have a good raise to 3♠ but this time, with all your points outside the spade suit, I recommend passing now and bidding 3♠ next time. This clarifies your hand to partner and in particular, indicates that you will want to defend if the opponents sacrifice over 4♠.

The cue-bid

This is a direct bid of the opponent's suit to show a very strong hand, but at the same time, denying the correct shape for a take-out double, which, as you will remember, has no upper limit in strength. Thus you will normally be showing a game-going or near game-going hand, one- or two-suited. The bid is forcing at least to suit agreement or no-trumps, and, more often than not, to game. It comes up very rarely so we shall give it very brief treatment.

Suppose 1♡ is opened against you and you hold:

♠ A K Q x x
♡ x x
◇ A K Q x x x
♣ –

To double is dangerous, in that partner with a long string of clubs and a weak hand may bid them at a high level, under the impression that it will be a cheap sacrifice against 4♡. Here, you should bid 2♡, forcing and showing the big hand, after which partner will realize you have a one-suited or two-suited hand. You can then have a quiet chat to finish in 4♠, 5◇ or a slam in either suit.

Similarly, with:

♠ A K Q J x x x x
♡ x
◇ A Q J x
♣ –

you are too close to a slam in your own hand to preempt with 4♠ immediately, so you should cue-bid 2♡ first and then (unless partner bids diamonds) keep repeating spades and partner will realize that you have this type of hand. When answering a cue-bid, just bid your longest suit at the cheapest level possible and if partner cue-bids again, bid no-trumps with a stop in opponents' suit or describe your hand further by repeating a long suit or choosing another. Never jump; there is no need to do so (except to give the clear message of a long, solid suit). Your partner has asked for a long conversation and as he has the big hand, you should respect his decision, keeping bidding space to a maximum. If you are strong, you can always bid on towards a slam if partner limits his hand with a non-forcing game bid, but remember that there is an opening bid against you.

The no-trump overcall

When we first learnt about bidding no-trumps, we defined an opening bid of one no-trump as showing a balanced hand with 12–14 points. This is, of course, completely arbitrary and the bid can be defined in other ways. Our method is called the *weak no-trump*. Some players prefer a *strong no-trump*, defined as 16–18 points and this is standard throughout America. (You should also be aware that they also insist that an opening bid in a major promises a five-card suit.) I do not intend to go into a long discussion on the pros and cons of the weak and strong no-trumps. For the time being, it will be sufficient to say that the strong no-trump is certainly safer but its frequency of appearance is very poor; indeed for that reason, many pairs prefer to define a strong no-trump as showing 15–17 points. A good compromise between the two is the *variable no-trump* defined as 12–14 non-vulnerable and 15–17 (or 16–18) vulnerable, which attempts to get the best of both worlds within the bounds of reasonable safety.

When overcalling in no-trumps, one has to be more careful in that at least 12 points are known to be held against you. The required point range (and this is accepted universally) varies according to where you are sitting. If you are sitting immediately over the bid (viz. one of a suit has been opened on your right), the hand over you is at present unlimited (or limited to 11 points if he has already passed) and you could easily be doubled if you bid on mere opening values. For that reason, you must be stronger to overcall a no-trump and 15–17 points is the accepted range (some insist on 16–18).

You should also have at least one stop (A x, K x, Q x x or J x x x) in the suit bid against you. However, the regulations on shape are not so strict as before. It is common to overcall 1NT on unbalanced hands, even including a singleton, if your hand is minor-suit-orientated and you are obviously angling for 3NT.

On the other side, if the bid is on your left and the hand on your right has already passed his partner's opening bid, then you know that your right-hand opponent has 5 points or less and therefore that it is less dangerous to bid on 12–14 points in the protective position (some pairs allow it on 11 or even 10). You should ideally still have the stop in the opponents' suit but you might get away with Q x or J x x. The question then arises of what to do if, taking your position into account, you are above your range for a normal 1NT overcall. In that case, you double for take-out first and then bid no-trumps afterwards unless partner produces a suit which you would prefer to have as trumps.

Another question arises if you are in the correct range but do not have a stop and your hand is unsuitable for a take-out double, viz. shortages in one or both majors. In these situations, it is reasonable to pass if you are at the minimum end of the range.

282 *The Expert Beginner*

If you have points to spare, you are justified in breaking the rules, either by overcalling on a four-card suit or making a take-out double. My policy is to prefer a pass if opponents are vulnerable, expecting at least 200 as a vulnerable undoubled penalty when there is no guarantee that my side has game, but to bid when they are non-vulnerable when the penalty will be expressed in 50s. This is very much a question of judgement and experts vary in their approach.

Let us try a test. Start your stop-watch.

(1) You are in second position at game all and 1♡ is opened by the dealer. What do you bid now on:

(a) ♠ Q x x
    ♡ A K x
    ◇ K x x x
    ♣ J x x

(b) ♠ Q x x
    ♡ A K J
    ◇ K x x
    ♣ K x x x

(c) ♠ A K x
    ♡ A K x
    ◇ A x x x
    ♣ J x x

(d) ♠ A x
    ♡ A K J x
    ◇ Q x
    ♣ Q x x x x

(e) ♠ A K x
    ♡ A Q x
    ◇ A x x x
    ♣ A x x

(f) ♠ x
    ♡ A K x x
    ◇ Q J x x
    ♣ A K x x

(g) ♠ K x
    ♡ x x x
    ◇ A K J x
    ♣ A K J x

(h) ♠ A K J x
    ♡ x x x x x
    ◇ –
    ♣ A K Q x

(2) The player on your left deals and the bidding goes: 1♡ Pass Pass ? What do you bid now on those same eight hands?

(3) Would any of your answers to those sixteen questions be different if the score was love all?

These should have taken you about seven minutes and you should be aiming to get under three. Let us work through the answers.

(1)(a) With 13 points and no long suit, you have no reason to bid over 1♡. Your honours are scattered apart from the ace and king of hearts, which are in the opponents' suit. Therefore, you are more suited to defending and accordingly, you should pass.

  (b) With 16 points and the hearts well stopped, you are well placed to overcall 1NT, hoping to finish in 3NT or game in a suit if partner turns out to be very distributional.

  (c) With 19 points, you are too strong for a simple overcall of 1NT and should double first, intending to bid no-trumps later. These hands cause a considerable problem in that you can express your hand with double followed by 1NT if partner responds to your double at the one-level, but should he reply at the two-level (and he might have to do so without a point in his hand) your rebid of 2NT shows a range of 18–22 points and it is difficult for partner to decide whether or not to go on to game. As we shall see later, it is even worse in the protective position.

  (d) Here, despite the 2524 shape, 1NT is the most descriptive bid on this hand. You are certainly angling to play in 3NT rather than 5♣.

  (e) With 21 points, you are strong enough to double and then bid 2NT over a one-level response, i.e. 1♠. If partner bids on the two-level, the problem discussed in (1c) arises. There are a number of involved solutions but if you doubled, intending to bid 2NT come what may, that is satisfactory for the moment.

  (f) This is another difficult decision. To double would indicate interest in the other major and should therefore be ruled out on this hand. It is thus a question between 1NT and pass. I prefer a pass against vulnerable opponents. With a bit of luck, one of the other players will manage a spade bid, putting you in a more informed position as to whether you want to play or defend. If partner bids, you can try for 3NT. If the partner of the opener bids it, the opener will have to bid again, after which you can either elect to defend or double for take-out to invite a minor-suit contract.

(g) Here the poor heart holding rules out no-trumps, but you are too strong to pass. As you have so many points, you can afford to break the rules by doubling, correcting a spade bid with a jump to 3♣. If partner repeats spades, you will, at least, have tolerance. It is still possible that 3NT may be on but it must be played by your partner.

(h) This is a very strong hand but the five small hearts are a distinct disadvantage and the diamond void makes a take-out double very dangerous although many players would take such action. I think it is best simply to overcall 1♠, then if the opponents bid diamonds, you can double for take-out to offer clubs and spades. If partner bids diamonds, then you will be glad that you underbid the hand anyway. Perhaps you can cue-bid hearts, inviting partner to bid no-trumps but being prepared to pass if partner has nothing to bid but diamonds, when the whole hand is a misfit and game is most unlikely.

(2)(a) We move to the protective position and now, as it is possible that partner has quite a good hand, you should protect with 1NT, showing 12–14 points balanced. Partner can take charge from there, using Stayman or a weak take-out, for example, if appropriate.

(b) Here you are too strong for a protective no-trump and should double. Now, if partner fails to jump, he denies 8 useful points and you can safely pass, confident that game will not be on, especially as your heart holding includes three honours in a trebleton, with the jack badly placed under the bid. However, if he replies 1♠, you may bid 1NT to show about 15–17 points in this position. However, it is debatable whether it is worth bothering on such a poor hand in this range.

(c) With 18 points, you should again start with a double, intending to bid 2NT whatever partner says, showing 18–20 points. You are primarily angling for 3NT.

(d) This is more difficult. If you double and partner responds 1♠, you can comfortably bid 1NT, but if he responds 2♦, this hand is not really worth 2NT. With six points in two doubletons, the hearts badly placed and the five-card suit of very poor quality in a minor, I would suggest devaluing it and bidding 1NT. This is the type of hand where, if partner is unable to make an effort over a weak no-trump, game will probably not be on.

(e) This time, you should start with a double. If partner responds 1♠, jump to 2NT, albeit a point over strength. With luck, you will get to 3NT or 4♠. If partner bids a minor, I suggest bidding 3NT, hoping that he has a few points and/or that his minor suit is long and will be brought in to make the contract.

(f) This is one of the most awkward problems of the lot. Many players would probably break the rules and double, hoping to correct a spade bid to no-trumps, and that is probably as good a solution as any. The alternatives are to allow 1♡ to play, devalue the hand and bid 1NT (although it is really too strong) or make an overcall with 2♣ or possibly even a jump overcall of 3♣. I feel it is better to mislead on the length of a minor than double with a singleton in the other major, and feeling the hand to strong for a simple protective overcall, would opt for 3♣. My view is that this is least likely to get you into trouble while still giving the chance of game in 3NT or five of a minor.

(g) Here you can double as your spades are not so bad and you have plenty of points to compensate. After partner's reply you will cue-bid hearts, giving partner the opportunity to bid 3NT.

(h) This time 1♠ is too modest; it either has to be a double or you might start with 2♠ or even 3♣, giving you the chance to bid both black suits with maximum economy. My choice would be 3♣, intending to bid 3♡ over 3♢ to give the chance of 3NT while partner can still bid 3♠ over 3♡ if he has a four-card suit.

(3) The only problem affected by the change of vulnerability is (2f). While, if the opponents are vulnerable, you might allow 1♡ to be played, this should not be considered when the penalty is unlikely to be better than a couple of 50s.

The jump no-trump overcall

Some players play this as natural (20–22 points balanced), and indeed that solves a number of problems in the section above. However, in practice, very big hands rarely come up when an opponent has opened and for that reason, the jump in no-trump has a better use. It shows two suits of at least five cards, being the lowest in rank outstanding. Thus:

If 1♣ is opened against you, you show diamonds and hearts;
If 1♦ is opened against you, you show clubs and hearts;
If 1♡ is opened against you, you show clubs and diamonds;
If 1♠ is opened against you, you show clubs and diamonds.

As such bids give a great deal of information away, it is unwise to make them unless you have serious aspirations of playing the hand. Your hand should be near to opening bid strength and the bulk of your points should be in the suits you are suggesting, the more adverse the vulnerability, the stricter you must be on these considerations. As the unusual no-trump is primarily orientated to the minor suits, sacrifices against game will usually be at the five-level.

This would be a reasonable minimum unusual no-trump against 1♠.

♠ x
♡ x x
♦ A Q x x x
♣ A K x x x

If you are more distributional, you can afford to be weaker:

♠ x	or even	♠ –
♡ x		♡ x
◊ A Q x x x		◊ K J x x x x
♣ K J x x x x		♣ K J x x x x

When replying to an unusual no-trump, you should choose a final contract based on partner's likely hand. Thus do not bid a long suit in the unbid major unless you are happy to play it opposite a singleton or void. The worst thing you can do with a

misfit is to advertise the fact to the opponents. Thus, after 1♠
2NT Pass ? With ♠ x x x x
    ♡ Q x x x x x
    ◇ x
    ♣ x x   bid 3♣, displaying no trace of anxiety.

Yes, I warned you that there would be situations where you have
to bid suits with two low cards!

With ♠ x x x
    ♡ K Q J 10 x x x
    ◇ x x
    ♣ x

you may bid 3♡ as you will not go many down playing single-
handed. Partner should respect your decision and will probably
provide a trick or two.

The penalty double and redouble

We have touched on the penalty double already in respect of
sacrifice situations, but must still look at those in competitive
situations and of freely-bid contracts. Briefly, when you are
considering doubling a contract for penalties, the following
should be taken into account:

1 The manner in which your opponents' contract has been bid. If
   it appears that they have strength to spare, do not consider a
   double unless you are absolutely sure that the contract is going
   down. If, however, they appear to have stretched to get there,
   then a penalty double is in order if you have an unpleasant
   surprise for the opponents, typically a very bad trump break
   or several honour cards badly placed for them.
      The sequence 1NT 3NT sounds confident. The 1NT opener
   may be maximum (his partner did not bother to ask) and the
   3NT bidder may have been just short of looking for a slam. Do
   not double unless you are sure of at least five solid tricks.
      Against that, the sequence 1♡   1NT
                                 2NT   3NT
   sounds like a crawl. You may well double if you are sitting
   with a stack, say A Q J x x over the hearts.

2 If you double a contract, are you sure that you will not push the opponents from a contract which they cannot make to another which they can! In other words, have you got them firmly by the scruff of the neck?

3 Whose lead is it? Particularly against a slam, it may be vital to indicate a specific lead to your partner. It is customary that a double asks for the first suit bid by the dummy hand. If you have bid a suit yourself during the auction, then you will normally expect partner to lead it, so a double indicates something unusual – probably another side suit in which you are void. This is known as the *Lightner slam double*.

4 A double tends to imply dislike of partner's bid suit and points in the opponents' suit(s).

5 If you double, you are undoubtedly giving away information to opponents which is almost bound to help them in the play. Is it worth it? You should be more worried on this point with broken holdings in opponents' suits like A Q 10 than with solid holdings like K Q J.

As far as redoubles are concerned, these are rare at a high level and are more often used over take-out doubles, as explained earlier, or after 1NT has been doubled and the redoubler is confident of at least 22 points between the two hands. Apart from that, I shall not discuss the use of redoubles any further at the moment.

Let us review the course so far. We have familiarized ourselves with the pack of cards and the scoresheet, and covered a little ground in the field of declarer play. So far, however, we have said little about defence. I have deliberately left that until after the bidding for reasons which will be explained in the following last short chapter.

Defence

This was briefly discussed in the play section earlier but further details have deliberately been left until now. If you go to any bridge school or teacher, these are the sort of tips you will hear:

1 Against no-trumps, lead the fourth highest of your best, usually longest suit.
2 If you are leading an honour, a solid combination such as K Q, Q J, etc, should be preferred to a broken holding such as A Q, K J, Q 10. In the latter cases it is better that the suit is led towards you.
3 Second hand plays low.
4 Third hand plays high.
5 Aim to lead through strength on your left and round to weakness on your right. This is another way of saying 'Lead from weakness through strength (visible or assumed) to strength.'
6 Never discard from holdings like K x, Q x x, J x x x, as the higher honours may then swallow up your honour.
7 If the contract has been bid against you in a confident auction and it looks as though the opponents have, if anything, points and/or trumps to spare, be prepared to take desperate measures to defeat them; i.e. get 'busy'. Any mistakes will, at the worst, give away overtricks of minimal value.
8 If, on the other hand, the opponents have just about crawled into their contract, your first priority should be to avoid giving anything away, i.e. defend 'passively'.
9 Cover an honour with an honour . . . and so the list goes on.

In fairness, all these guides are reasonably sensible and are applicable a fair proportion of the time, but there are so many exceptions that it is almost better not to know them in the first place. A top-class player spends a great deal of his time breaking the above rules and if you are going to learn to play the game to even intermediate standard, you will have to understand what you are doing rather than purely follow the above guides, parrot fashion.

At the beginning of the course, heavy emphasis was laid on familiarity with the pack and now you are going to put your acquired skill to use.

If you are on lead, you can only see your own thirteen cards but the bidding should have given you a fair amount of information about the shape and strength of the opponents' hands. From that, you should ask yourself how the opponents intend to make their contract and from where the defenders' tricks are most likely to come.

With no-trumps, it is almost invariably a race to develop long suits, so you should attack your longest suit, even if it means leading away from an embarrassing honour holding. The three exceptions arise if:

1 That suit has been bid against you, in which case you may want to consider another suit.
2 Your partner has bid a suit, when you should consider preferring your partner's suit to your own.
3 Your hand is desperately weak and therefore short of entries. You might try to find your partner's long suit in preference to your own, which, in the absence of other information, often means leading your shortest suit.

Let us try some simple examples. Suppose the hand on your right deals and the bidding goes: 1NT Pass 3NT All Pass. What would you lead from:

(1) ♠ K J x x x
     ♡ A x
     ◇ x x x
     ♣ x x x

(2) ♠ K J x x x
     ♡ x x
     ◇ x
     ♣ K J x x x

(3) ♠ Q J 10 9 x
    ♥ x
    ♦ x x x x x x
    ♣ A

(4) ♠ x x x x x
    ♥ 10 x
    ♦ x x x
    ♣ Q x x

In (1) with a good suit and an outside entry in the ♥A, you have every reason to attack with your long suit, starting with your fourth highest spade.

In (2) you have two suits to choose from and in this situation, it usually pays to favour the major. The 1NT opener has denied a five-card major and his partner made no attempt at Stayman. 3NT hands are more often than not minor-suit orientated and spades thus offers your best chance. Again start with your fourth highest spade.

In (3) you have six cards in diamonds against five in spades but the spades are so much stronger that they are far more likely to bring in tricks than the very poor diamond suit. There is no guarantee, but even ignoring the fact that the spades are a major and the diamonds a minor, the spade opening lead gives you the best chance. When you have a solid run, you should start with the top of that run in preference to the fourth highest, i.e. the ♠Q. With Q 10 9 x x, you should start with the ten and with K J 10 x x, choose the jack. In each case the lead *denies* the card immediately above it but *virtually promises* (except with a short-suit lead as in (4) below) the card immediately below it.

In (4) you have only two points and, giving the opponents about 25, that leaves partner with 13. So, as he is likely to have the side-suit entries, it is *his* suit you should attack. On the bidding and your hand, it is most likely to be hearts and you should start with the ♥10, playing the standard higher card from a doubleton.

Against a trump contract, there are countless considerations and I do not favour making rules. A few guides, however, may help. If any of the following apply then it is likely that the declarer is going to try to make his contract by ruffing and you should therefore lead a trump, even if it has to be from an embarrassing holding. The trick given up will usually be returned to you, often with interest.

1 The opponents have bid three suits and are now playing in the fourth;
2 A suit has been bid and supported; the opener offers no-trumps but his partner insists on the trump contract;
3 You have made a take-out double and it has been left in;
4 An opponent bids two suits and his partner prefers the second and you are either very long or very short in the first suit;
5 It is clear that you and your partner between you have all three side-suits strongly held.

Where these do not apply and your partner has not suggested a lead, you should prefer unbid suits to bid suits. It is often a mistake to lead dummy's long suit on the pretext of 'leading through strength'; you are also leading through length and possibly helping to set up the suit. Avoid leading away from aces at trick one but do not be too afraid of leading away from lower honours except round to a bid suit. Many beginners are told: 'Never lead away from a king.' Remember that, if your partner has the queen, you are effectively leading from K Q, which is strong.

The best leads in the absence of solid honour holdings are short suits of small cards, doubletons and singletons. Here you are leading from weakness with the possibility of setting up ruffs for yourself. However, you should refrain from trying to get ruffs if you have trump holdings which are unsuitable. For example, if your trumps are Q J x, you have an almost certain trick and will not a gain by a ruff, although you could gain with two ruffs. Where you are very long in trumps, you should consider leading your longest side suit to try to force the declarer to ruff and reduce his trumps to your length or less – he may then lose complete control of the hand.

Try a few more examples. Say the opponent on your left deals and the bidding goes (with you and your partner silent):

| 1♠ | 2♡ |
| 2♠ | 4♠ |

What would you lead with:

(1) ♠ x x x
♡ K Q J 10 x
◇ K x
♣ J x x

(2) ♠ x x
♡ Q x x
◇ x x x x
♣ K J x x

(3) ♠ x x x   (4) ♠ x x x x
     ♡ J x x x   ♡ K 10 x
     ◇ K Q J x   ◇ A Q x x x
     ♣ x x   ♣ x

In (1) the dummy hand has shown at least a five-card heart suit and you know that the suit will not yield any tricks apart from the ace. You also know that the dummy is short of at least one minor and possibly both and that declarer, unable to capitalize on the heart suit, will have to resort to ruffing minor-suit cards on dummy. Try to prevent this by leading a trump. That ♡K looked such lovely solid lead, didn't it? It is unlikely to run away.

In (2) the heart situation is disastrous from your point of view. The suit appears to be dividing evenly and your queen is probably well placed for the declarer. This is the time to take desperate measures and you must get your side's tricks going first. You are clearly most unlikely to get rich on those four small diamonds and must attack clubs, starting with the fourth highest. Hopefully, you will find partner with an honour. If he fails to oblige, you are probably not going to defeat this contract anyway.

In (3) the heart position is less clear and you have an excellent solid lead in ◇ K with no reason to consider anything else.

In (4) the heart position is again unfavourable for you but your best chance this time is to find your partner with the ♣A and/or a quick entry in trumps and defeat the contract by club ruffs. The singleton club stands out.

Note, in each case, the way to think about the hand; the same applies to the rest of the defence.

One important point arises with solid honour holdings. It was explained earlier that you lead the top card from a run: K from K Q or from K Q J; Q from Q J or Q J 10; and the top from an *interior sequence*, viz. J from K J 10, 10 from Q 10 9, etc. This applies when you are the first or second to lead to a trick and wish to indicate to your partner what you have. When a low card of a suit is led by your partner towards you and you are the third player to play to a trick, you need play no higher than necessary. Thus you choose the lower or lowest from a run and the card you play denies the one immediately below it but does not exclude (you cannot be more definite than that) the card or cards above. So, if partner leads a low card and the next player also plays low, you play 10 from Q J 10, J from Q J or K Q J or A K Q J, Q from K Q or A K Q, etc. Where you have a broken holding and there is nothing to finesse against on dummy, you should play your highest card. Play the K from K J 10, and if this loses to the ace, your partner will know that you do not have the queen; A from A Q J, denying the king; Q from Q 10 or Q 10 9, denying the jack.

You can also indicate solid holdings if partner has led a card higher than your top card in that holding. Thus, if partner leads an ace and you hold something like Q J 10 9 x, you should play the *queen*. This denies the king but strongly suggests the jack, ten etc. Similarly, if partner leads the king, you can play the jack from J 10 9 x, denying the queen but suggesting the ten, etc.

From the last two paragraphs, you can see that the guide is:

To show a solid holding, go as near to the card led as you can.

These are all ways of indicating your holding to partner and is the initial scratch on the surface of the sphere of defensive signalling, the purpose of which is to help your partner to place the unseen cards. This is an enormous subject but can be divided into four broad categories:

1 Encouragement or discouragement of partner's led suit;
2 Distribution – in principle an odd or even number of cards in the suit led;
3 Suit preference – in principle higher- or lower-ranking;
4 Other relevant information.

For the time being, however, the first two will be enough – the others are a little advanced and can be studied later. Here are two simple examples:

```
              ♠ K 5 3
              ♡ A 4 3
              ◇ Q 7 5
              ♣ J 10 7 5
  ♠ A 4 2      ┌─────────┐      ♠ 9 7
  ♡ Q J 10 5   │    N    │      ♡ K 8 2
  ◇ J 10 9 2   │  W   E  │      ◇ 6 4 3
  ♣ A 8        │    S    │      ♣ 9 6 4 3 2
               └─────────┘
              ♠ Q J 10 8 6
              ♡ 9 7 6
              ◇ A K 8
              ♣ K Q
```

South deals at game all and opens 1♠. West passes and North bids 2♣. East passes and South rebids 2NT showing 15 points, perhaps a poor 16. West passes and North bids 3♠. Remember that this is forcing and offers 3NT and 4♠ as final game contracts. South is wide open in hearts and with his strong club holding and five-card spade suit, he prefers the trump game and signs off in 4♠.

West has two solid suits to lead from and prefers the stronger, starting with the ♡Q. North plays the ♡A and the spotlight falls on East. He plays a high card, the ♡8, to encourage a heart continuation. South knows that he will lose two heart tricks as well as the two black aces immediately if he tries to draw trumps so he attacks clubs at once. He hopes that the opposing clubs will break 4–3 so that he can enjoy one discard on the third round of clubs before either opponent can ruff or they can cash the two heart tricks. West wins the first round of clubs with the ♣A and continues with the ♡J and the ♡10. The defenders will also take the trump ace as their fourth trick – one off.

Now let us exchange the positions of the red kings while keeping the distribution unaltered (see overleaf):

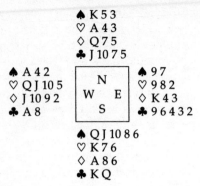

```
                    ♠ K 5 3
                    ♡ A 4 3
                    ◇ Q 7 5
                    ♣ J 10 7 5
  ♠ A 4 2          ┌─────────┐      ♠ 9 7
  ♡ Q J 10 5       │    N    │      ♡ 9 8 2
  ◇ J 10 9 2       │  W   E  │      ◇ K 4 3
  ♣ A 8            │    S    │      ♣ 9 6 4 3 2
                   └─────────┘
                    ♠ Q J 10 8 6
                    ♡ K 7 6
                    ◇ A 8 6
                    ♣ K Q
```

As it happens, 3NT may now be a better chance but let us assume the bidding is the same and South is still in 4♠ against the lead of the ♡Q. When North rises with the ♡A, East discourages with the ♡2 so that West now realises that the ♡K is in the South hand. When he gets in with the ♣A, West will switch to the ◇J and set up two diamond tricks to go with the black aces to defeat the contract. Play it out for yourself to be sure that you understand that it is crucial for West to know what to do when he gets in with a black ace early on.

Information about distribution is important for a number of reasons, the most common being to organize a ruff and to know how long to hold up an ace. Here is a simple example of the former:

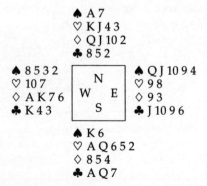

```
                    ♠ A 7
                    ♡ K J 4 3
                    ◇ Q J 10 2
                    ♣ 8 5 2
  ♠ 8 5 3 2        ┌─────────┐      ♠ Q J 10 9 4
  ♡ 10 7           │    N    │      ♡ 9 8
  ◇ A K 7 6        │  W   E  │      ◇ 9 3
  ♣ K 4 3          │    S    │      ♣ J 10 9 6
                   └─────────┘
                    ♠ K 6
                    ♡ A Q 6 5 2
                    ◇ 8 5 4
                    ♣ A Q 7
```

Again South deals at game all and opens 1♡. West passes and North shows his good diamond suit with 2◇. South rebids 2NT,

showing his 15 points, and North signs off in 4♡. West leads the
♢A and when North follows with the ♢2, the spotlight again
falls on East. It should be clear to him that his partner has led the
ace from ace-king (he would have no reason to lead an unsupported ace of an opponent's suit) and therefore with the queen
and jack visible on dummy, encouragement/discouragement is
irrelevant and distribution is required as a ruff is possible. To
show an even number (here two), East *peters* with the ♢9. West
continues with the ♢K and then a third round, which East ruffs.
He switches to the ♣J, leading through strength to strength and
the ♣K provides the fourth trick for the defence to defeat the
contract.

Now let us change the diamond distribution and the positions
of one or two of the other honours:

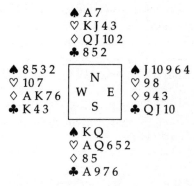

```
            ♠ A 7
            ♡ K J 4 3
            ♢ Q J 10 2
            ♣ 8 5 2
♠ 8 5 3 2       N       ♠ J 10 9 6 4
♡ 10 7                  ♡ 9 8
♢ A K 7 6   W     E     ♢ 9 4 3
♣ K 4 3         S       ♣ Q J 10
            ♠ K Q
            ♡ A Q 6 5 2
            ♢ 8 5
            ♣ A 9 7 6
```

With the same bidding as before, South reaches 4♡ and West
leads the ♢A. This time, East shows an odd number by playing
his ♢3. This could be a singleton, but that would leave South
with four when he would have been more likely to support the
diamonds rather than bid no-trumps. It is therefore very likely
that East has a trebleton. That means that, once the ♢K has been
knocked out, South, having drawn trumps first, will be able to
enjoy two discards on the ♢Q and ♢J. West should realize that
he has found a poor lead and go for desperate measures. It is
obvious that, at best, only one trick will be available in spades
and he will need to find his partner with honours in clubs for the
defence to have a chance. He must therefore switch immediately

to clubs and hope to set up two tricks in that suit in addition to the two top diamonds. Notice again that the signal on trick one helped West to work out what was required.

It is also important to give count to tell partner how long to hold up a control (usually but not necessarily the ace) when declarer or (more often) dummy has a long suit to set up and is short of outside entries. Suppose this is the diamond suit in a no-trump contract:

$$K Q J 10 8 6$$

$$7 2 \qquad\qquad\qquad A 4 3$$

$$9 5$$

The North hand has no outside entries and South leads the nine. West plays the seven, high to show an even number, and North the ten. Now, if East wins immediately, South will be able to enjoy the rest of the suit. But if East realizes that the cards he cannot see are divided 2–2, he will refuse this round and win the next, isolating dummy's remaining winners.

Change the position to:

$$K Q J 10 8 6$$

$$7 5 2 \qquad\qquad\qquad A 4 3$$

$$9$$

and this time, East plays the two. Now West has to decide whether the indication of an odd number means that the layout is as above, in which case he can win the first round, or whether it is:

$$K Q J 10 8 6$$

$$2 \qquad\qquad\qquad A 4 3$$

$$9 7 5$$

in which case he must hold up his ace to the third round. It will often be obvious from South's bidding.

Regarding the remainder of defence, my advice is this. Bear in mind the guides at the beginning of this chapter but far more important, observe the following:

1 Do not lose interest if you have a very bad hand. A ten could make all the difference.
2 Make a positive attempt to watch every card that goes, particularly the trumps and high cards. We spent a lot of time

practising that at the beginning. It is crucial to know which cards are left towards the end of a hand. This point is worth stressing as, while you might be forgiven for making mistakes during the early tricks of the play, there is usually little or no excuse for erring in the later stages when the deal will very often be what is termed an *open book*, i.e. the position of every outstanding card is known.

3 As soon as the dummy goes down, make a positive attempt to place the important cards you cannot see, using the bidding (and later on, defensive signalling) as information – that is why I left defence until after bidding had been discussed in full. Ask yourself 'Who has got it?' and answer, not worrying if you get it wrong; it is better to do that than not try at all. Once you have placed all the missing cards, check that the bidding and play so far make reasonable sense on your assumptions. If they do not, try placing the cards again.

4 If there are several reasonable alternatives, place the cards so that they are just enough for you defeat the contract.

5 Make a mental note of the distribution of a suit which is confirmed every time a player fails to follow a suit for the first time.

6 Now play as though you can see all four hands. It is so much easier!

You are encouraged to go through the ten problems on declarer play discussed earlier and note the way the defence was conducted. The fact that it was not successful is neither here nor there. Note particularly the comments I made regarding discards.

On that note, I think we have done enough. If you have mastered everything in the book and brought your times for the exercises down to those recommended, you are well placed to start playing the game with a reasonable knowledge of what it is about.

As far as thinking is concerned, there are a lot of rules on this point but the most important is to try and predict how the bidding is going to proceed so that you can avoid long trances. It is particularly embarrassing to think a long time and then pass, but it is quite legal, bearing in mind that partner must not take advantage of the information that you were close to a bid. Equally, during the play, try to predict which cards the opponents are going to play and do your thinking in advance so that you are ready at the critical moment. Never, in any circumstances, hesitate before following suit with a singleton; just play it in even tempo without undue haste.

Finally, the important thing is enjoy the game and treasure your mistakes, remembering them and learning from them.

Index